Growing Up In Riverside

Growing Up In Riverside

a Lifelong Accumulation of Essays

Gary C. Layton

Growing Up in Riverside: a Lifelong Accumulation of Essays
Gary C. Layton

The essays in this book are based on the memories of the author. Names of actual people and entities have been changed. Any likeness to actual persons, either living or dead, is strictly coincidental.

ISBN-13: 978-1730967078

Cover design by Gary Layton
Edited by Gary Layton and Jenny Margotta, editorjennymargotta@mail.com

Printed in the United States of America

Dedication

To Doyalene:
my lifelong companion, friend, lover, and wife, whose love, understanding, and patience helped me defeat my demons.

To Douglas W. Baker:
my lifelong friend whose love of life and spirit of adventure helped me through some trying times.

To my dear friend Mary Ogren:
for all the help correcting my grammatical errors.

Table of Contents

Prologue

I was born in 1938, the last of four children. Being the only boy in the family, after the death of my brother, meant I relied heavily on friends for my adventures, "doing what boys do." We were poor and, out of necessity, most of our adventures cost nothing or next to nothing. We used our imaginations. We spent days and evenings outdoors, exploring. We had something to look forward to each day. We formed lasting bonds. We not only had fun, but along the way friends became family, and those relationships have lasted a lifetime. How many people can say they are still in regular contact with their friends from 70 years ago?

I grew up in Riverside, California—a Riverside that, because of years of progress, is unrecognizable today. Gone are the many open fields and large lots. Gone are the country roads. Gone are the times when you could play freely without worrying about whose property you were on. Even though I no longer live there, Riverside will always hold a special place in my heart. It is a place of fond memories. A place where a boy became a man. A place where I learned what's important in life. A place where I learned that family and friends are treasures to be cherished.

As I get older I find that I like to reflect on some of my adventures and remember some of the good times and the people who have been so important in my life. It gives me joy to sit and write essays about those days. I hope it will give you joy to read my stories.

Exploring Highgrove

Even as a little kid I loved the outdoors. I would leave the house early and explore the canyons and hills around Highgrove. The area was loaded with ravines and rolling hills and was always green with foliage in the spring and early summer. Most of the ravines had running water in them that you could safely drink, and the orchards of oranges, peaches, and plums were plentiful, so water and food were available most of the time. I remember one year eating so many oranges that I broke out with red, itchy, splotches all over my skin. I had to give up oranges for several weeks to get the splotches to go away.

A lot of the time it would be dark by the time I made it back to the house. I don't recall my parents ever voicing a concern over my absence. There were a couple of times, somewhere between the ages of five and seven, that it got too dark to find my way back, so I just settled down alongside the road and waited for someone to come along who would take me home.

One time they sent a search party out to find me. I remember that one well; I should say I remember the look on my dad's face when he grabbed me. I remember the licking that followed as well, but nothing, not even a good licking, could curb my desire to go exploring.

The Ravine

This was the first essay I ever wrote, and it deals with my early childhood in Highgrove. I believe I wrote it over 50 years ago. I kept it in a file folder and transcribed it to MS Word a few years back.

Highgrove was very rural in the early '40s, and a block south of our house was a ravine where I did most of my exploring. I was very adventurous in my youth and would explore tirelessly all day, only returning home to eat and sleep. This ravine supplied me with many adventures, up to the age of seven when we moved away. Some adventures were nearly tragic.

I used to dream very vivid dreams when I was young. One night I dreamt I was able to run down the cliff into the ravine, jump into the air, and soar away over the ravine. I could see the rabbits running under me, and I could clearly see the landscape of the ravine beneath me. The dream was so vivid that I actually believed I could fly. The next morning I hurried down and stood on the cliff overlooking the ravine. I started running down into the ravine with all the confidence in the world that I was about to go soaring. I lifted off and soared right down the cliff and hit the bottom. The pain in my right ankle was so excruciating that all I could do for a while was just sit and wait for the pain to go away.

No one ever came near the ravine in those days, so I had no choice but to get myself out. It took me several hours to crawl back to the house and get help. The ankle was not broken, but it was badly sprained and would plague me for the rest of my childhood.

One day I was playing around a drainpipe that went from the roadway down into the ravine. I haven't any recollection of the drainpipe's size, but it might have been approximately 12 inches in diameter and maybe 20 feet long. There must have been something in it that attracted my attention because I reached down into the pipe and all of a sudden realized that I couldn't back out. I was stuck in that pipe.

Looking back on it now, I probably would have been better off if I had just stayed put in the hopes someone would drive down the road and see my feet sticking out of the pipe. But at that time my only thoughts were to get out of the pipe. It was full of brush, rocks, insects, spiders, etc. I started to crawl down through the pipe, pushing all the debris in front of me as I progressed. I finally made it out of the pipe at the bottom with only a few scratches but in desperate need of a bath.

That incident could have been tragic if I had become stuck near the middle of that pipe. Nobody knew where I was, and finding me in that pipe would have been very difficult.

As I said, I was a very adventurous boy, and search parties were sent out several times to find me while we lived in Highgrove. A good licking followed all of the recoveries, but they never seemed to stop my need to explore.

That ravine in Highgrove supplied me with numerous adventures until the day we moved to Riverside from Highgrove after my brother died in 1946. Ironically, we moved back into the same house on Lime Street that my brother was born in 12 years before.

That was when I met my friend Doug, who had an adventurous spirit as strong as mine. We began a new life in Riverside of exploring and enjoying a lifetime of adventures together.

Bebe's

There was a place in Long Beach called Bebe's. It was a place where the elderly people would go to replenish themselves. My Grandmother Hoagland and Aunt Norma would go there quite frequently, and my sister Joyce and I would always ride down with them, often staying for a couple of days. We would have a great time playing and running around, and there were always children of our age to play with. Bebe's used to show movies there by using the wall on the side of the building for their screen.

I think that Bebe's was a scam. They had a lot of patio space, and instead of having a roof on top of the patio structure, it was covered with copper wires running horizontal across it. There were wires connected to the horizontal wires, and they would come vertically straight down and stop about three feet off the ground. The elderly people would sit at the benches under these wires and hold onto them. I guess the ions coming off those wires were curing the ailments in their bodies. My grandmother always brought several gallon jugs of water and would set them on the picnic tables under the wires. She would put the wires into the jugs to purify the water—or whatever it was supposed to do—and haul them home for later use.

My biggest memory was lying on the sand late at night and listening to the B17s and B25s flying over to fight the war in the Pacific. Every time one of the old borate bombers flies over now, it reminds me of those warm nights, lying in the cool sand at Long Beach.

Camp Haan

Camp Haan was located across the interstate from March Field. It was originally a quartermaster depot, but in 1940 it was set up to be a coast artillery antiaircraft training facility. My dad was 4F from the military because of injuries suffered when his gun turret blew up while he was stationed on the USS *Mississippi*. He wanted to help with the war effort, so he drove a bus out at Camp Haan and hauled the GIs around. I used to ride with him during those trips.

One of my memories is of sitting with my parents at the base, watching a USO show. I still remember several entertainers walking back and forth across the stage, holding up a cardboard jeep as if they were riding in it and singing away. I couldn't have been more than five or six, but it tickled me so much that it is etched in my memory.

Near the end of the war they realized there wasn't any need for antiaircraft batteries, and a lot of men were being lost in the Pacific Theater. They started replacing the fallen troops with the men from Camp Haan who had been trained to operate the antiaircraft batteries. My dad would haul those GIs to the troop trains when they were shipped to the Pacific. There would be women and children there to send them off. I remember it quite well because there was a lot of crying and ruckus going on. I was too young to realize why everybody was crying and that the men were possibly going to their doom.

Childhood Memories

It's funny how childhood memories work. You think you remember something from your youth, but you're not sure if it's an actual memory, dream, or just your imagination. Following are some of my recollections.

We moved from San Bernardino to Highgrove when I was an infant. I have no knowledge of when, but I believe I was too young to even walk. People say you have no memories of your infancy, so my memories may just be dreams.

The Chair: I remember with extreme clarity being on the front porch of the Highgrove house. I believe I was sitting in an infant chair of some type, because I wasn't moving around. There was a Ford pickup taking off across the front yard with a dining room chair in the bed of the truck. Somebody yelled and the pickup stopped abruptly. An arm reached out from the driver's side window, grabbed the chair, lifted it out, and set it on the lawn. Then the truck took off, speeding away.

I guess the event was so unusual that it stuck in my mind. I asked my mother many years later about the incident, but she just said I was too young to remember anything during that time, and I must have overheard someone talking about it. One day I was looking through an old family picture album at my grandmother's house and there was a picture of my dad with another man I didn't recognize standing in front of a 1935 Ford pickup. That pickup looked just like the one I remember seeing during that incident.

Beekeeper: I remember watching my dad and his mother looking over and discussing the repair of a bunch of rabbit hutches in the back yard of the Highgrove house. I have no idea if I was able to walk at that time, but I do remember I wasn't able to talk, although I was able to understand what they were talking about.

Our next-door neighbor came walking by in a beekeeping outfit. He was apparently going down to the ravine to maintain some beehives. They started talking about him; they thought he was just a bum walking by. Now, I have no idea how I knew it was our neighbor in a beekeeping outfit, but I just knew. I tried to tell them who he was, but they couldn't understand my baby talk.

I always encouraged my children to talk to their babies in plain English, never baby talk. I feel from my experiences that babies understand you perfectly but just haven't developed speech patterns yet.

Boy in Drag: I was, as a baby, very pretty, with long, curly blond hair. One day, in Highgrove, my parents assigned some neighborhood girls to babysit me. After my parents left, the girls put me in a highchair, put my hair in curlers, and dressed me up like a girl. They then took me out on the street and, with each one holding a hand, walked me up and down the street for everyone to see. (God, I wish I could get rid of that memory.) That episode traumatized me so severely that I cannot watch a movie or newsfeed or be around where men are dressed like women.

Planes, Trains & Tools: I used to dream a lot about toy electric trains loaded with tools coming through the walls. And I dreamed about airplanes. (The old boxcar types of airplanes.) I have no idea why I would have any knowledge of old airplanes or tools, but possibly the transfer of memories can come through genetic transfers, as some scientists have suggested, or maybe re-incarnation does exist. I do know I dreamed about a lot of stuff that I shouldn't have had any experience or knowledge of for a person my age.

Lying

When I was young my big sister, older than me by 15 months, was a daddy's girl. To say she was spoiled would be an understatement. I must say that to a point I was spoiled as well. My father was adamant, however, that a man is never to strike a girl, and I have held to that standard throughout my life.

My sister held Daddy as a club over my head to get whatever she wanted. If I had a toy or a treat that she wanted, she would tell me to give it to her, and she would start crying and screaming that I hit her if I refused. The response from my father was always the same: I knew a severe beating was to ensue.

During a couple of these beatings, he yanked so hard on my arm that it tore the ligaments in my shoulder, and that shoulder has hurt throughout my life. Dad would always start the punishment in the same manner. He would yell, "Why did you hit her"

I would always respond with the truth, stating, "I didn't hit her."

This would infuriate him even further, and he would scream, "I hate a liar worse than a thief," and the punishment would become even more severe.

The beating would go on until my father got tired and or decided that I wasn't going to admit that I hit her. I would never have given in and said I had hit her, even if it meant me being beaten to death.

I ran away after one of the beatings and hid out pretty well for a couple of days until a search party found me. It wasn't pleasant having to return home.

One day, when we were living in the Riverside house, I was chopping firewood. I was using a hatchet, making kindling, and my sister was at the back of the yard. The yards were at least 300 feet deep in those days, and she was clear at the back near the alley that ran behind the yard. I can't remember what was said, but she started crying and running towards the house, screaming that she was going to tell Daddy that I hit her. I got so angry and scared that I threw the hatchet at her, and it hit her just above the right eye. The blood started gushing out of her head. Fortunately, the hatchet had turned in the air, and the back of the hatchet hit her. If the sharp end had hit her, it probably would have killed her.

I ran over and just as I picked up the hatchet, Mom and Dad came running out to see what all the commotions was about. My parents were horrified, looking at my sister lying on the ground with blood gushing out of her head and me standing over her with that hatchet in my hand. My dad screamed, "What are you doing?"

I answered back, "Every time I have something she wants and I won't give it to her, she runs to you and says I hit her, and you beat the heck out of me. This is the first time I have ever hit her, and now I am going to kill her. That way this will be the last beating I will ever have to receive from you."

I have never seen my dad move so fast in my life. He tackled me and got that hatchet away from me so fast I didn't even see him coming. He scooped my sister up, and he and Mom rushed her to the hospital.

I figured I would be dead when they came back, so I packed up a few possessions and literally headed for the hills. A few days later a search party found me and took me home. I feared for my life, but when I got home nothing was said about the incident. My sister never accused me of hitting her again, and I can't remember my dad ever punishing me for anything after that day.

A few years ago I was visiting my sister and we were sitting there talking, and I noticed the scar over her eye. I said, "My God, I forgot about that scar."

My sister looked at me with the most pitiful look on her face and said, in a most sorrowful voice, "I hope you don't hate me, because I really do love you."

I couldn't help it. The look on her face and her voice was so forlorn that I burst out in hilarious laughter. I realized that she has been carrying guilt from that incident her entire life.

This trauma in my early life has left some lasting imprints on my personality. Every time someone accuses me of lying, all the feelings of helplessness and despair return, and I become so angry that I want to lash out and hurt somebody for the hurt that I feel. I find that I have to retreat and get away from the situation before someone does get hurt, because it's not likely to be me.

Cardboard Boxes

My best friend Doug lived in a trailer behind his grandparents' home on Orange Street in Riverside. There was a large lot next door that we spent a lot of time playing on. This lot was located on the southwest corner of Orange and Russell streets and was fronted on Orange Street to the east and Main Street to the west. The lot went back level about 200 feet and then dropped abruptly for another 200 feet to the level of Main Street. This drop-off created a steep embankment and was a virtual playground for a bunch of young kids.

There was an electric shop and an appliance store on this property that fronted on Main Street. The appliance store always had large cardboard boxes that had housed washers, dryers, refrigerators, etc. These boxes were a godsend to a couple of adventuring boys. We made forts out of them; we put them on the old paper wagon and made army tanks out of them. They had a multitude of uses that only a young boy's imagination could come up with.

One of the fun things we used to do was seal each other up in one of the washer or dryer boxes and then push the box over the edge of the steep embankment. It was a blast, tumbling over and over as we rolled down to the Main Street level. Fortunately, we were never hurt in such a stupid endeavor.

Meeting my Lifelong Friend Doug

My big brother died in 1946 while we were living in Highgrove, and by the time I was seven we relocated to a house on Lime Street in Riverside. I guess the memories of the Highgrove house were too much for my parents to bear. When I became an adult, my Grandmother Layton told me that my brother was born in the house on Lime Street. I look back at pictures of my brother when he was two or three years old and realize that the hedges behind him in those pictures are the same hedges that grew along the south property line at the Lime Street house. My parents were possibly trying to relive old and happy memories by moving back.

Looking back today, I realize there were a lot of pictures of us taken while my big brother was alive, and none after that. The only pictures I have of our childhood in Riverside are the ones I took.

Somewhere around the age of seven or eight, I met my lifelong friend Doug. From then on, my exploring was done in partnership with him. We would explore all over the Riverside area. Nothing was left to chance.

Riverside was changing in those days. The orange groves were starting to come down, the land was being cleared, and every time we saw the smoke from a bulldozer we went to investigate.

Doug had some problems at home that were very sad, and I won't deal with his hardships, but after his mother's accident in 1955, he moved to San Bernardino to live with his dad. We didn't see much of each other after that for a few years.

I went on playing with cars and built the old camping truck that I have written about in another essay. I took that camping truck on adventures all over California and Mexico. I was only 15 at the time, yet I drove that truck thousands of miles without ever getting caught.

I believe I was about 17 when I wrecked the truck and destroyed it.

The Radio

In the days of my youth, from the '40s to the early '50s, radio was the means of distraction in the home, much as TV is today. We had a console radio in the living room that was a good four feet high and two feet wide. There was only AM in those days, and some of the broadcasts came in pretty noisy.

There were always children's shows on in the afternoons after school, so we would hurry home to listen to "The Lone Ranger," "The Cisco Kid," "Gene Autry," and my favorite, "Bobby Bensen at the B-Bar-B Ranch." I found out later in life that Bobby Bensen, the young kid who ran his own ranch, was actually a 40-year-old actor, but he really stirred the imagination of an 11-year-old boy.

I had many adventures riding along with Bobby as we captured cattle rustlers and helped the damsel in distress. I discovered later in life, after driving trucks through the Big Bend country, that my imagination didn't produce the same topography as actually existed there. In my imagination the Big Bend country looked more like the topography around southern California.

In the early '50s I acquired a table radio. That little radio, about the size of a microwave oven, afforded the opportunity to listen to the radio in bed. I would listen to "Inner Sanctum" and "The Shadow." "Inner Sanctum" always started with a screeching door opening, accompanied by a horrid, evil laugh. "The Shadow" always started with the lines, "What evil lurks in the heart of man? Only the Shadow knows." Those programs always scared the heck out of me, and I would cover my head with a blanket to keep the boogeyman from getting me.

Many evenings we would sit on the living room floor around the radio in that Lime Street house, listening to our parents' favorite programs. There was "Fibber McGee and Molly." It was always a laugh when Fibber McGee opened his closet and you heard all the stuff falling out. Your imagination would run wild, seeing all those pots and pans, golf clubs, suitcases, etc.

falling out onto the floor from that overstuffed closet.

Then there was the "Jack Benny Show" with Jack and Rochester. Jack was supposed to be a tight, penny pincher, but in real life he was a very generous man. It was always fun when he would go down to his safe in the basement to get a dollar from the safe. You would hear him walking down the stairs into the basement. It seemed like a hundred steps, and your imagination would take you deep into a dingy, musty basement.

Then he would go through a half-dozen locked, creaking doors—you could see them in your mind—until he finally arrived at the safe. You could just visualize that huge safe door with the big combination lock clicking as he turned the dial and you heard the tumblers falling into place. Finally, the door opened, and in your mind you could actually see that big door opening as you heard the scraping of metal and the rusty creaking of those old hinges.

A lot was said about Jack's Maxwell automobile. When Rochester fired up that old Maxwell and they headed to town, you could almost see that old car, Rochester sitting in the driver's seat and Jack sitting in the back as they headed downtown. It's amazing that you were sitting there in your living room, listening to a radio, but your mind could visualize what was happening. The imagination is an amazing thing.

Then there were the variety shows. The "Blondie and Dagwood Show," "Amos and Andy," "The Bob Hope Show," and so many more. It was definitely a golden era. I often wish I could climb into a time machine and go back to that living room floor and do it one more time and just savor it.

A Halloween Scare

The Halloween holiday nears and brings back a flood of memories of my youth. During our younger years, my lifelong friend Doug and I had many adventures on Halloween. One that comes to mind happened when we were about 12 years of age.

My parents' home on Lime Street in Riverside had a large lot with a walkway of about 60 feet in length from the sidewalk to the front porch. I was always a techno nut, so I put a couple of jack-o-lanterns along the walkway. One was located near the intersection of the sidewalk and the walkway; the other one was located on the porch near the front door. I hooked up speakers to an amplifier and placed one behind each jack-o-lantern.

I had hooked up a recorder to the amplifier and it emitted cricket sounds and moans and groans that I had recorded from some Halloween programs on the radio. I had also hooked up a microphone so that we could add comments for special occasions.

Doug and I hid behind an old couch that had full view of the porch and walkway. The couch was located under a tree and sat far enough back in the yard that it was unnoticeable in the darkness.

We started hooting and groaning into the microphone as the evening progressed and were having a great time scaring the little kids. Doug was really getting carried away and became quite good at making these really scary sounds. One little guy came to the porch dressed as a ghost, and Doug started in on him. I don't remember the exact words, but it went something like, "Hey, little ghost, you look yummy to me. I think I will eat you."

The poor little guy let out a scream, dropped his candy, and ran back towards the sidewalk. As he approached the other speaker, Doug said, "You cannot get away from me, yummy little ghost." The poor kid was panicked by then, realizing the monster was all around him and he couldn't get away. He went screaming and running down the sidewalk, heading out of sight.

We grabbed his bag of candy and went running after him

to give him back his candy and assure him that everything was all right and that there weren't any monsters. Our running with the bag of candy attracted a bunch of older guys who confronted us and accused us of stealing candy from children. We had to do some fast talking to explain what had happened before we got our lights punched out by those guys.

The little ghost was far out of sight by the time we convinced the guys that it was a harmless prank. (Hopefully, it was harmless.) We searched all over for the little ghost, but he was gone. The poor little guy never did get his candy back.

We went back to the house and gave up for the night. It was getting late, and all the trick-or-treaters had cleared the streets. My mother commented later that we didn't have nearly as many kids that year as the year before. I didn't tell her we scared most of them away.

Andulka Park

My lifelong friend Doug and I were constantly exploring the area around Riverside. I think we knew every nook and cranny in the area. There wasn't a ravine or a cave we didn't explore. The population of Riverside was less than 50,000 in the days of my youth, but a rapid growth started in the mid-'50s.

At that time much of the area in and around Riverside was covered by citrus groves. The local tax collector started raising taxes on the groves to the point that the citrus industry was no longer able to make a reasonable profit, so the grove owners started selling the land to developers for huge profits, and the building boom began. Soon the groves started coming down and the land was being cleared.

When we were young the Canyon Crest area was just groves with an occasional mansion here and there. There was hardly any smog and you could see for miles. Every time we saw black smoke, we knew bulldozers were clearing land and the citrus trees were being burned. We would follow the smoke to see where the latest action was.

The whole area around Chicago Avenue was orange groves in those days. There was a bowling alley—I believe it was called Tava Lanes—on the southwest corner of Eighth and Chicago, but there was nothing but orange groves farther south on Chicago.

One day Doug and I found this old, burned-out house west of Chicago Avenue and south of Eighth Street. We explored the house and the area around it. We went back several times and played around the old house. I took a picture of Doug standing in front of the house, and he took one of me standing in the doorway. The pictures are dated December, 1956.

One day we went back to the house to play. It was gone and the bulldozers were clearing the land. We went back over the next few weeks to watch the progress of the construction. It became obvious they were creating a bowl for a lake, complete with an inlet and outlet for an aeration system. They were planning to build high-end housing around the shore of the lake, and they planted huge palm trees around what was going to be the shoreline. I took a picture of Doug standing in the bottom of the lake near the suction for the aeration system. This picture is dated December, 1956 as well. It was taken just a few days before they were to start filling the lake.

I was looking at my pictures a few months ago and ran across these pictures, and I started wondering whatever happened to the lake. I got on Google Earth, looking for a lake in the area, but I couldn't find one. I called Doug and asked him if he had any recollection about the lake and the area. He told me they couldn't keep water in the lake. The ground was too porous and the water would drain out so quickly that it was too expensive to maintain, so they just abandoned the project.

Doug told me he thought the Curcis and several other families, possibly including the Tavagliones, were involved in developing the lake. I can't remember what the project name was, but Doug said there is a park there now where the lake was. He couldn't remember the name of the park, so I looked in the area off Chicago Avenue and found Andulka Park. I called Doug back and described what I found, and he said, "That was it."

So there you have it. Andulka Park is sitting smack dab in the middle of what is a defunct lake.

(Photographs on pages 207 and 208.)

Riverside's New Phone System,

I don't know how many remember the old party line telephone system in Riverside. You used to have to pick up the phone and listen to make sure someone on your party line wasn't using the phone. If no one else was on the line, the telephone operator would come on the line and say, "Number Please." You would then say a number, like, "Overland 6234," and she would reply with, "Thank You" and would connect you.

The old phones were plain and had a smooth face with no dial and a small round ring with a plastic window in it. This ring was about an inch and a half in diameter and was located in the center on the front of the phone. You unsnapped the ring and put your phone number under it and when you snapped the ring back on, the phone number showed through the plastic window.

I had "tinker-i-tis"—my dad's word—and couldn't keep my hands off anything mechanical or electrical. I was soon moving around and adding phones to our house. (There was an ample supply of old telephones in the surplus stores in those days.) I was only about ten or 11 years old and didn't really have an understanding of a phone system at that time, but how hard could it be. Right? Only two wires. How could you mess up with only two wires?

Well, some of the phones would ring and the others wouldn't. I couldn't figure it out. Then, when you answered some of the ringing phones, it would be the party line. How come the party line's phone was ringing from my phone, and some of the other phones would ring when it was for our party line phone?

It took a while, but I finally figured out that the two wires needed to be one direction for the party line, and I needed to reverse them for our phones. I finally got all the phones in the house working right.

Somewhere in the early '50s—I don't remember the exact date—they converted our phone system to a rotary dial system. These phones looked identical to the old phones, but on the front of each phone was this funny-looking, round thing, about three and a half inches in diameter.

This odd round thing had ten holes in it, numbered from one to zero. It had a little stop in it so when you put your finger in the hole, you could only spin it so far. It was called a rotary dial. (I guess because it dialed and it rotated.)

The phone company spent months going to each home and changing out the old phones with the new, rotary dial phones. We continued using the new phones in the same manner as the old ones until the change-over to the new system was completed.

The phone company installers were shocked when they showed up at our place and saw the mess I made of our phone system. They ended up ripping out all my hard work.

When they finally got all the phones installed and tested, they scheduled a date to switch over to the new system. Everybody in the city was so excited to get this new technology, and the new phones were the talk of the town. (I believe this date was October 17, 1954)

At five p.m. on the arranged date, the system switched over. I think everybody in the city picked up their phones that evening at five p.m. and started dialing. The system overloaded and blew every fuse in the system, taking down every phone in the city. Chaos ensued, and it was pretty hectic until the phone company got the system restored. I had a sister who was an operator and a brother-in-law who was a lineman, and they said all hell broke loose for a while. What a day, what a memory.

(Photograph on page 209.)

Saturday Matinees

Every Saturday morning they would have a matinee at the Golden State Theater on 7th Street in Riverside. The admission cost was 10¢ and a Doctor Pepper bottle cap.

We used to go by the soda pop vending machines and look in the pulled-bottle-cap drawer to find the Doctor Pepper bottle caps required for admittance, and then we would head for the show.

It was a lot of fun at the theater because they showed one movie and then an intermission, and they always had contests and door prizes during intermission. You could win money or candy during those intermissions, and the contests always created a lot of fun and excitement. I can still see us running up on the stage and doing the required stunts to earn the prizes. Then we would stick our hands into bags full of money or candy to retrieve our prizes.

I remember eating the candy in those boxes of Raisinets and then blowing in the empty boxes after the candy was gone. The noise those empty boxes produced was like the whistle on a train, and it was very annoying to the audience trying to watch the movie. It was even worse when you had four or five of us blowing in those empty candy boxes at the same time.

They always showed a Tarzan movie, followed after the intermission by a Western. (Usually, Roy Rogers or Gene Autry.)

It was a great time at the Saturday Matinees, and it has left me with fond memories of all the wonderful friends and the fun and laughter we shared on those Saturday mornings so long ago.

I started a growth surge when I was 11 years old; I was over six feet tall before I turned 13. At the time I was about a foot or so taller than all of my friends. I never realized I was that much taller than everybody else until later in life when I saw pictures that Doug's mother had taken of us at that age. It dawned on me, when I saw the pictures, that the theater manager must have thought that I was possibly over 18 and just wanted to start trouble with the little kids.

The manager would always pull me aside and threaten me with eviction from the theater or possibly even calling the police and having me arrested. I didn't understand at the time and told him I just wanted to come to the movies with my friends. I tried to convince him that I was only 12, but I don't know if he ever believed me. The manager always made me promise not to cause any trouble, or I would suffer the consequences. He would let me in after I promised I would behave. I went through that every week. You would think he could have figured it out after a couple of weeks.

(Photograph on page 210.)

Shooting the Rabbit

Back in my early teens my Uncle Jack and Aunt Ruth lived on some acreage at the top of Pigeon Pass, which is now Moreno Valley. Uncle Jack knew of my love for hunting and invited my best friend Doug and me up to hunt rabbits on his property. Doug and I strapped our shotguns to the handlebars of our bicycles and rode up to Uncle Jack's home for a day of hunting rabbits.

Uncle Jack was showing us around his property when a rabbit was startled. I popped off a shot and dropped the rabbit. Uncle Jack walked over, picked it up, and commented, "There isn't a mark on it."

Doug, always being quick witted, commented in his smart-aleck way, "We always shoot them in the head, that way the meat isn't ruined."

Uncle Jack pondered the statement for a few seconds and handed the rabbit to me.

I doubt I could have ever duplicated that shot!

The Burning Tail

Life was different in the '40s and '50s. We didn't have all the government restrictions rules and regulations that we have now. The law was pretty much ruled by common sense—something we now seem to be lacking

The yards were large in those days, and houses were barely within shouting distance of each other. Backyards didn't butt up to each other like they do now. There was always an alley between the backyards so you had road access to your backyard and separation from your neighbors.

Most homes had small animals in their backyards, mostly chickens, rabbits, and goats. People didn't run to the store for meat on a regular basis. Your mother would tell you to go out and get a rabbit or chicken for dinner, so you would go out back, grab a chicken out of the chicken coop, or a rabbit out of the rabbit hutch, kill, clean, and dress it, and take it to Mom to cook for dinner.

This proliferation of backyard animals meant the yards were always littered with trash. There were always piles of wood from dilapidated chicken coops, rabbit hutches, goat pens, various sheds, and small out buildings. It provided us kids with an endless supply of firewood. In the days of our youth, we often built a fire near the rear of the yard in the evening and sat and enjoyed the companionship of good friends around the warmth of those fires.

Our next-door lady was a drunk and crazy. Her son was killed in the war, and the grief apparently drove her crazy and turned her into an alcoholic.

The war was barely over, and I hadn't experienced the carnage and mutilation that war brought, so I was still romanticizing our great victory. In later years I would experience such horrors and soon realized there was no romance in war.

One night we had a fire going, and we were standing around the fire, watching and enjoying the red glow of the embers as they slowly drifted toward the sky. All of a sudden the quiet of the evening was broken by the wailing of a dog running down the alley towards us. The lady next door came running out to see what the ruckus was all about, and the dog spotted her and ran to her back door for help. She comforted the dog and then started screaming obscenities at us. We all stood around dumfounded and confused at this display of emotions. But we just attributed it to the fact that she was crazy and went on about the business of talking and enjoying the evening.

A little while later a group of cops showed up and separated us. They took me aside and asked me why we set the dog's tail on fire. We were all about 11 years old at the time and pretty intimidated by these large officers of the law. My response was apparently the same as everybody else's. I told the story about the dog running down the alley and running to the lady's house and her screaming at us. I told them the dog had never come near us, and we had no clue why the lady was screaming at us or that the dog's tail had been burned.

We must have all told the same story, because the cops just cautioned us about the fire and left. We never did find out how that dog's tail got burned, but I know none of the kids in our group would have done anything like that.

The Tank

During the '40s and early '50s, Food Machinery Corporation in Riverside manufactured small tanks that were called water buffalos. They used to test them in the lake and surrounding woods around Fairmont Park in Riverside. Doug and I used to go down to the park and watch the tests in amazement. They would run around the wooded area in the Santa Ana riverbed and mow down brush and small trees with those things. Then they would come over to the lake and run around in the lake with them. We were amazed that they could drive those things in the water without sinking them. I guess the government contract for making and testing them ended, because they stopped coming to the park for testing.

Doug and I were riding our bicycles around Fairmont Park one day in the fall of 1950 and discovered they had built a cement platform coming up out of the lake, right across the street from the American Legion Hall, and one of those tanks was sitting on the platform. We immediately had to do some exploring.

We got up on the tank, opened the hatches, and climbed inside. We were fascinated by all of the levers and controls inside. We immediately started playing war. We were busy operating all of the controls when all of a sudden we realized the tank was moving. It scared the heck out of us. We bailed off the tank and got out of the area before anybody saw us.

We went back a few weeks later, and the tank was back in position on the cement platform, so we decided it was time to play tank some more. We were really disappointed when we climbed back up on that tank and found all the hatches had been securely welded shut. This ended our ability to play tank, except in our imaginations.

We went back in October of 1953 and took three pictures of us on top of the tank. One was with Doug standing on the tank, one was with me squatting on the tank, and one was of us both squatting on the tank. We had to take the picture of both of us with the camera sitting on the tank, using a time-release shutter, and unfortunately, the tank isn't in the picture.

Doug and I have talked about going back, getting up on the tank, and taking a last picture 60 years later. But Doug is getting frail and is suffering from cancer, so I doubt he would be able to get up on the tank. I told him that if nothing else, we should get a picture of us standing in front of it.

My younger grandson, Hunter Layton, and I went to the tank in September of 2013 and took a picture of us standing in front of the tank. Hunter climbed onto the tank, and I handed him the camera. He took a picture of himself squatting on top of the tank, emulating the picture I had taken 60 years ago.

To this date Doug and I have never made it back to the tank for that picture. I have a feeling we shouldn't wait much longer.

(Photographs on pages 211 through 214.)

Doodlebugs

Most people don't have a clue what a Doodlebug is, but in the '40s and early '50s, they were very popular. They were a very small scooter with a 1.5-horsepower Briggs and Stratton engine in them. They would haul a small adult or a child with ease.

Doug and I had a couple of them, and I was always messing with things. I was able to build them up so they would perform fairly well. We could get 3-horsepower engines off old lawnmowers and adapt them to the Doodlebugs. Doug actually hooked his lawnmower up to his Doodlebug and towed the darn thing all the way to Highgrove on the weekends to mow lawns.

We used to ride all over Riverside on those things. We usually took the canal road to stay off the streets with them. I don't know if the cops were more lenient in those days, or we were just lucky, but I have no memory of being hassled riding those things around. I remember cops going by us and looking at us and just smiling. Doug did have one stop him one day. The cop checked him out, told he couldn't ride it on the street, and to go straight home with it.

As I have mentioned before, Doug lived next to a large vacant lot that was fairly level. It was fronted by Orange Street and went clear to Main Street on the back. It went back about 200 feet and then there was a cliff that dropped off about 30 feet to the level of Main Street. The grass and weeds would get about a foot high during the springtime and were very slippery when wet.

We used to go out there on the Doodlebugs and try to ride on the weeds and grass. It was extremely difficult to control them on that surface. If you cranked the throttle just a little too much, the things would just spin around in circles and throw you off. We used to go out there and have contests to see who could stay on the longest. We had more fun spinning those Doodlebugs. We would get thrown off on our rumps and laugh ourselves silly.

My dad had a friend named Berky. (That's the only name I knew him by.) He heard I was good at fixing up the Doodlebugs, so he bought one for his son and brought it to me to modify. I built the thing up by putting a 5-horsepower engine in it and changing the sprockets. I checked it out and it ran pretty good, so I took it out for a test drive. I went flying up Lime Street, and I think I was going about 50 miles per hour on that little thing. It was really flying, and about the time I got to Popular Street the thing went out from under me.

Later inspection showed the rear wheel had disintegrated. I guess that little wheel just couldn't take the stress of the horsepower and going that fast. I told Berky that he didn't want it for his kid and I would just put it back to stock as soon as I got back on my feet.

The accident tore the hide off the outside of my left leg and took the ankle down to the bone. I had to go to the hospital and get fixed up, then I had to go back every few days and have the scabs scraped off the wounds. I saw the brush they used; it just had regular soft bristles, but it felt like a wire brush. They kept putting antiseptic and a numbing agent on it while they were brushing those scabs off, but it didn't help much. I sure didn't look forward to my hospital visits.

Everybody in the hospital asked what happened every time I went in. I was too ashamed to admit I fell off a Doodlebug, so I just told them I crashed a motorcycle.

(Photograph on page 215.)

The Raft

One day when Doug and I were around 13, we were walking through the alleys in Riverside when we came upon some peeler cores that were being discarded. Now if you don't know what peeler cores are, they are wooded poles about three inches in diameter and six feet long. They are used for fences and borders for landscaping. The minute we saw them we knew they would be perfect for making a raft. We went back and got the wagon and used it to haul them back to my house.

We spent the next couple of days building this really cool raft. We mounted the mast, loaded the raft onto the wagon, and hauled it to Fairmont Park to launch it and have a great adventure rafting around the lake. One of the park officials saw us just as we reached the entrance of the park. He drove over and told us that we couldn't put the raft on the lake, so we just hung our heads in disappointment, turned around, and headed for home. But we kept our eyes on the park official as we were walking away. We turned around and headed back toward the park as soon as he drove out of sight.

There was an inlet on the northeast edge of the lake where the water emptied into the lake. We decided to launch the raft at that location. We pulled the wagon down to the edge of the water and slid the raft off and into the water. The raft floated and looked beautiful.

Doug was the first to step onto the raft. It immediately started to sink. Doug bailed off the raft and jumped onto the shore, suffering only a wet pair of shoes. We were immensely disappointed with our failure as raft builders. The raft had already drifted out onto the lake, so we were unable to retrieve it. There was nothing we could do but head home. Our rafting adventure had come to a close.

Over the next few weeks we would see the raft floating around the lake as we rode our bicycles around the park. One day the raft just disappeared.

One day in the spring of 2011, Doug called, all excited. He was watching the local PBS station, and they were doing a segment on the early days in Riverside. They were showing pictures of Riverside, and there was a picture of us launching the raft. Unbeknownst to us, someone had taken a picture of us that day. Doug called the station to see if he could get a copy of the picture, but they were unable to retrieve it. So even though I don't have the photo to prove it, Doug and I and our raft are part of Riverside history.

Flares

In the early '50s the mail was brought into Riverside by helicopter. There was a landing pad next to Radio Station KPRO on Russell Street, just inside of the curve where La Cadena Drive turns into Russell Street. The helicopter would always arrive after dark, and they would lay highway flares out to mark the landing pad. We would always await the arrival of the helicopter, and as soon as everybody had gone, we would retrieve the flares, extinguish them in the dirt, and save them for later.

We had more fun with those flares. You could break them apart and make fuses out of them and pretend that you were blowing up buildings, bridges, etc.—anything your mind could conjure up. You have to remember that back then only the rich had a television in their homes, and the only stimuli you had if you were poor were comic books, radio, the Saturday morning matinee at the movie theater, and your imagination.

One night we got the brainy idea of lighting several of the flares and placing them across the main highway into Riverside, which at that time was Russell Street. We placed them across Russell Street at the corner of Orange Street. That way we could lie in the bushes in our friend Johnnie's front yard and watch what might happen.

It wasn't long before all the cars were stopped, and people were getting out of their cars and walking around, wondering what was going on. We could see headlights stopped clear around the curve past the KPRO radio station. Man, it was "cool." We were having a good time until all of a sudden police cars started arriving. The policemen got out of their cars and started fanning out and checking the area. It scared the heck out of us, and we all slipped around the back of Johnnie's house and hid in his parents' wine cellar until everybody was gone and the area quieted down.

I suppose no one would have suspected us if we had just walked out of the bushes into the street and acted like we were curious as to what was going on, but our guilt made us run and hide. It scared us so badly that we never pulled another stunt like that again.

Gary the Gopher

When I was 12 years old, I was walking home after finishing my paper route, and I passed by a trench that had just been dug for a pipeline. I spotted a gopher running around in the trench, trying to get out. I went down in the trench and picked him up. He immediately bit me on the thumb and I dropped him. I took off my shirt and wrapped it around him so I could pick him up without getting bitten again. I put him in the wagon and went home, with him running around in the wagon.

I made the gopher a home out of a large box and filled it with dirt. I put a board over the top of it with a couple of holes in it. I would put a carrot in one of the holes and watch as he pulled it down. I would pull the board off the top every few days and examine the tunnels he had dug. I was able after time to actually pick him up and play with him without getting bitten. I played with him every day, and he seemed to enjoy playing with me. I ended up naming him Gary.

One day I put a carrot in the hole, but he didn't pull it down. I lifted the board off—he was dead. I buried Gary alongside the house, then I etched his name in a rock and put it on top of his grave.

I went by Lime Street after I grew up to see if I could retrieve the rock, but the house was gone and there was a large apartment house in its place. So it is all in the past.

Ice Cream Wagon

The industrial complex in Riverside had large factories that were built to support the war movement, and after the Second World War, they utilized these factories for domestic production. They built everything from washers and dryers to refrigerators. They were able to bring the prices down on these items to the point where the average working family could afford them. People started changing out their iceboxes for the more efficient, new-fangled refrigerators, and soon every yard and alley had these iceboxes piled up.

Doug and I were about 11 years old, and one day we spotted a really nice, double-door icebox. We loaded it on the wagon and hauled it over to my house. We took the wheels off an old wagon, put them on the icebox, and made it so we could pull it around.

In those days we didn't have freeways. All the traffic was confined to city streets and rural highways between cities. In Riverside the traffic would come in from Colton and Redlands on La Cadena Drive, make the turn onto Russell Street, and then down to Main Street. There was a stop sign at the corner of Russell and Main where the traffic would turn left to First Street then right to Market Street. They would then turn left on Market Street and go all the way through Riverside, heading for Corona and the beach cities.

Now, Doug was a real salesman. He could, as the old saying goes, "sell an icebox to an Eskimo." We went over to the Swift packing plant on Main Street. Doug talked the plant manager into selling us ice cream bars and dry ice. The Swift plant was about halfway between Russell Street and the railroad underpass on North Main Street, so it was an easy pull with the homemade ice cream wagon back to the intersection of Russell and Main streets.

Cars back in those days did not have air conditioning, so on hot summer days, you drove around with your windows down and just suffered. There was nothing between Colton and the intersection of Main and Russell streets in those days, so people were pretty hot and tired by the time they made the long journey from Colton to the stop sign to turn onto Main Street.

We would wait until the heat of the day, go by the Swift plant to pick up the ice cream bars and some dry ice, and head for the Russell Street stop sign. We sold a lot of ice cream to the travelers. Almost every car would purchase ice cream from us. We made some pretty good money until one day a local businessman drove by and saw what we were doing. He went to the Swift plant and raised heck with the manager and they refused to sell us any more ice cream. We were out of business; time to go on to another venture.

Mulberry Street Ravine

Riverside in the '40s was a small city and was still rural. We lived on the north end of town, and most of the population was south of us, so there was a lot of rural area to explore. I remember one ravine quite well. It was south of us about a half mile, near Mulberry Street and the railroad tracks. The tracks are gone now, and the freeway runs over the top of where the ravine was. Mulberry Street now veers to the right where the ravine was and the land is all level now.

That ravine must have been somebody's private property, because it was all terraced with beautiful rock walls and had all kinds of vegetation planted on the terraces. It was about 150 feet wide, with rock-and-mortar terraces on both sides, and was only about 25 or 30 feet deep. Rose bushes, vines, and flowers abounded. The fragrances of those flowers filled the air with sweet smells. There were springs with water flowing everywhere.

I used to love to hang out in there, mainly in the summer. It would get over 100 degrees in Riverside in the summer, but the ravine would be cool—in the '80s—so I spent a lot of time playing down there.

Freemont Elementary burned in 1948, and I attended Longfellow Elementary while Freemont was being rebuilt. I walked to Longfellow every day, and I would always walk through that ravine on my way to and from school. To this day I still remember the smell of the vegetation in that ravine. It is one of my fondest memories.

I did not like riding on school busses, and I walked to school my entire life. One day while I was attending Longfellow, I decided to ride the bus. I got on the wrong bus and rode it to the last stop, which was near Arlington. The bus driver would not let me ride the bus back to the school. He made me get off the bus eight miles from my house. You have to remember that Longfellow Elementary was probably less than a mile from my house. It was a long walk home, and that was the last school bus I was ever on, even when I went to Central Jr. High School, which was a two-and-a-half-mile walk.

I used to ride my bicycle or walk to Central Jr. High. I enjoyed the walk because it always afforded me time to explore. The evening walk home would sometimes take several hours, due to getting sidetracked by my endless curiosity.

I started walking to Central Jr. High with a girl who lived near my home, and we would walk to and from school together. There was a soda fountain in Kustner's on Main Street. We would always stop there and share a cherry Coke together. I never cared much for the cherry Coke but sure enjoyed the company it afforded. We would just sit there, sucking on that cherry Coke and enjoying some good conversation. I am not sure of her name, but it might have been Lucy. She paired up with another girl from the neighborhood, and they started walking together and I was out. Our relationship, like all my others, fizzled. As with all my relationships, I often wonder how her life turned out. I hope she had a happy, long life.

My friend Doug was attending Lincoln Jr. High, so we weren't seeing much of each other during those times. I palled up with a guy name Iden. Iden live up on Hoover Street and was an electronic nut like I was. We would ride up to his house after school and play with his radios. I would then ride home on the canal road all the way down to my place, which kept me from having to ride my bike on city streets.

Iden and I built crystal sets and mounted them on our bicycles. We had these long, whip antennas so we could get reception. People would stop us and inquire about the long antennas and the fact that we were wearing earphones. We would let them put the earphones on, and they would be amazed when they heard music coming out of those earphones. You have to remember that not a lot of cars had radios in them in those days, and portable radios were non-existent until years later.

During those days, we used to go back and forth between each other's houses on that canal road. We would, on a weekend, ride several times a day back and forth. I plotted it out recently; it was a nine-mile trip, and we didn't even think about it. Most kids nowadays would complain if they had to ride a bicycle more than a block!

Iden and I have remained friends throughout the years.

My Athletic Ability

First let me state that I am not an athlete, I am a mechanic. I can fix almost anything, I can build almost anything, and I can make almost anything, but I am so uncoordinated that if you throw a ball at me, it will hit me in the face.

That did not stop me from playing sandlot baseball and football ball with my friends. We used to play football on the front lawn at Radio Station KPRO on Russell Street in Riverside. I was always the favorite player and each team would argue about getting me on their team. I was much larger, heavier, and stronger than the other kids my age, so that afforded me the honor of being the star football player.

The football games were always one sided. The opposing team could never get a player through me to get a touchdown, and I always carried the ball when we were on offense. My friend Doug still laughs to this day about me running for those touchdowns. He said it reminded him of an opossum running with all of it babies clinging to its back.

The radio station had a nice, large front lawn, and there was a hedge on the west side of the lawn that ran all the way from the street to the building. That hedge was the goalpost, and I would just run right into the hedge for the touchdown, with all the guys piled on my back. Every once in a while, they would trip me and I would fall down. I would lay the ball down to get up, and one of the guys would kick the ball and holler fumble, and they would scramble to take possession. I was such a lunkhead that I fell for it every time.

I had such a rapid growth spurt at 11 that I developed a heart problem. I think my heart was just too small to pump the blood through that big body, and when I exerted myself too much, my heart would go into double time, and I would get lightheaded and start passing out. The guys were all used to it, and when it happened, they would just drag me off the field and continue playing until my heart went back to normal and I could continue.

We always drew a crowd when we played, and one day this guy decided to start coaching us. He was a pretty good coach and was quite helpful, but when my heart started acting up and the guys started dragging me off the field, he came running over to see what the injury was. The guys just said, "No problem. He just has a bad heart," and they just dropped me and went back to playing like nothing happened. I will never forget the look of fear on that guy's face. He never came back to coach us again.

We always played baseball at the Fremont Elementary School baseball field off North Orange Street in Riverside, and I always played right field. I played deep because I couldn't catch the ball, so if the ball was hit to me, I could run up, pick it up, and throw it in. I had a good arm and could throw the ball a good 300 feet, and I was quite accurate with my throws. I was a good batter and could easily knock it to the fence almost every time I got up to bat.

Doug was a good pitcher but he only had a fastball. He had pretty good control, and that thing zinged as it went by. I used to be his batter when he practiced pitching. Or maybe I should say "his target." I was hit quite often. One time one of those fastballs hit me square on the right bicep and it hurt. I had a baseball-size bruise on that bicep for weeks.

Doug then started practicing with tennis balls because they didn't hurt as much when they hit me. I got to the point where I could hit those fastballs pretty well. Our friend Johnny lived across the street from Doug, and I would try to hit those tennis balls into his swimming pool. It was about 200 feet over to his pool from Doug's driveway, and I got to where I could put them in the pool pretty accurately. Doug often talks about me hitting those tennis balls into Johnny's pool.

One day a bunch of us were down at Fremont Elementary playing ball, and a couple of kids about our age came by and asked if we would like to play a game against their team. We didn't know who these guys were, but we said sure, so they set the date, time, and place to meet. We didn't think any more of it and went on playing.

I was attending Central Jr. High School at the time, and a few days later I started hearing people talking about how some guys were going to play a game at a particular field. The time and date coincided with our game. I noticed as time went on that the talk all around school was about how these guys were going to kick our butts. There was a lot of trash talking going on, and I still didn't know who these guys were.

Doug attended University Junior High and wasn't hearing the talk, so I told Doug about it and he was really surprised. We thought this was just going to be a bunch of guys getting together to have a friendly game.

I can't remember where we met for the game; it might have been De Anza Park, but I'm not sure. I do remember I was surprised at the field. There were actual lines, a batter's box, coaches' boxes and, of all things, real base bags and an actual home plate. That was a far cry from the torn-off pieces of cardboard we used for our bases and home plate. There were bleachers, and they were half full of people there to watch the game. We all huddled together and started talking, wondering what the heck was going on. We finally decided we had come to play ball, and we were going to stick around and play.

This church bus came driving up, and all these kids got off, wearing these really nice uniforms, complete with bags full of equipment, and they all even had cleats on. It was quite a clash with us standing there in torn Levi's and T-shirts. Most of us were wearing worn-out tennis shoes, and I don't think even half of us had baseball caps. Our gloves were worn out and secondhand, and mine didn't even have the trap or web in it. It had rotted off years before. The final straw was when these two guys in their late teens or early twenties stepped off the bus in full umpire uniform regalia, including chest protectors and facemasks. We thought we were screwed. But there was no way we were going to quit.

We all lined up on the field, and the umpires went over the rules and did the coin toss. We lost, so the other team got home field advantage. The other team took the field, and we took our turn at bat. We ended up getting the bases loaded without any outs.

I got up to bat and couldn't get used to the pitcher. I got a couple of strikes and balls on me. The pitcher had little control and no speed on the ball, and it was difficult to time my swing after being used to hitting Doug's fastball. I finally hit the ball up against the fence, and with the outfielders playing up short, I was able to make it all the way to third. The next batter hit me in, and several more runs were scored before they got us out.

We took the field and the other team came up to bat. Doug threw his fastball to the first batter, and you should have seen the look on his face. He lowered the bat, looked at his team, and shrugged his shoulders. We could see him saying, "What the heck was that?" Doug was in tune and threw two more right down the pipe then struck the next two batters out. This went on for four innings until finally, Doug's arm gave out and he started walking guys, so we took him out and put Early in as the pitcher.

Early wasn't that great of a pitcher, so they started getting hits and runs off him, but we always made them up when we came up to bat.

Our little rag-tag team humiliated those guys in front of a bleacher full of friends. That's why you shouldn't start trash talking until the contest is over.

The Boy Scouts

At the south end of the riverbottom near the 7th Street Bridge in Riverside was the local Boy Scout camp. Doug and I both joined the Boy Scouts and spent quite a bit of time at that camp. We would spend our summers in a place called Camp Emerson in the Idyllwild area.

I always had a natural ability to do just about anything that was mechanical, so I always did well in the competitions when it came to building shelters, basic rope-tying competitions, etc. I got so many merit badges that I was finally given the first class rank. I could tie a knot so fast that some of the scoutmasters would protest when I beat their troop members. They would inspect the knots and sometimes have me tie them again to see how I tied them. My knots always turned out to be tied correctly.

I stayed with the Boy Scouts for quite some time and, with the first-class rating, ended up being invited to join the Tahquitz Council Order of the Arrow. I remember the initiation and it was quite hard. The first night they ran us around in the dark with blindfolds on and then released us and told us to count to 100 before we took the blindfolds off. The idea was to be able to find our way back to the lodge. That was a piece of cake. We just followed the lights back. The only problem I had was running into a water faucet right at the groin area. The faucet cut me and I was in pretty bad pain during the ordeal.

When we found our way back to the lodge, we were given this Indian chant to memorize, and we had sit on the lodge floor and chant until we knew what it meant. We then would advance to the podium and tell the chief our words of wisdom. When we had learned the great words of wisdom, we were allowed to sit in the pledge chairs on the stage.

We were all down on the floor, chanting away, when I heard a perfectly clear, "I am a fool" from one of the guys behind me. I went to the chief and repeated it. He said yes and let me sit in the first pledge chair on the stage.

One by one most of the guys figured it out and were moved to the pledge chairs. They finally gave up on some of the guys who just couldn't get it and just let them come up and take a pledge chair.

The next day we had to do some community projects around the camp, and I remember having to dig this one deep long trench for what I remember was to be for a sewer line. (I could be mistaken about that.) We had to make a vow of silence for that one day, and every time we spoke we had to put a notch in this little wooden arrow we had to carve by ourselves and then carry in our mouths. The purpose of the arrow was to remind us not to talk. Too many notches and we would flunk out.

I remember this one poor guy who couldn't keep his mouth shut, and every time he spoke he would start crying as he pulled out that arrow and put a notch in it. I think by the time the day was over, there wasn't enough room left for any more notches in his arrow. They really took great pleasure in picking on the poor guy.

The Order of The Arrow guys would come over and ask us a question, and if we answered them, we would have to remove the arrow and put a notch in it. They never said how many notches we could have before we flunked out.

That night at the council fire before the rock of the great Tahquitz, they held a ceremony before the entire camp and invited the accepted pledges into the Order of The Arrow. They would go to each pledge and yank him out of his seat and place him before the council. I think they purposely let the poor guy suffer who couldn't stop talking. He was the only guy left before they finally went over and yanked him out of his seat. He was so darn happy that he started crying again.

I don't remember what happened to Doug with the Scouts. I don't remember seeing him around the Scouts, and I have no recollection of anything after that last campfire at Camp Emerson.

(Photograph on page 216.)

The Neighborhood Bully

My friend Doug and I were standing on my front lawn on Lime Street in Riverside one warm summer afternoon when we spotted a couple of younger kids fighting on the sidewalk next door. We went over and realized that one kid didn't know how to fight and was getting pretty well pummeled by the other kid.

Doug and I were about 14 or 15 at the time, and these kids were about nine or ten. We took pity on the kid who was getting pummeled and broke up the fight. We brought the kid over to my house and proceeded to teach him how to defend himself. Doug and I showed him how to properly clench his fists and punch straight, putting his body weight into each blow.

I held up my hands and had him practice his aim by striking my hands. I moved my hands around so he would learn how to punch a moving target. We also showed him the proper places to hit a person to be an effective fighter. The kid got very good in no time and had really quick hands.

We worked with him for a while, building up his confidence, and then told him he didn't have to take any guff from that bully anymore. We sent him on his way, feeling pretty good about helping this poor boy learn how to defend himself.

To our surprise he went right down the street and picked a fight with the boy who had been pummeling him earlier. He thoroughly thrashed the kid and sent him home, crying. We stood there dumbfounded. Wow, that kid learned quickly; we had turned him into a real scrapper. I said, "That other boy will never pick on him again."

We noticed in the next few days that "our student" was getting into fights all over the neighborhood. One day he got into a fight with a kid a couple of houses down from my house. He sent that kid home, bleeding and crying. Doug and I went down the street to talk to him. We talked to him about getting into fights and asked him how he had hurt that kid. He proudly proclaimed, "I hit him with my Gene Autry ring."

"What?" we asked.

He proudly held up his fist and showed us a big ring on his finger. We looked at the ring and saw it was a Gene Autry decoder ring.

I told Doug, "We just created a monster." We had turned this kid from a victim into the neighborhood bully.

The Rabbit

Somewhere around the age of 12 or 13, Doug and I decided to take some of our paper-route money and buy 410 gauge shotguns to replace my trusty old .22 rifle. We felt it would be better to have two shooters instead of one, and bagging rabbits and small fowl would be easier with the shotguns. We went out to the foothills quite often and got quite good at bagging rabbits with the shotguns.

On one memorable trip we went out early and walked a couple of fields without spotting any rabbits, which was quite unusual. While walking one of the fields, a large dog came up to greet us. I don't remember what breed of dog it was, but it was about the size of a golden Lab. The dog was quite friendly, and we petted it and played with it for a while before continuing on our hunting expedition. We continued looking for rabbits, and the dog followed along with us. We made jokes about having a hunting dog for a companion.

We walked through another field, still without any luck spotting rabbits, and we commented on the fact that there were no rabbits around. That was very unusual for that time of the morning. Rabbits are usually out early in the cool of the morning, feeding on the vegetation.

We were standing in the field, contemplating whether to take off or continue. Doug was standing approximately two feet from a large bush, and still wondering where all the rabbits were, when the dog walked up, stuck his nose in the bush, and pulled out a rabbit. We both burst out in laughter.

We headed on home, completely satisfied, knowing that we hadn't been skunked, because at least the dog got a rabbit.

The Wagon

I started delivering the Los Angeles *Herald Examiner* when I was about 12. The money from this paper route afforded me the opportunity to buy a new, 410-gauge shotgun and the new, latest-design, 3-speed bicycle with 26-inch tires, among other items. If you developed your route up to more than 150 papers, they would supply you with a *Herald Examiner* wagon. They felt you would not be capable of delivering that quantity of papers very easily, so they gave you one of their wagons to make your job easier and quicker.

The wagons had large tires with roller wheel bearings, heavy-duty suspensions, and well-built steering systems. That wagon was great for all kinds of uses. When I wasn't delivering papers with it, Doug and I would haul all kinds of projects around in it. We picked up scrap metal to sell to the scrap metal yard. We hauled our raft to Fairmont Park with it.

Our favorite game was to put a large cardboard box on it and pretend it was an army tank. We would mount a smaller cardboard box on top for a turret. We would mount a BB gun in the turret for the cannon. We got into all kinds of trouble with our tank. I was always the propulsion and Doug was always the driver. I asked him later why I was always pushing the tank and he was always driving. He said it was because I had longer legs and was stronger.

I think maybe it was because I was stupider than him. (Duh!)

Uncle Jack

My paternal grandmother's younger sister was married to a man named Jack. Jack was a large man with a barrel chest who spent his life working as an iceman. Uncle Jack and Aunt Ruth were a warm, loving couple, and we spent many hours visiting with them when our older daughter was an infant.

Uncle Jack spent his life delivering ice. When we were young, refrigerators hadn't come into use yet. Most homes, except the most affluent, had iceboxes. They were nothing more than heavy, insulated wooden boxes with a compartment to hold a block of ice and a couple of compartments to hold food. Some fancy iceboxes had two compartments to hold ice. Each home had a blue card they would put in their window to signal the iceman that ice was needed.

On hot summer days all the kids in the neighborhood would wait in anticipation for the arrival of the iceman. He would pull up in front of a house that was displaying the blue card and climb into the back of the truck. He would use an icepick to separate a 25-pound block of ice from the large block in the back of the truck and deliver the block to the house. This procedure always left little splinters of ice lying in the back of the truck. All the hiding kids would rush the truck as soon as the iceman walked into the house. They would grab handfuls of the ice splinters and delight in the coolness of the ice on a really hot day. It was really refreshing to have those pieces of ice to suck on. All the kids thought they were really pulling a fast one on the iceman.

Years later, while I was visiting Uncle Jack's home with my family, I related the story of stealing ice chips from the back of the truck. Uncle Jack said he always kept track of the number of kids in each neighborhood; that way he could make sure to leave enough ice chips behind for everybody. He said he would turn and watch out the door as soon as he entered a house. He got great delight in watching the kids scrambling to the truck to steal the ice chips.

Exploring and Camping in the Santa Ana Riverbottom

Somewhere between the ages of seven and eight, I met my lifelong friend Doug. From then on my exploring was done in partnership with him. We would explore all over the Riverside area, and nothing was left to chance. Riverside was changing: the orange groves were starting to come down, the land was being cleared, and every time we saw the smoke from a bulldozer, we went to investigate.

I remember one time when we were about 11 or 12, they were clearing a grove near Spruce Street and Chicago Avenue in Riverside. There was a beautiful mansion right in the middle of the orange grove. We had not known it was there, because it was hidden from view by the grove. Once they cleared the grove and we found the mansion, we explored it and it was beautiful.

You have to remember that we were a couple of poor boys living in very small, plain houses. The woodwork in that house was beautiful. We went back a couple of days later to do more exploring, and the house was gone. The only things left were the foundation and the basement.

The most fascinating thing we found was a safe in the basement. With the house gone, the safe was open to full view. The door had already been removed from the safe and was lying on the basement floor. There was a large bookcase that looked like it had hidden the safe, just like in the movies.

The interior of that safe was darn near as big as the living room in our house, and it had all kinds of shelves and compartments. There were still some papers on the shelves, and we had a great time going through them. I remember thinking we should do something with the safe door. It was really cool and we decided to move it. That darn thing was so heavy that both of us couldn't even budge one corner of it.

Doug and I both had paper routes by the time we were 11. We were making some money, so we both bought 410 shotguns.

We would pack up a bedroll, throw the shotguns over our handlebars, and ride up to Box Springs Mountain to spend a couple of days hunting and camping. We would take minimal supplies with us and would pretty much live off the game we hunted. I remember one time we were riding along and a police officer was standing alongside the road. He commented as we rode by, "Those shotguns aren't loaded are they, boys?"

We said, "No, sir, they're not."

"Good," he replied. "You boys have a good time."

We thanked him and kept riding on our way. If that incident happened today, we would have 15 cops and two helicopters swarming over us, and we would be on the ground, getting the crap beat out of us. Wow! Have times changed.

We would also take our fishing poles and bedrolls and head down to the Santa Ana riverbed west of Riverside near Fairmont Park. The area was heavily wooded and afforded us a great place to camp and explore. It was a very easy, short walk up to the lake, where we could catch a couple of perch or bluegill and take them back to camp for dinner. In the photo section of this book, there is a picture Doug took of me at one of the camping outings in the riverbottom. I was apparently cooking something when Doug snapped the picture. The picture is dated November of 1953, so I would have been 14 at the time.

(Photograph on page 217.)

Klure and Harris

Just north of the railroad underpass on North Main Street in Riverside was a business call Klure and Harris. They dealt with metal products of all kinds and bought and sold scrap metal. They had a yard behind their location where they would store all the scrap they hauled in. The road was a washboard, and the small scraps of metal would bounce off the trucks and spill onto the roadway as the trucks hauled the scrap metal in.

Doug and I used to go over to the scrap yard and pick up all the small scraps that fell off the trucks on that washboard road. We would fill our wagon full of those small pieces of metal then go around to the front and sell the scrap back to Joe Klure. We always went away with our wad of cash, chuckling about how we fooled old Joe. We always had money for the movies and the skating rink, thanks to Joe Klure.

Eventually, we grew older and went on to different things.

I was working many years later at the local Motorola service shop on North Main Street in Riverside when Joe Klure walked in with a handheld radio to be serviced. I related to Joe how we had scammed him by picking up his scrap and reselling it to him. He said he had known what we were doing and had been really disappointed when we quit. He stated that he had to hire an extra man after that to pick up the scrap, and he had to pay the man about four times what he had been paying us.

I guess we weren't so darn smart after all!

The Fort

Ever have a fort as a kid? Forts are special places where you can go and be anything you want to be. A kid who never had a fort never really lived a complete childhood. A fort can be anything from blankets thrown over a table or chairs to an elaborate tree house. Anywhere you can go to release your imagination is a fort.

Doug and I used to build some pretty elaborate forts in our day. We would take appliance boxes and tape them together to make multi-room forts, and they were pretty cool. We would cover them with brush to camouflage them. We even converted a chicken coop in my back yard on Lime Street to a fort, complete with a watchtower.

Our favorite forts were underground. Doug's grandparents lived next to an empty lot on the corner of Russell and Orange streets. It was a large lot, as were most of the lots in Riverside in those days, and we made excellent use of that lot in our youth. There was a cliff near the rear of the lot that dropped down to the elevation of Main Street, and about 100 feet from the cliff, or drop off, were some buildings that fronted on Main Street. One building housed an electric motor rewinding shop and the other one was an appliance store.

The appliance store afforded us all the large boxes we needed for fort material, boxes for making a tank out of the *Examiner* wagon, or boxes we would seal each other up in and push over the cliff. So many uses that only young boys' imaginations could dream up.

The motor rewinding shop supplied me with old, discarded electric motors which afforded an endless supply of magnet wire. I used the wire to make up the coils and antennas for crystal sets so we could listen to music on Radio Station KPRO. I even built my first amateur radio, 40-meter transmitter with the wire from those discarded motors.

But back to the forts. We decided an underground fort would be the ultimate achievement. We dug several underground forts, and our expertise improved with every one we dug. Finally, we started digging a very large fort near the bottom of the cliff. We dug trenches deep enough for us to walk in and dug rooms off the main trench, or hallway. We ended up with a five-room fort.

I was always a techno nut, and I ran wiring to each of the rooms and hooked up a telephone system in each room, using WWII field telephones that were readily available at the war surplus store. We assigned a certain number of rings to each room.

After I finished up the wiring to all the rooms, we laid flattened appliance boxes over the trenches and covered them over with dirt. We now had an underground fort. It was a really great fort. We were the envy of all the guys in the neighborhood.

We would let the guys go into the different rooms and we would call them on the telephones. They were excited and amazed, and everybody wanted to join our fort.

We had more darn fun playing in that fort. The guys would go to the different rooms, get on the phones, and dream up some of the craziest scenarios. Then we would come charging out of the fort in full force to attack the enemy. We spent a good part of our days, playing in that fort.

Our forts were so popular that the guys always wanted to join our fort, so we would come up with initiations they were required to complete in order to join. I'm sure Doug must have come up with them, because I can't imagine me being that mean.

When we had the fort in the chicken coop in my back yard, we decided it would be an Indian fort. One of the initiations was you had to wear an Indian breechcloth and run around the block. One kid decided to do it, and he took off around the block. About halfway around, the breechcloth came off, and I don't think he even realized it, because he just kept on running. He was probably the first streaker in history. The neighbors got quite a kick out of it, and Doug and I still laugh about it to this day. We remember his name but swore to each other never to divulge it.

The Mission Inn

The Mission Inn encompasses the entire city block between 6th and 7th streets and Orange and Main streets in the downtown area of Riverside. Frank Miller's father built it in 1876, and Frank inherited it after his father's death in 1902. Frank changed the name to the Mission Inn that year and started some major renovations.

The Inn has several architectural styles and is a fascinating place to visit. There are rumors that an escape tunnel from the basement goes all the way to the base of Mount Rubidoux. The basement is huge and consists of tunnels and alcoves with barred doors covering the entrances to these alcoves. In our childish imaginations we saw these alcoves as cells in a huge dungeon and were fascinated by their existence. I realize today that they were just storage areas for all the expensive and rare antiques and art Frank Miller collected over the years.

At the southwest corner of the Mission Inn, which would be the corner of 6th and Main streets, is a huge rotunda that houses office rentals. I once sold life insurance for the Independent Order of Foresters out of one of those offices in the 1960s. In the rotunda are small alcoves with statuary in them. Doug and I discovered a small stairwell behind the statues, and being adventurous, we immediately began exploring. The stairwell led to the "dungeons" mentioned above.

The dungeons were definitely off limits to the public, but we didn't let that stop us. We visited the dungeons many times during our youth and were never discovered. We explored and let our imaginations run away with thoughts of prisoners chained and being tortured in those alcoves. We searched tirelessly for the escape tunnel to Mount Rubidoux, but sadly, we never found it. Eventually, as we matured and grew, our fascination with the exploring ended, but the memories of those fascinating days of exploring those dungeons has been imprinted onto our memories forever.

Doug and I talk often about our adventures in the dungeons, and I am sure that over the years our imaginations have expanded those memories. Doug related to his wife about our adventures in the dungeons, and I am sure she just thought he was bloviating about the experiences.

A few years back the Mission Inn opened up a tour of the dungeons for a fund-raising event, and Doug took his wife on the tour. I imagine she was amazed when she found that Doug's tales of dungeons and secret places wasn't just bloviating but were based on a boy's real adventures and memories.

McDermont Fruit Packing Company

My mother packed oranges most of her working life. She would follow the fruit harvest all over California during the early years before we were born. After we were born, my parents settled in Riverside, and she worked exclusively at McDermont's.

McDermont's was located along the railroad tracks at about 10th Street in Riverside. When I was 14 years old, my mother got me a job there. I was over six feet tall by then and nobody questioned my age.

My first job was in the lug shed. The lug shed was a very large building about 60 feet wide by 120 feet long, and instead of having solid walls, the walls were all open, with chicken wire covering where the walls would normally have been.

The lugs—large boxes—were shipped out to the groves to be filled with oranges by pickers and returned to the packing shed. The filled lugs were put on conveyer belts and sent inside the packinghouse, where the oranges were automatically dumped onto washing and sorting trays. The lugs would take a return route on the conveyer belt out to the lug shed. They would come through a hole high up on the wall and drop by roller conveyers down to my station.

My job was to take the lugs off the conveyer as they came in, stack them seven lugs high, and store them in the shed. I would truck the lugs over to the loading dock when the trucks came in for a load of empty lugs to take back to the groves for the pickers. I would load the trucks with the lugs and tie them down for travel.

I was the only one working in the lug shed, so there was nobody to talk to unless the trucks arrived for loading. At times I would just sit, waiting for lugs to come through the wall. It seemed like hours before a lug came through, and I was so bored I would use the stacked lugs to make a maze to truck through when I finally got seven lugs to stack. I tried anything to keep from going nuts with boredom.

It seemed like I worked in that darn lug shed for years, but I am sure it was only a month or two before I was promoted and was able to start working inside. What a change. I was able to talk to people. It was cooler inside, too, and I was always able to stay busy with something to do. My first job was to supply the packers with wrapping paper and cardboard boxes to wrap and pack the oranges for shipping.

I stacked boards and nails in a machine that automatically nailed wooden boxes together. Those boxes were used to pack oranges for overseas shipping. That machine was fun to operate.

One thing that fascinated me was the large room downstairs. It looked like a huge cooler with a big, thick door on it. We would put lugs of green oranges inside that cooler just before quitting time, seal the door tightly, and inject an ethylene-type gas into the room. The next morning when we opened the door, all those previously green oranges sitting there had turned into the prettiest ripe oranges you have ever seen. We would put them on the conveyer and send them upstairs to be packed and shipped. I was always amazed every time we opened the door and saw all those ripe oranges.

I was pretty strong when I was young. I could handle the 60-pound boxes of packed oranges with ease, so I was assigned the job of packing the railroad cars with lugs of oranges. The packing shed was on a railroad siding, and there were always boxcars on the siding. It was a lot of fun to take one of the old trucks, push the boxcars up alongside the packing shed, and load the boxcars with oranges.

I was put in charge of making sure the boxcars were properly loaded and the box count was correct. I would then put the manifest on the door of the loaded car after we sealed the door. We used an old truck to pull the boxcar out onto the outgoing siding. I always felt uncomfortable telling people two to three times my age what to do, but they never seemed to question it. I guess my size and my ability to operate all the equipment gave them confidence in me.

I always rode with my mother to work, and I always drove. I wasn't old enough yet to get a driver's license, but nobody really cared in those days. One of the guys who worked with me asked if she was my wife. I was dumbfounded that, with my baby face, he would ask such a stupid question, but my mother got quite a kick out of it when I told her.

I had one humorous situation occur when I was in charge of loading boxcars. One of my classmates came to work for the summer. I remember him because I ran track with him. He was all excited about his new summer job. He talked about all the money he was going to make and thought about quitting school to continue working.

We had an unusually hot summer in Riverside that year, and those boxcars got pretty hot inside, making loading them a hot, miserable job. About the time school was going to start, he announced to me that he was going back to school. He said he was going to finish his education so he never had to work that hard ever again. I think that summer job was the best thing he ever did for his education.

One final thing from the memory of my packinghouse days was handling the "rots." When the lugs of oranges came in from the groves, they would be put onto conveyer belts and transported inside the packing shed. The conveyer would turn the lugs over, dumping the oranges onto sorting tables and then sorting them by size. This sorting was done automatically, but the oranges were manually inspected before they hit the sorting tables. Any cuts or rots were tossed on the conveyer behind the sorting table, and they were sent to a large bin attached to the outside of the building.

We backed a dump truck under the bin when it was full and dumped the rots and cuts into the dump truck. We had to get up in the back of the truck and move the oranges around to level the load. This meant walking around on top of the oranges, squishing them down with our dirty boots. We would then drive the load of oranges over to the Sunkist Orange Juice plant and dump them into their hopper. The smell was horrid and now, every time I buy a bottle of orange juice, I swear I can smell those rots.

The 36 Ford

I believe I was about 12 years old when my dad brought home a 1936 Ford 4-door sedan. A group of marines was heading back to their base when their car broke down. My dad made them a deal. He would take them all back to their base if they would give him title to the old Ford. They agreed and Dad hauled the old Ford home. He told me it was my car and to quit messing with his.

I played around with the car and eventually found that the distributor wasn't turning. I went to my friend down the street who had a little fixit shop and talked to him about it. He said the timing gear had to be out. He explained how the timing gear worked and how to get to it.

I went home and tore the engine apart, and sure enough, the timing gear was stripped. I pulled the gear off and took it to him. He took me to the parts store and made sure I bought the right timing gear and gasket. I came home and put the car back together, and I'll be darned, it started right up.

I practiced pulling it forward and backing it up, trying to get used to using the clutch and gearshift lever. Then I practiced turning it without running into anything. I didn't have any problem with size; I was almost six feet tall by then. The yards were extremely large in Riverside in those days, and you could easily drive around in our backyard. I practiced steering it for several days and got used to driving it around in that huge backyard. That lot is so large that there is now an apartment complex on it.

One evening I pulled the car up next to the house and waited for my father to come home from work. When I saw him turn the corner, I started the car. I pulled around the house and into the driveway just as he was pulling in. Man, was he shocked.

I told him what I had done. (I didn't mention the neighbor's help.) He was absolutely flabbergasted that I could get the thing running, but he made me promise not to drive it on the street. (A promise I would later break.) He bragged to everybody

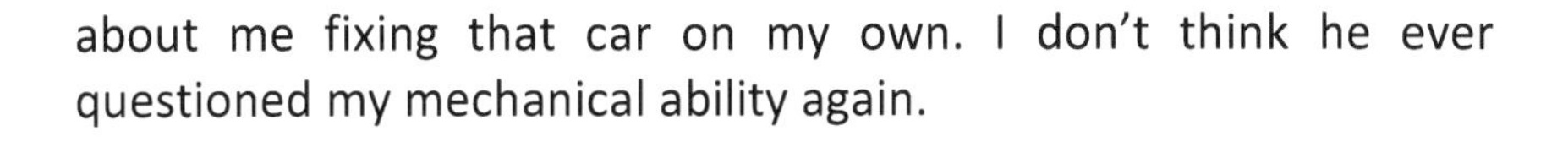

about me fixing that car on my own. I don't think he ever questioned my mechanical ability again.

My Harley

I need to mention the motorcycle. I bought a Harley when I was 16. It was a '45 Flathead, and I rode it constantly. I had trouble sleeping as a child and would go to bed about midnight or one a.m. and would wake up around four or five. (Actually, I still do. The only difference is that now I take a nap in the afternoon.)

I would take the motorcycle out early in the morning and ride it through the hills around Central Avenue and Alessandro Boulevard in the Riverside area. That area was made up of rolling hills in those days, and the road had unending curves and up and down hills. I used to ride that motorcycle wide open through those hills, sweeping down low around those tight turns.

For some reason it gave me a feeling of peace and tranquility. The dew was always on the grass that covered the hills in those cool early morning hours, and there was the sweet smell of the dew in the air. Whenever I encounter that smell, it always brings back those feelings of tranquility and peace. That is why whenever I lose a loved one, I will look for a large field of grass to walk on. If I am at a cemetery, I will walk around on the grass. I think the smell of the grass brings back those memories.

My Mechanical Ability

I brought all kinds of clunkers home in the next few years, tore them apart, and fixed them. My friends came over with their cars and we would work on them. None of us were old enough to drive, but we did it anyway. The police just never seemed to bother us in those days. We all became pretty good drivers by the time we were old enough to get drivers' licenses.

My Dad died when I was 16, and my Mom took off to pursue a career in staying high. I was left homeless, so I packed up my tools in my car and hit the road. I went everywhere trying to get a job, with no luck. You had to be 18 to work in industry. I was too young, but I was over six feet tall by that time, so I would tell everybody that I was over 18. They would say I was about to be drafted and wouldn't hire me. I couldn't tell them I wasn't old enough to be drafted, so I was out of luck.

One day I stopped at a car lot in San Bernardino where my friend Doug was working as a lot boy and told him about my plight. While I was talking with him, I noticed some nice looking Chevys sitting in the back row. The early Chevys had Babbitt rods with scoopers on them to pick up the oil and spray it up into the bearings. All other makes of cars had pressure oiling systems. The spray system was very inefficient, which is why a lot of Chevys had knocking rods. Chevy was the only one that had this problem, and it could be very easily repaired by filing down the rods, cleaning out the spray nozzles, and re-aiming them.

I asked Doug why they were sitting there, and he said they were rattling so bad that the owner of the car lot was going to take them to auction. Ray Hilton, the lot owner, came out to see what I was doing there talking to Doug. I told him I could make the Chevys sound like new cars for $7.00 apiece. He didn't believe me, but Doug assured him that I could do it. Ray told me to go ahead and try one, and he would pay me if I could make the engine quiet.

I picked a really nice, cherry, '41 Chevy coupe. I pulled the pan and filed the rods down, cleaned the nozzles, and aimed them. Then I put the pan back on and poured the old oil back in. Mr. Hilton came out and started the engine. He about flipped when he heard that engine purring like a new one. He immediately told me to do all the rest and said he was going to go out and buy a bunch more just like them. He told Doug to wash the coupe, polish the hood, and put it on the front line.

Mr. Hilton told everybody around what I was capable of. and pretty soon I had all of the work I could handle. There was a 3-stall garage on his lot next to the street with an upholstery shop in the front half. He told me I could use the garage if I would service his cars. We agreed, and I was in the automotive repair business.

In about a year I had two mechanics working for me, and business was good. There I was, 17, and I didn't know anything about running a business and being very successful. I would take my profits and use them to buy new tools and equipment. I had a really nice, fully equipped shop and could do about anything, but I didn't have a dime in the bank. Along came a recession and business really dropped off. I didn't even have enough money to pay the utilities or the help.

One day Doug's dad, Woody, came in with a truck that needed to be fixed. I fixed it right away, and he told me he would pay me a $100.00 a week if I would take my tools with me and drive his trucks down into Texas and Mexico and repair them if they broke down. I told the guys that we were closing the shop, and they could take anything they wanted to cover their wages.

I was now a truck driver. I spent the next couple of years hauling palm trees and cycads out of Mexico and South Texas and bringing them into California. I honestly believe that half the palm trees in Palm Springs were hauled in by me from South Texas. I was too young to drive truck in-state and inter-state, but we got away with it by putting my name on the trucks' titles. Apparently, if I owned the truck, they couldn't stop me from driving it.

Woody took on a partner after a couple of years, and I

believe the partner put a lot of money into the business. The company was now Baker and Lloyd Nurseries, instead of just Baker Nursery. Mr. Lloyd, the new partner, wouldn't stand for having my name on the titles, so I signed off on them. I was stopped at the Arizona border by DOT on my second trip back from Texas after my name had been removed from the titles. That ended my driving career.

Mr. Lloyd wanted me to stay on and work in the nursery until I was old enough to drive again, but I left their employment and joined the Forestry Department.

I worked for the Forestry for about five years and then went to the Riverside City Fire Department for another six years. I made little use of my mechanical skills, except for the last three years with the fire department. They put me on the rescue truck, and my mechanical skills really helped out when responding to auto accidents. It is a lot easier to cut someone out of a crushed car when you understand the structure of an automobile.

I was highly praised for my work with the rescue crew, but I got really fed up with the politics in the fire department and decided to pursue a career in, my first love, electronics.

I bounced around between a couple of small companies before settling in at ComSerCo in Riverside. It was a Motorola service shop that specialized in two-way radio communications. Working on radios was the same as working on an automobile. You had to break a trouble down to a section and then to the specific location. My natural mechanical skills made me really shine in that industry. I was sent out as a last resort when no one else could solve the problem, and I was quite successful at it.

People would comment about how good I was and always asked where I got my training. I had to make something up because they wouldn't have believed I only had a ninth-grade education with no training and that it just came to me naturally. I worked at ComSerCo for seven years and again got fed up with the politics, so I started my own communications business.

I ran Layton Electronics and Hi Desert Communications for

15 years. I started both companies and eventually built them up to 12 employees and radio repeaters on several mountaintop sites. I also leased radios to small businesses. Again my mechanical skills afforded me the ability to build these businesses and make them successful. I got so fed up with dealing with the egos of some of the technical people that I sold the businesses in June of 1985 and took a long vacation.

My wife and I got bored with traveling, so we came home and I went back to school and earned a degree in business. I walked away with a 3.95 GPA. It should have been higher, but I got fed up with an idiot professor and told him so. My grade suffered for that indiscretion.

I went back to work as a general manager for the company that bought me out. I brought them out of the red and into the black in 11 months. I continued to work for them until they decided to do a realignment. I wasn't interested in dealing with their idiotic ideas, so I left and went to work for the County of Los Angeles as a senior communications technician, supervising the high desert shops around the Lancaster area. It was a good move because the previous company I had worked for went bankrupt in two years because of their ill-conceived realignment.

In December of 1989, I went to work for the County of Los Angeles Communications Department and worked there until retiring in October of 2002. Fortunately, I was able to apply my fire department time to my county retirement, so I ended up with a fairly good retirement income.

The last few years with the county were hard to do, as the politics were terrible. I don't know why people can't just go to work, do their jobs, and go home in the evening and enjoy their family. Why do people always let their egos get in the way and try to start trouble? I pretty much hid out the last couple of years and was really happy when I retired.

Thanks to my natural mechanical ability, I was able to get through life relatively easily. I had good jobs and made pretty good money. I see so many people struggle today, trying to get through life, and I wonder why they don't have any common sense. I guess I am just fortunate.

What Learner's Permit

My dad brought home a broken-down, old 1936 Ford 4-door sedan. (See the previous essay, "The '36 Ford.) I couldn't stop tinkering with things, so he thought if I had my own car to keep me busy, I would leave his stuff alone. I repaired it, got it running, and my friends and I would drive it around the back yard.

Back yards in those days were different than they are today. The average back yard was 300 feet deep and 100 feet wide, so there was plenty of space to drive the car around. We would siphon a couple of gallons of gas out of my father's car, put it in the Ford, and drive it around for several days.

We let our imaginations run wild while driving around that yard, pretending to go to the mountains, the beaches, or other exotic places. We all got pretty good at driving. We learned how to clutch and shift and turn with ease. After a while we grew brazen and started driving the car up the alley behind the house when no one was around.

Eventually, we started driving it after dark on the streets in our neighborhood. With all that practice, we all got to be pretty good drivers. One day we ran out of gas about four blocks from home. My dad was at work, so we didn't have a source of gas, and we ended up pushing the car all the way home.

When I started taking drivers education in high school, the teacher asked me on the first day out how long I had been driving. He knew I had been driving for quite a while and relegated me to the back seat while the less experienced kids got to drive. That made drivers education pretty boring for me.

The day I turned 16 I used my Aunt Laura's jeep to take my driver's test. It was one of the little military jeeps that were completely open with no top or doors. The driving inspector had me take a couple of turns and then told me to parallel park. That was a piece of cake in a jeep. He said ok and had me take another couple of turns that ended up with us back at the DMV office. He signed my temporary driver's license, stepped out of the jeep, and handed me the paperwork. “Here,” he said. “Now you can drive legally.”

My Old Triumph Motorcycle

I had an old Triumph motorcycle in my younger years. The old Triumphs didn't need a battery; instead, they relied on a generator to produce the voltage to run the bike. They had a large capacitor and a Zener diode to protect the electrical system from over voltage. The old bikes didn't have electric starters like they do now, so a battery was unnecessary. You used a kick-starter to start the old bikes. The only problem was that there was no electricity to run the lights if the motor wasn't running.

My problem with motorcycles in my youth was that they had only two speeds: stopped and wide open. This was a malady that often got me into trouble. One night I was riding down Highway 395 at about two in the morning. It was pretty desolate on that stretch of highway in those days, and without lights, on a moonless night it was pitch black.

I was heading south, back to San Bernardino, on one of those moonless nights, cruising at a comfortable speed of about 90 miles per hour. I would have been going faster, but 90 was as fast as that old bike could go. All of a sudden the engine seized and everything went black. My first thought was, "Holy crap." I pulled the clutch in and started applying the brakes. I tried hard to keep from leaning or causing the bike to turn. Luckily, I was on a straight stretch of road at the time.

I kept expecting to feel the bumping as I went off the road and then my crumpling body flying through the air. (As had happened many times before.) Fortunately, I came to a complete stop. I didn't know where I was because of the darkness, but I did have asphalt under my feet, and that was a welcome feeling.

I should have known better, because I had bored that old Triumph out wrong, and it would often seize when it got hot. It was a cool night, so it didn't take long for the engine to cool down and I was able to restart it. I headed back south towards San Bernardino, this time at a much lower speed. I obviously made it, or I wouldn't be here writing this. (See photograph on page 218.)

Radio Station KPRO 1440

Radio Station KPRO was located on Russell Street in Riverside, just west of the Mulberry Street intersection on the north side of the road. It was a high-quality station and could compete with any big-market radio station in any of the large cities in the United States.

KPRO had broadcast studios that were capable of seating an audience of 30 people very comfortably. The walls were covered in drapes, and the stages were large enough to do live radio shows. If you have ever seen movies showing people doing a radio broadcast show, you have an image of what KPRO's studios looked like. They were first quality, which was surprising, considering the size of the market in the Riverside area.

There was a gentleman named Joe Pine in the mid-'50s who, I believe, was the first talk-show radio host. Joe drifted into town and started broadcasting from the radio station. He was quick witted with his responses and became sort of a fad with all the teenagers in town. We would go to the station and watch him sit up there on that stage and insult callers with his quick wit.

One night one of the guys called in and asked him his opinion of car clubs. He quipped back that he thought it was a good idea. "Everyone should have a club in their car to beat off unsavory people." That's the only remark Joe made that I can still remember. Joe eventually went to the big time, heading for Los Angeles to broadcast from KFI and, later, television. The "Joe Pine Show" was the only program I ever attended at the KPRO studios.

Living at the north end of Lime Street put me right in the ground wave of the station. I think you could have heard the broadcast from an old coffee can if it was aimed just right. I was always tinkering with stuff and was very inquisitive, and I discovered that I could stick a couple of razor blades upright on a piece of wood, hook one razor blade to one side of a pair of headphones and an antenna, hook the other side of the headphones and a ground to the other razor blade, take the lead out of a #2 pencil and lay it across the razor blades, and "voila," I had a radio. I would carefully roll the lead over the razor blades until I could hear the station. I would lie there at night and secretly listen to the radio with those headphones. I showed my "radio" to my buddy Doug, and he wanted one, so I made one for him. For his I used a crystal so he wouldn't have to tune it. Doug used to lie there at night, listening to the station as well. That was over 70 years ago, and he still tells everybody that story when we are together.

I left Riverside from 1955 to 1962, so I didn't see the demise of that grand old radio station. I did see pictures later of the tower lying on the ground, destroyed. Apparently, they tried to use a sky crane to take it down, and it went out of control and the antenna crashed to the ground, destroying the tower. I understand the station was moved out on North Main Street somewhere.

That was a grand era, and it's a shame it had to end.

The '47 Plymouth

My friend Doyle Miller's parents had this 1947 Plymouth. (I am guessing at the year.) We used it all the time for running around. We would try to pick up girls in it, but I can't remember that we ever succeeded, even though we sure tried.

I remember one time we went over "thrill hill" in it. Thrill hill was in the Bloomington area, paralleling what is now the I-10 freeway. It had a large drop-off, and if you were going really fast, you would get airborne as you went over it, and it would feel like your stomach was coming up. Several kids were killed going over thrill hill, so the road department finally went in and redid the road, leveling out the drop-off and spoiling all the fun.

I remember the night we went over. We must have had girls with us, because I remember being in the backseat, holding a vanilla milkshake. All I remember is watching that milkshake come out of the cup as we came down the drop-off and going back into the cup without spilling a drop when we landed at the bottom.

One night we went over to Lakeview in the Plymouth and raided a watermelon patch. We scrambled around that watermelon patch, grabbing the biggest watermelons we could find and stuffing them into the back seat of the Plymouth. It was a really dark night, which made it difficult to see, so occasionally, we would step on a watermelon, busting it open. We would reach down and pull the heart out of it and eat it while searching for more big watermelons to load up.

The Millers had this large kiddie pool in their back yard, and when we returned home, we filled the pool up with all those watermelons. Doyle's parents were really surprised when they got up the next morning and found that pool full of watermelons. I don't remember the Millers being upset at us for stealing those watermelons; I actually think they were amused. I do remember eating a lot of watermelon for the next several days. Watermelons are not my favorite thing anymore, and I can't remember being fond of them since that time.

We used to go over to the Bloomington area a lot. There was a trailer park there that was loaded with girls, and I faintly recall us having "the hots" for a couple of them. Being a gentleman, I will not relate any more details about that. One night, very late, as we were returning to Riverside from Bloomington, we ran out of gas near Fairmont Park. Gas was usually not a problem, as Doyle's dad worked for the Riverside County Road Department, and he always had 5-gallon jerrycans full of gas on his county truck. That usually afforded us an unlimited supply of gas, but that night we ran a little short. I remember we pushed that car all the way home. We must have been in good shape in those days; I doubt I could push a car even to the side of the road now.

I don't recall what happened to that Plymouth, but I do recall Doyle buying a 1942 Ford Coupe. That was the last car Ford produced until the end of WWII. I remember that car being a lemon—we spent more time working on it than riding in it. I think he finally gave up and junked it.

I have a lot of pleasant memories of us cruising around in that Plymouth. It was probably one of the happiest times of my youth.

(Photograph on page 219.)

The Hubcap Affair

Back in the '50s, Dodge Motor Company came out with the Dodge Royal Lancer. The Lancers had a set of hubcaps on them that were the rage, and everybody who was anybody had a set of those hubcaps on their ride. I have a picture of my 1952 Mercury with a set of Dodge Royal Lancers on it.

Those hubcaps were so popular that you had to guard your vehicle at all times. If you parked your car and went into a store for more than a few minutes, the hubcaps would be gone by the time you came back out. It was a constant round robin with those things.

We had a four-man team to get the hubcaps. If we saw an unattended car with a set of Dodge Royal Lancers on it, our driver would drop the team off a little way down the street from the car, and then the driver would pull the car a little bit up the street past the target car. The guys would walk up the street, two guys on the driver's side and two guys on passenger side. The driver's side front-tire man was the group leader. Our four guys would walk up to the car, and if the coast was clear, each person would kneel down at his station. The lead man would say, "Ready. Screwdrivers in. One, two, three." On three, everybody pops their hubcap, sticks it under their coat, stands up, and keeps walking up the street to the pickup car. The whole procedure only took a couple of seconds.

Doug got so tired of having to replace his Dodge Royal Lancers that he decided to screw them onto his wheels. He went to the hardware store and got some sheet-metal screws. He drilled holes through the hubcaps and into the rims and used the sheet metal screws to secure the hubcaps to the rims. It worked great; there was no way you could get those hubcaps off without destroying them.

Doug drove home and parked his car with the secure feeling that his hubcaps would be there in the morning. When he got up the next morning, the hubcaps were still there, but two tires were flat. The screws were too long, and the drive home had worked them through the tires and punctured the inner tubes.

One night we spotted a parked car with a set of Dodge Royal Lancers on it. We were dropped off, and we walked up on the target car. One guy on our team was a kid named Vince. Now, Vince was a nice guy, but he was, as they say, not the brightest bulb in the chandelier. Vince was on the passenger-side rear tire. As we walked up to the car, there was a guy in the back seat with shoulders as wide as a Mack truck. He had this cute little blonde girl under him.

We signaled each other and kept walking up the street. We got at least a half a block away from the car when we heard Vince saying, “Are you guys ready? Hey, where is everybody?”

About that time the Mack truck guy came flying out of the car. He was angry and it got real ugly. We waited for a while like the cowards we were, then we went back, picked up Vince after the beating, and took him home.

(Photograph on page 220.)

Blueberry Hill

In 1956, Fats Domino had a hit song called "Blueberry Hill." Some of the guys found a small hill on the outskirts of Riverside that was very secluded. It made a great spot to go and park with some degree of privacy. You had to go up a long dirt road and then drop down into a bowl to get to the spot. That made it virtually impossible to be seen by anyone except an airplane, and you were afforded complete privacy.

I have tried to reconstruct the location with a fading memory and Google Earth. I believe the location to be somewhere near what is now the Indian Hills Golf Course near Limonite Avenue and Camino Real near the Pedley area. Our code name for this secret location was "Blueberry Hill," and it became a very popular spot for the teenagers in the area to congregate on Friday and Saturday nights.

All we had to hear was "Blueberry Hill," and everyone was off to our secret spot. The guys would bring their girlfriends and park their cars, open the doors, and everybody would turn their car radios to the same station and dance or just stand around and talk and enjoy the music and the camaraderie.

Some of the guys who were there without girls would consume beer and get a little stupid while having a good time. Occasionally, a couple of guys would get really stupid and get into a fight, but nothing serious ever came of it. The '50s were different than now. Guys didn't carry guns and knives like they do today. A fight usually continued until the guys got so tired they would just give up due to exhaustion, or their friends would intervene and get them calmed down.

Some of us would stop at Tuxie's in Rubidoux on the way up and pick up some French fries and Cokes to take with us. (French fries and Cokes were the only things on Tuxie's menu.) I haven't been able to find out if the old Tuxie's in Rubidoux, or West Riverside as it was known in the '50s, is the same Tuxie's that is now located on Magnolia Avenue in Riverside.

The culture of the '50s was different than the culture of today. Drugs didn't come into use until the hippie generation of the mid-'60s. We did have a few individuals using drugs in the '50s, but they were ostracized by the rest of the teenagers of the era and pretty much stayed to themselves. I had one good friend of many years ask me if I wanted to smoke some weed with him. I told him no, and he never talked to me again. All my friends were like me. We were too busy building and racing cars and chasing girls to be bothered with staying high on drugs, although we did consume a lot of beer.

Drive-in Movie Theaters

The drive-in movie theater was very popular in the '40s and '50s, and many a warm summer night was spent watching the movies in the comfort of our cars. Since we were young and had limited funds, we devised many ingenious ways to get access to the drive-in without paying.

One of the fun ways was to back in the exit, but this strategy was often a failure. One night Doug, Gerry, and I tried backing into the drive-in theater on Mission Blvd. in what is now known as Rubidoux. We had just pulled around to find a parking space when this guy who obviously worked for the theater came running up, hollering and blowing his whistle at us. The jig was up—we had been discovered.

Doug pulled out and started driving up the aisle, with the guy running right behind us, blowing that darn whistle. Doug continued driving, just keeping the guy close to us. He drove around the drive-in, up and down the aisles several times, before heading for the exit. Just as we got to the exit ramp, Doug stopped and let the guy catch up to us. As the guy got next to the window of the car, Doug said, "We were just leaving."

This poor guy was totally out of breath, panting and gasping. It took him a minute to catch his breath before he replied, "Oh. Ok. Have a nice evening."

We drove off, laughing hysterically. We laughed about the incident for months.

We would often find a blind spot on the rear wall of a drive-in. We would slide over it and look around for somebody we knew to sit in their car and watch the movies with. The drive-ins were set up with benches and speakers near the screen so you could sit outside and watch the movie. People would sit up there if it was too hot in their cars, or kids sat there if they just wanted to get away from their parents. The benches were hardly ever used. We would walk up and sit on those benches if we were unable to find any friends in the cars.

One of the most common things was to have everybody pool their money and then pile into the trunk. One guy and girl would drive in and pay the admission. The cashier would just assume it was a couple on a date.

You had to watch out when getting the people out of the trunk because the theater people would watch for trunks to open. I solved the problem in my Mercury by setting the rear seat on hinges and opening up the back wall into the trunk. That way, when we pulled in, the guys could push the seat down and crawl into the car without opening the trunk. That Mercury had a large trunk and could hold a lot of people. It was a favorite with everybody on movie nights.

I used to hang out at Tommy's house on 4th street in San Bernardino. Tommy was married to Millie, and Tommy's sister Jo and her husband lived there as well. One night we all decided to go to the movies. Everybody but Millie climbed into the trunk. She was so claustrophobic that she just couldn't get in the trunk, so my girlfriend climbed in the trunk, and Millie was to ride with me up front and pretend she was my date.

Everything went well until we arrived at the drive-in with Millie sitting next to me, pretending to be my date. There was always a line of cars two abreast, lining up to get into the theater. The ticket booth was located in the center of the roadway to take the admission from the two rows of cars. They would take the admission money through the driver's side window in one row and the passenger side window in the other row.

We were about two cars back from the ticket booth when Millie noticed that Tommy's parents were sitting in the car next to us in the other row, and they were staring at us. Mille went into total panic and started screaming, "Tommy's in the trunk."

We were so close to the cashier that I was afraid they could hear her, so I started revving up the engine to try to drown out her voice. The more I revved the engine, the louder she screamed. I yelled at her to shut up, that she could go over with Tommy to his parents' car after we got in and explain what was going on.

I finally got her calmed down by the time we got to the cashier, and fortunately, they hadn't heard her over all the noise. We all went over to Tommy's parents' car after we got settled in and explained the situation. Tommy's parents got quite a kick out of the incident.

Flashing Red Light

Doug had this really cherry, '57 Chevy pickup. We got the brainy idea of putting a red light bulb in his dome light. We hooked it up to a turn-signal flasher, and when Doug flipped the switch, the cab of his pickup was filled with a flashing red light. We would get some unsuspecting guy in the truck with the idea that we were going cruising. We would grab some beer and drive around, and about the time our guest got comfortable, Doug would flip the light on and we would shout, "Oh crap, it's the cops."

It was hilarious, watching the poor sucker trying to get rid of that beer.

Grandmothers' Boarding House

My Grandmother Hoagland ran a boarding house and she had several elderly guests. Salesmen would come by and sell them worthless stuff that was supposed to cure their ills. They bought a box from one of these salesmen that was approximately 14 inches wide, 6 inches high, and 12 inches deep. It had a metal plate covering the top that looked like a ferrotype tin that I used in developing photographic prints. You put your feet on top of the metal plate and plugged it in. It warmed your feet and supposedly cured your lumbago or something. One day the box quit working, and everybody in the house panicked. I took the box apart and all it had in it was a 60-watt light bulb. I replaced the light bulb and it was working again. Everybody in the house was relieved and almost instantly started feeling better. I never disclosed what was in the box or what I did to fix it.

I stopped by the boarding house one day for a visit, and a traveling foot doctor was there. This guy claimed he could diagnose health problems—and cure them—by pushing buttons on the bottom of your feet. (Of course it took several visits to do this.) I thought, *Oh my God, here's another one. These guys must have this place on a sucker list*.

He had just finished giving treatments to all the elderly ladies in the house and was preparing to leave. My loving, gullible grandmother insisted that I get a treatment. The foot doctor assured me that the first treatment was free, so I decided, *What the heck*. I pulled off my shoes and socks and exposed my stinky feet to him. He started prodding around on the bottom of my feet and found this spot that hurt when he pushed on it. "You have a sore throat," he commented.

I thought, *How the heck did he know that?*. I did have a sore throat, but I had never told anybody that I did. Kind of makes you wonder doesn't it?

***

I remember when Grandmother got her first TV. All the little old ladies would put on their finest, do their hair, and put on their make-up. They would all be chattering and excited that Monte Hall was on. One day when they were watching the show, he made the comment, "I see all you wonderful ladies sitting out there on that couch and those chairs. Thank you for watching, and I hope you enjoy the show." They all sat there, all giddy, talking to him and giggling like a bunch of little schoolgirls. They were absolutely convinced he could see them. There was no way I was going to try to convince them otherwise.

***

Grandmother bought some of the most ridiculous stuff after getting that TV. I would ask her, "Ma, why did you get this?"

She would answer, "That man on TV showed it to me. Isn't it wonderful?"

I told her, "Ma, those guys on TV are salesmen. You can't trust them."

She would just look at me with those beautiful, trusting eyes and say, "No, he was the nicest man."

Oh my God, what do you do?

***

Years later, I was going through my mother's papers and found the receipt for that worthless box with the light bulb in it. The guy charged my grandmother $250.00 for the darn thing. That was in the '50s; it would probably be a couple of thousand in today's dollars. That thing couldn't have cost more that a couple of dollars to make: $50.00 would have been a rip off, but $250.00 was just plain thievery. I wonder how those snake oil salesmen slept at night!

Hush-Hush

There is a ravine in Riverside between Saunders Street and Terracina Drive just east of Magnolia Avenue and bordered again on the west by Saunders Street. This ravine housed the gymnasium and football and athletic fields for Riverside Polytechnic High School.

We would often park on Saunders Street, located on the north side above the ravine, and watch the football games from our cars during cold weather. In warmer weather we would sometimes climb down the north side of the ravine and sit on the dirt and watch the games from there.

One night when we were about 18 or 19, Doug and I were sitting in his Fordillac on Saunders Street, watching the game and having a beer. (Fordillac was the term we used to describe a 1950 Ford with a Cadillac engine in it.) Two girls came up the street, walking by the car. I had previously dated one of the girls. The girl I had dated recognized me, so they stopped and we started talking. The girls were getting cold standing outside of the car, so they decided to get in to warm up. The one I had dated got in the back seat with me, and the other girl climbed into the front seat with Doug.

The girl with me was a really nice girl, and we exchanged pleasantries. We inquired as to how each other had been and what we had been up to. We just chatted and had a nice conversation, but I noticed Doug was getting uncomfortably friendly with the girl in the front seat.

After a while the girls decided it was time to leave, so we bid them farewell, with me promising I would call the girl I had dated and we would go out again. (Which for some reason I never did follow through on.)

Everybody would hang out at Ruby's on Market Street in Riverside. All of us would cruise through, looking for friends to hang out with. It was quite warm a few nights later, so I got the motorcycle out, and while riding around I decided to pull through

Ruby's.

There was a group of motorcycle riders parked there. I didn't know who they were, so I stopped and started talking to them. They all decided to go for a midnight ride, so I joined up with them for the ride. One of the guys wanted to stop by his fiancés house and take her with him. We pulled up to her house, and his fiancé came running out of the house, skipping down the front porch steps, all excited and ready to jump on his bike, when she spotted me and started to panic.

I will never forget the look of surprise, horror, shock, and every emotion that flashed across her face. I can't even begin to describe the look on her face. It was the girl who had been in the front seat with Doug. She ran over to me and started begging me, pleading, "Please don't say anything about the other night."

I responded by saying, "You must be confused. I don't have a clue what you're talking about."

She smiled, thanked me, climbed onto her fiancé's bike, and we all rode off for a late night ride. She must have thought her fiancé and I were friends since we were riding together, but I didn't have a clue who he was. He was just another rider in the group.

I always had a habit of staying out of other people's business. I had enough problems of my own without getting involved in everyone else's. And I wouldn't have been responsible for destroying someone's relationship, even if I had known her fiancé.

I never saw either of them again.

Safeway Contest

While we were living on Russell Street, my wife shopped at the local Safeway at, I believe, around 4th and Market streets. They had a contest going where they would give you this little paper token with a number on it. It was a scratcher, and you would scratch the coating off it to expose the number. The idea was to collect the year 1962 with four of the tokens. She just kept getting ones, nines, and twos, so she got discouraged and just kept throwing the darn things away. One day at the check-out she got a six and commented, "Darn, I had all the others and I threw them away." The clerk asked what number she had and she told her, "The six."

The clerk said that was the key number, and all the clerks in the store started going through trashcans and found the other numbers. They gave them to her and told her to take them to the manager.

The management had her come in the next day and they made a presentation of giving her the check. They took pictures—one you'll find in the photo section of this book—and put them on their promo material. The prize was only $100, but you have to remember that rent in those days was around $60 a month.

My wife was really excited and even more so when I told her to save the money for Christmas. The family had a pretty good Christmas that year.

(Photograph on page 221.)

Lifting the T-Bucket

Back in the '50s a lot of guys would take a '20s-series Model T, put the body on a later model frame, and put a small truck bed on it or just hang a beer keg gas tank over the rear differential. They would put a V-8 engine in them and have a pretty cool hot rod. The modified cars were commonly referred to as T-buckets.

My friend Sammy and I put one together using an Oldsmobile 88 engine and a LaSalle transmission. It was pretty cool to cruise around in, and it would really scoot.

We needed to put a block under the front axle when we were putting it together, and I discovered that I could put my legs against one of the front tires and, by using my back, lift the tire off the ground. This came in handy later and also provided us with entertainment.

We would occasionally be stopped by law enforcement to check us out, and they would always question the fact that the vehicle had no fenders. We knew we were not required to have fenders if a vehicle weighed less than 1,400 pounds. If the police officer was insistent that we needed fenders, I would jump out and lift the front end off the ground. That usually ended the conversation.

We had one CHP officer pull us over one time just to show his buddy that I could actually pick the darn thing up. He had stopped us earlier and was telling the guys about it, and they were skeptical.

It got around that I could pick up the car, and it sometimes created chaos when we were around a bunch of guys who had been drinking. The guys would try to pick it up—unsuccessfully—and insist that it couldn't be done, so I would pick it up. Their egos would take over, and they would darn near tear the front end off that T-bucket, trying to lift it. Nobody was ever successful at picking it up except me.

I lost track of Sammy and often wonder if he is still alive. He could verify the truthfulness of this story if he is.

Outrunning the Law

Back in the late '50s I had an auto repair shop on Baseline Street in San Bernardino. I was approached by the San Bernardino County Sheriff's Reserve to fix up a jeep for them. The jeep had been donated to them and was in pretty good shape. I volunteered to fix up it in my spare time at no cost, with the understanding that they would supply the parts.

Over the next few months, I tuned up the engine, checked out the running gear, and changed out all the fluids. I was able to get the upholstering shop located in the front of my building to reupholster the seats as a donation to the Sheriff's Reserve. I got Holly's Auto Body on 5th and Tippecanoe to paint the vehicle.

I installed red lights on the jeep and set up flashers. They did not provide a siren. The sheriffs came out and put their emblems on the jeep, and I turned it over to them. They seemed pleased with the work I had done and put it into service.

A year or two later Doug Baker and I attended the drags at Morrow Field in Colton. We were probably just there as spectators, as I don't remember we raced that evening. Doug was driving his Fordillac—a '50 Ford coupe with a Cadillac engine in it—and it could scoot pretty well. Doug got into the spirit of racing, and as we pulled out onto Valley Boulevard after leaving the drags, he punched it just a little too hard. About that time the a sheriff's deputy pulled up alongside us in the jeep, shone a spotlight on us, and announced, "Sheriff's Department. Pull over."

Doug shouted an explicative and punched the Fordillac. As we were speeding up Valley Boulevard, he commented, "What did those jerks in the jeep think they were trying to pull."

I told him he should turn south on Rancho and get across the county line as fast as he could because it had been the Sheriff's Department all right. I said, "I know because I built that jeep up for them."

Racing in Redlands

In 1956 and 1957 I was living in San Bernardino, running an automotive repair shop on East Baseline. All my friends were still in Riverside, so I would constantly drive to Riverside from San Bernardino to hang out with them.

We spent most of our time at King's on Jurupa and Magnolia and would sometimes drift down to B&B's or Ruby's. The usual thing was just to hang out, talk with everybody as they drove through in their cars or on their motorcycles, and spend time with our girlfriends. It didn't seem like we were doing much, but it was enjoyable. Occasionally, someone would start bragging about his car, and a race would soon ensue, which meant a quick trip out to Alessandro or Auga Mansa for a race.

One night at King's one of the guys came up with a small hydraulic jack. When someone drove in, the guys would surround the car and just start talking with the driver. We would kind of lean on the car so it rocked a little bit, and while we were doing that, the guy with the jack would crawl under the car and jack up the rear wheel enough that it just cleared the ground. Pretty soon we would all say our goodnights and walk away. The look of shock on the driver's face was priceless when he stepped on the gas and that car wouldn't move.

One time a police car drove in, and I thought, "Uh-oh, this is not a good idea." But before I noticed it, the jack guy had slid under that police car and jacked it up. We talked with the policeman for a while, then bid him farewell and stepped away. He put that car in gear and stepped on the gas. Nothing.

Everybody started laughing and he knew he had been punked. He was smiling when he said, "Ok, guys, what's going on?"

We told him to take the car out of gear and put the brake on and we would fix it. He did and the guy crawled under the car, came out with the jack in his hand, and showed to him. The cop started laughing then he waved and drove away.

I thought we were all going to get busted over that stunt, but the police officer seemed to get a kick out of it.

One night some guys from Redlands came into King's and challenged us to some races. The prize was that the loser had to give the winner a case of beer. I was still at the shop in San Bernardino, so Doug called me and told me to get a case of beer and see if I could find Butch and have him bring his Deuce and meet them in the orange groves at California and Barton Roads in Redlands. I found Butch, we got a case of beer, and we headed for Redlands.

There were quite a few cars there when we arrived, so we parked and got into a rules discussion with everybody. We made up the rules, and Butch ended up with a couple of cases of beer rather quickly. Doug did pretty well with the Fordillac as well. I think we were drinking more beer than we were winning.

All of a sudden these cop cars came driving out of the orange groves and lit us up. Nobody had a clue where they had come from. They lined us up, took our IDs, and started writing down our information.

We all ranged from 17 to 19, but there was one guy who was over 21. We figured he was going to jail. They asked him if he bought the beer, and he said no, that we all had it when he arrived, and we were using it for prizes. Of course we all confirmed his testimony.

Next they asked about all the open containers on the floorboards of the cars. We told them that we found them on the street and didn't want to run over them and puncture our tires, so we picked them up and just threw them in the cars.

The police officers really got a kick out of that one. One of the officers said, "That's a pretty good story." They were both trying to be stern, but you could tell they were about to burst out laughing.

The police officers' final decision was that it was our lucky night. They were going to let us go because of all the paperwork we would have created, but they were going to have to confiscate the beer. They told us to place the beer in the trunk of the patrol cars, which we immediately did. Then they told the guys who lived in Redlands to go straight home, and the guys from out of town to get out of the city limits as fast as we could. We all hopped in our cars and headed home.

The guys from Riverside headed straight out Barton Road for home, and we headed up California and went over to Alabama to get across the river into San Bernardino. We were only about 300 feet from leaving the Redlands city limits when we got stopped again.

The cops got us out of the car and shook us down. They searched the car and found nothing. We had already thrown all the empty beer bottles away in the orange grove off California Avenue.

Then the cops did something I had never seen before. They made Butch bend over and put his finger on the street. They told him to walk in a circle around his finger three times, leaving his finger in the same spot. He made one revolution and fell flat on his face. They looked at me and asked if I had been drinking and I said, “No sir.” They told me I had two minutes to get Butch back in the car and past the city limit sign or we were both going to jail.

They must have gone back to their car and sat there and laughed at us. I had one heck of a time getting Butch back in the car. I’m sure it took me at least 15 minutes. I finally got the car started and past that city limit sign into San Bernardino, post haste.

It is a good thing we didn’t get hauled in that night, because the guy who was 21 eventually ended up being the police chief of the City of Riverside. If he had been busted that night, he would never had been able to have a career in law enforcement.

Street Racing

Back in the '50s we did a lot of street racing. Back then a lot of the roads in the Riverside area were rural without any houses, and those were the roads we would race on. One night a couple of guys chose each other off—challenging each other to a race. They started heading out to where we always raced, with about 20 cars following them. Doug and I were about nine cars back, and when the guys turned onto Cemetery Road, we noticed the fifth car back was a police car. The police officer was following us, but nobody was paying any attention.

Doug and I didn't turn the corner; we just went straight. We were the only car that went straight, and I never heard what happened later that night.

***

I had a 1952 Mercury coupe that I had fixed up, and it would move pretty well. I hung out at Holly's Body Shop and would do sanding for him in return for work on the Mercury. I had 155 louvers punched in the hood, had nosed the front down two inches to put it on a rake, and one night Holly and I painted it Sierra Gold Metallic.

We both had several beers that night, but the paint job tuned out pretty well until you got down on the ground and looked at the rocker panels. Somehow, we had neglected to bend down and spray the bottom of the car. We had used the bottom of the pot to paint the car, and finding a color match would be difficult. I decided you would have to lie down to see it, so the heck with it.

I worked the night shift at a chrome plating shop in San Bernardino, and every night I would take a metal piece off that Mercury and drive off in the morning with another item chromed. It didn't take long before every interior metal part of that Mercury had been chromed. One day they shut down the night shift and laid us all off, so that ended a good thing.

There was a straight stretch on Agua Mansa Road where we marked off a quarter of a mile. There was literally nothing out in that area in those days, so it made a great place to race. We actually used white paint to paint a starting line and the quarter mile mark across the road, and we would go out there and race.

Saturday nights were race nights. I don't know what it was with that Mercury, but after a few beers I just couldn't get that Mercury into second gear without blowing the transmission. Every Sunday morning would find me out back, replacing the transmission. I had that transmission out so many times that it almost came out by itself. Monday mornings would find me in the wrecking yard, getting another transmission. They would ask me what kind of car I had. I would tell them any Ford transmission from 37 up would work. The gears were the same, and all I needed was the gears. I would replace the cluster, second gear and the syncro rings during the week and have another spare tranny ready for the next weekend. After a while when I walked into the wrecking yard on Monday mornings, they would throw a transmission up on the counter without asking. I would give them $15.00, thank them, and walk out.

***

One of our friends—his name was Jack—bought a new 1957 Oldsmobile Tri-Power, and it was fast. Gerry's older brother Nick had a 1940 Ford sedan that we had reworked, and Nick wanted to see what it would do against that Oldsmobile J2, so we headed out to Agua Mansa to try them out. We had built that flathead up, and the stock fuel pump couldn't keep up with those three Strombergs on the flathead. The carburetors would flat run out of gas when you really got on it.

We solved the problem by installing a pressure tank between the passenger's legs on the floorboard, just in front of the passenger seat. The hand pump to pressurize the tank was mounted to the left side of the tank so the driver could reach it. I think back about that tank now after spending years as a firefighter; my God, you were sitting inside that car with a firebomb between your legs.

We got all lined up and started off with engines screaming and tires smoking, and we were racing. I was sitting there, pumping that hand pump like crazy, trying to keep the pressure up in the tank. We were screaming and were quickly up to about 85 miles per hour and still accelerating. We were doing a good job staying up with that J2 when all of a sudden the sky lit up with a red light, and we heard a siren wailing. We pulled over and faced our fate. The CHP officer was a really nice guy I knew from previous incidents. I asked him how he could catch up to us so quickly in his Dodge.

He was really proud of himself and explained what happened. He knew what we were going to do, so he followed us with his headlights off and stayed back a few hundred feet. Then he started accelerating and was already doing about 60 miles per hour when we took off. He flipped his reds on when he got near us. Thank God I was a passenger that time and didn't get a ticket.

***

I had this '36 Chevy coupe, and one day I somehow got upside down in it. We got it back on its wheels and got it home. The wheels were bent, but otherwise, it was in pretty good shape except for one minor problem: the car's top was below the doors. I contemplated cutting the roof off, but the body was so badly crunched that I ended up cutting the body off and selling it for scrap. I had a Model A roadster pickup cab just sitting in the yard, so I bolted it on the Chevy chassis. There it sat, just the running gear with that Model A cab sitting on it. No fenders, no bed with the rear differential, and the gas tank just exposed to view. I wish I had taken a picture of it because it would have been the first original Rat Rod that is so popular today.

I fired it up and it ran terrible. I checked it out and found that the carburetor was broken in half. It must have happened when I rolled the Chevy. I had a carburetor off a '47 Dodge that was close to fitting, so I modified it to fit on the Chevy engine. I don't know what happened, but that thing turned into a bomb. Nothing could keep up with it, even the new '55 Chevys couldn't out-accelerate it. All the guys nicknamed it the "go bomb."

I had a lot of fun racing guys with that thing. They had a hard time believing that six-cylinder engine could accelerate that quickly. I ended up selling it to Doug when he moved to San Bernardino, and he had more fun racing the guys in San Bernardino. He tried to take it over to Morrow Field to race it in the drags, but they told him, "Get that death trap out of here."

I can't remember what he did with it, and when I asked him, he can't remember either. I guess it will always remain a mystery.

(Photograph on page 220.)

The '40 Ford

Doug, Gerry, and I were pretty much like the three musketeers. We were all on our own as teenagers and were constantly running together. Gerry liked '40 Fords. He had purchased a pretty clean '40 sedan, and we spent a lot of time cruising in it. I was, at the time, running an auto repair shop on Baseline Avenue in San Bernardino, and the guys would usually stop by the shop in the evening, and we would consume massive quantities of beer.

I used to collect items in the shop for later projects. I had collected a Mercury crank, a set of 3/8 x 1/4 pistons, a set of high compressions heads, an Iskendarian cam, and a 3-jug manifold with Stromberg 97s on it.

We were all standing around one night, consuming beer, and came up with the brilliant idea of hopping up the engine in the '40 sedan. We pulled the car into the garage and proceeded to pull out the engine. I bored the block out 3/8" to fit the new pistons, set the Iskendarian cam in, and adjusted the valves. We put the Mercury crank in and started setting up the clearance on the wrist pins and putting the rods on the pistons.

You have to understand that by this time we had consumed a lot of beer, and while reaming out the rods for the wrist pins, one of them fell right through the rod. Now, the wrist pins are supposed to be a push fit into the rods and should not just fall through. Doug gave me a funny look as the wrist pin hit the floor, and I knew we had screwed up big time. Not having a spare rod to replace the screwed up one, I just winked and said, "Racing clearance."

We have used that as a cliché for years. It quite often fits many situations, and we just say, "Racing clearance," laugh, and go on.

We finished putting the engine back together and had it back in the car and running by daybreak. We fired it up and that wrist pin did give a pronounced tapping while the engine was idling. We decided it gave the car a distinct character.

It turned out the car was like a bomb. We went around choosing people off, and they would laugh when they heard the engine knocking. They would be shocked when we blew them away.

Back in the early '50s, Fords were dominant; they were hard to beat in a race. In 1955, Chevy came out with a 265 V-8, and it was a high-revving bomb. They were really fast. All the guys started buying them. Most of them were cheap, 210 coupes with a stick shift. Some of the cars were so cheap they didn't even have back seats in them, but they would go like a bomb.

Some of the guys' egos would get so big that you couldn't even stand to be around them. A lot of the guys thought they were speed racers, but they didn't know an air bleed screw on a carburetor from an air bleed screw on a wheel cylinder.

One Saturday night we decided to take the sedan to Morrow Field in Colton and run it through the drags. Gerry pulled up and entered it in the stock class. They didn't even bother to look under the hood and check the engine. I think the knocking engine fooled them into thinking it was a stock clunker. We ran a few practice runs and found that the rear wheels spun so badly that we couldn't even get it off the starting line.

In those days it was cool to have the nose down and the rear end sticking up in the air. All the cars running around in those days looked like stink bugs going down the street. One of us came up with the idea of taking the small front tires off and exchanging them with the larger rear tires. This helped level the car out, and we discovered we could take off in second gear without losing too much traction.

We started the competition and were doing really well. Doug would drive in one race, and then Gerry would drive in the next race. They kept up just enough to win but not excessively, so as not to attract any attention. They finally ended up winning all the races and found themselves running off as top eliminator with a little punk in a '55 Chevy who thought he was a speed racer and had an ego as big as Mount Everest.

Gerry was driving and creamed him big time. Doug and I were in the pits, waiting for Gerry to return, and didn't witness what happened, so the following is as told to us by Gerry.

That guy was hopping mad and came out of his car, screaming that nothing could beat his Chevy. He started protesting and hollering for the officials. Gerry just started driving back toward the pits with this guy screaming, honking his horn, and following him. The officials stopped Gerry before he got back to the pits to see what all the ruckus was about and had started questioning him when the little jerk drove up. He insisted on seeing the engine, so Gerry lifted the hood. The jerk pointed to the engine and started screaming, "That's not stock."

Gerry always was a man of few words. He just slammed the hood, said, "No shit," and drove off. He drove back to the pits to pick us up and told us what happened. We drove home laughing. It turned out to be a really fun evening.

The Girl from Desert Hot Springs

In the days of my youth, I dated a girl from Desert Hot Springs. I have no clue how I met a girl that far from the Riverside area and took her out on a date, but I did date a Native American girl from the Morongo Tribe in the Banning area, so possibly I met her during my times of being around the area.

We went out for dinner and dancing and had a nice time. Later that evening we just drove around and looked at the sights. We ended up parked on a peak overlooking the desert and were talking and enjoying each other's company. She started telling me about one of the areas we could see from where we were. She told me about another evening when she had been out here, and a cigar-shaped craft came flying over. It hovered for a while and then landed.

She described how these golden-skinned, golden-haired people, wearing wrinkle-free clothes, came out and escorted her into the craft. She described the people and the craft, but I wasn't able to absorb too much of it because the "Twilight Zone" music was playing so loud in my head that it was drowning her out.

Everybody knows that aliens are green not golden.

Another thing that stayed with me was the comment about their clothes. If you are my age, you will understand what I mean. If you are from the perma press generation, you will not understand.

When I was young our clothing was either wool or cotton. If you sat down, your clothes would be wrinkled when you stood up. The only way to keep this from happening was to starch your shirts. You had to use heavy starch on the shirts to keep them from wrinkling, and the heavy starching made them stiff and feel like cardboard. That made your dress shirts very uncomfortable.

When the girl made the statement about their clothes not wrinkling, I knew she was in la-la land. I decided I needed to get her home immediately. I took her straight home, dropped her off, said goodbye, and never looked back. I didn't leave her any contact information and never saw her again.

A few years later I married and joined the Riverside Fire Department. One morning I came home from work, and my wife showed me a new shirt she had just purchased for me. I commented it was nice and didn't think any more of it. She started wadding the shirt up in a little ball, and I said, "What are you doing? You're going to have to iron it again."

She just smiled and threw it in the dryer. When she pulled it out a few minutes later, there wasn't a wrinkle in it.

My mind drifted back to the girl from Desert Hot Springs. My God! I impugned that poor girl, perhaps in error. My hasty judgment kept me from dating a nice girl who was fun to be with. She would have been an interesting person to be around, and my stubbornness ruined what could have been a great relationship.

Because of that experience, I have found that I am much less judgmental and more open-minded. I guess the little green men actually are golden.

The Manure Pile

Back in the late '50s I was working for Woody Baker as an equipment operator, mechanic, truck driver, and jack-of-all-trades in his nursery business. I have written other essays of my exploits with Woody as we traveled around Mexico, Texas, Louisiana, and California in search of palm trees, cycads, yuccas, and other exotic plants for his nursery operation.

I was pretty full of myself at the time. My job was delivering plants and trees around California and running back and forth between Texas and Mexico, hauling trees back to California. I was feeling pretty important about my status in the nursery business.

We usually had a couple of individuals working around the yard, doing odd jobs, weeding, planting, trimming, etc. I had talked Woody into hiring one of my friends to do yard work around the nursery. The friend, whose name was Billy, was married to Jesse, another friend I have written about. They had a baby, and they really needed the money, but Billy was a lazy cuss, and it took a lot of prodding to keep him going.

One day I walked into the office and Woody was sitting there, looking out the window, watching Billy. Woody said, "That kid has been leaning on the shovel out there for over an hour. Go out there and fire him."

I told Woody that Bill had a family and asked if it would be all right for me to go out there and talk to him and tell him to get to work. Woody agreed. I walked out and approached Billy to try to give him a pep talk. When I walked up to Billy, he said, "This work is too hard. I'm going to have to have a raise if I'm going to work this hard."

I was stunned at what he had just said. I had just come out to try to save his job and see if I could motivate him, and he comes up with a comment like that. I told him there wasn't going to be a raise, so he might as well pack it in and go home. I hated firing people, but Billy made that firing real easy.

***

One day Woody was in a grouchy mood and told me to take one of the pickup trucks over to the dairy and get a load of manure. Now, at the time, I felt this was beneath me. I realize now that I was being ridiculous, but back then I took it as an insult to my position. I went to the dairy and told the guys I needed a load of manure, but I wanted the fresh stuff. They looked at me like I was nuts but directed me over to the fresh pile. I loaded the truck up and headed back to Woody's place, the urine pouring out the back of the truck.

I arrived back at the nursery in time to unload the manure just before quitting time. I unloaded the truck, and as I was leaving for the night, I looked in my rearview mirror and saw Woody leaning on a shovel, gazing quizzically at that pile of wet, urine-oozing, fresh manure. I thought to myself, *This is it. I'm going to be fired when I get to work in the morning.*

I arrived at work the next morning expecting to be fired, but nothing was ever said about the manure. After that I was never asked to go pick up another load of manure. I thought I was being very clever, but now that I'm older, I realize he probably thought I was too stupid to know you don't pick up the green manure.

The Old Camping Truck

I had this 1936 Chevy 4-door sedan that I had cut off the body from the top of the windshield back. I built a wooden bed on it with side compartments to hold food and supplies like sleeping bags, camping equipment, etc. I had built a rail up over the front of the bed of the now truck where you could stand and hold on while going down the road. This rail had another purpose as well that I will describe later.

The guys would all get together, pile all their equipment in the truck, and we would haul off on adventures to the mountains for fishing and to the desert for hunting. We had some great times in that old Chevy.

The Mojave Desert was pretty barren in the '50s. Victorville was probably no more than a square mile in size, Hesperia was just beginning, and Apple Valley was in its infancy, as well. There were very few paved roads, except for the main arteries, and this made it a virtual playground for adventurous kids like us. The mountains were virtually uninhabited, with lots of open space, and all of the lakes were accessible, so you could camp on the lakeshore pretty much anywhere you wished.

We would drive up the hill to Big Bear and spend a few days camping on the edge of the lake. We would go exploring and would fish for our meals. The old mining camps around Holcomb Valley were still pretty much intact and hadn't been destroyed by the off roaders yet, so going through the old ruins was pretty fascinating. Some of the buildings were still intact; some of them even still had silverware and condiments sitting around.

My grandfather and great uncle had some mining claims up in the Stoddard Mountains northeast of Victorville, and each year they would have to do $100 worth of what they called assessment work on each claim. They would then file a report with the county about what work had been done and the approximate value of that work. This had to be filed before June 1st of each year; otherwise, the claim was considered abandoned and any other person who was interested could legally jump the claim.

Each spring before the hot weather set in on the desert, we would load up the truck, and a bunch of us would go up to the mines. We would spend several days exploring the mines and basically just camping out. The mines consisted of three claims: the Mojave Girl, the Mojave Boy, and the Tarantula. The Mojave Girl was the one closest to the access road to the mines and was just above the crusher and the mining cabin. The Mojave Boy was over on the face of the next hill, and the Tarantula was a vertical shaft on top of the ridge.

The Mojave Boy was a horizontal shaft that went back about 300 feet into the mountain, and it didn't look like there had been much activity. On one trip up to the mines, my friend Gerry and I were looking around the entrance to the Mojave Boy and spotted something sticking up out of the ground. We dug it up and discovered it was a bunch of rock drills wrapped in a piece of burlap. That area is pretty dry and the burlap was intact, so the drills looked like new. We assumed by the find that the Mojave Girl had petered out, and they had been starting on the Mojave Boy, hoping to find a new vein.

We had made several trips to the mines, and the curiosity about the Tarantula kept building. It was too dark down there to see how deep it was, and throwing rocks down to listen for them to hit bottom was inconclusive. One year we devised a rope-and-pulley device, made a Bosun's chair out of rope, and the guys lowered me down into the shaft. We had great expectations of finding something spectacular down there, but we were very disappointed.

The darn shaft only went down about 30 feet before it turned off at an angle and went another 25 feet or so straight down. That's why we couldn't judge the depth by throwing a rock down the shaft. The sad finding was the mummified remains of what appeared to be a mountain lion on the floor of the shaft. Judging from its size and canines, I'm sure it was a mountain lion.

The poor thing must have fallen into the shaft in the dark and starved to death. There would have been no way to climb out of that shaft.

The Mojave Girl was another story. This mine went back into the mountain several hundred feet and had several tunnels branching out from the main tunnel. There was one tunnel that emptied out into a large cavern that was big enough to park a B-25 in. They must have found a major vein in that area. Some of the tunnels were partially blocked by rockslides, and we had to crawl over them to get through to the other side of the tunnel. We even had to dig out some of the rockslides in order to get over them.

We spent a lot of time exploring the Mojave Girl and had a great time doing it. I pulled an ore sample off the wall of the Mojave Girl and sent it in to have it assayed. The report came back at $600 per ton. In those days $200 per ton was considered worth mining, so the Mojave Girl was still very rich in ore.

On one trip to the mines, my friend Gerry found a couple of sticks of dynamite back in one of the tunnels in the Mojave Girl. I had a lever-action Winchester rifle at the time. My memory tells me that it was a 32/30. I have looked through several gun digests and have never found any mention of a 32/30, but I remember that the cartridge case was much larger than the 30/30-carbine cartridge.

I was a good shot in those days and was known to be able to shoot the eye out of a squirrel at 100 yards. We got the brainy idea of stuffing one of those sticks of dynamite in the crack of a large boulder. We got back about 60 feet and crouched down behind some bushes, and I aimed at that stick of dynamite to see if we could blow it up. I'm sure glad we didn't put both sticks in that boulder. When we came to our senses, it looked like we had the chicken pox. We had red spots all over us, we were bleeding, and it took hours to get all the sticks and rocks out of our teeth and hair. We very carefully carried the other stick of dynamite to a remote location and buried it.

One year we were up there in the evening. It had just gotten dark and we were all sitting around the fire, talking. If you have ever been on the desert at night, away from city lights, you know why Indians never attacked at night. It gets so darn dark that you can't see your hand in front of your face.

All of a sudden that night, it started getting very light. It just kept getting brighter and brighter. Then this horrendous roar started, and it kept getting louder and louder. Pretty soon this huge fireball that was literally glowing white came roaring right over us. The noise was so loud that I don't think we could have heard each other if we had screamed. The object then disappeared behind the mountain to the left of us. It scared the holy you know what out of us. We thought the world was coming to an end. I think the ground even shook.

We had no idea what the heck just happened, but about 20 years later some miners made the discovery of the Old Woman Meteorite in the Old Woman Mountains, 40 miles west of Needles, California. That meteorite is the second largest meteorite ever discovered. It is 38 inches long, 30 inches wide, and 34 inches high. I just wonder if that was what we saw that night. If it was, it appeared a lot bigger than that.

Now I will tell you about the top rail on the truck. We would chase animals all over the desert. We would chase anything that would run from us: coyotes, rabbits, foxes, anything. The guys would stand up on the truck with rifles resting on the rail and shoot at the animals as I chased them. It was great fun at the time.

Fortunately, the truck bounced so much that I don't remember anyone ever actually hitting anything. It really makes me feel ashamed, looking back on it now, knowing what we did, but it is part of the past and needs to be mentioned. I just hope God will forgive me for it.

As to the fate of the mines, I was the only one in the family who was willing to go up and do the assay work. There were many cousins who had a share in the mines, and I tried to get them to help, but to no avail. I couldn't even get them to chip in on the gas to help pay my expenses to get up to the mines. But I bet they would have had their hands out for their share if I started mining one of those mines.

One year I just decided to skip going up there. Two years later I took a friend with me to look at the mines. There were new monuments up. I looked at the paperwork and found that the claims had been jumped the day of expiration of our claims. Somebody had been watching the mines, possibly for years, ready to pounce. There were armed guards at the mine road, we could see bulldozers working, and they had a large, commercial crusher going. It was a big mining operation working up there.

As to the fate of the camping truck, one night my friends Don, Gerry, and I were chasing jackrabbits in the Central Avenue Hills just east of Riverside. I failed to miss a huge olive tree. I hit it dead center. If you have ever hit a solid object at 30 miles per hour, you will know that it knocks the snot out of you.

I went through the windshield, Don went over the windshield, and Gerry, who was standing up on the rail in the back, went right over the top and landed it the dirt behind the olive tree. I am happy to report that the olive tree remained unhurt, but my poor truck was a mess. I ended up with a major goose egg on my forehead. Everyone else was just bruised or scratched.

We were very lucky, but we were miles from nowhere and in no condition to walk. Luckily, we were able to rip the radiator away from the engine and drive the thing back to my house. It was steaming like a locomotive, and the engine was red hot by the time we got it home. The engine really started losing power a couple of miles from home, and I thought it was going to seize up, but the old girl got us home. It had gone its last mile, though. I pulled it over on its side, cut it up, and sold it for scrap metal. I just wish I had a picture of it for posterity. It was about the ugliest thing you have ever seen, but it served us well.

My Love of the Outdoors

My love of the outdoors began very early in life. As a small child I enjoyed playing outside, and I made friends who were my partners in exploring the fields, ravines, orchards, and springs in the area where I grew up. Every day was an adventure with little but the "great outdoors" and our imaginations to entertain us. We would spend the entire day engaged in these explorations. We would wander freely and only return home when the sun began to set and supper called us. And when I became an adult, it was only natural that I wanted to share the wonders of Mother Nature with my wife, family, and friends.

But being a responsible family man meant that my trips and explorations were limited by the constraints of earning a living. My working career was varied and interesting, with many detours along the way. In fact I began earning a living at an early age. I earned money with a paper route, I picked up and sold scrap metal, and I sold ice cream bars to overheated travelers from my ice cream wagon, all between the ages of ten and 14.

I went on to do odd jobs after my dad died and my mother took off, leaving me homeless. I worked in a butcher shop for a while. I started going back to the junior college to try to finish school. I worked during the summer as a carny for Ritter United Shows. I ended up in San Bernardino, running an automotive repair shop and then hauling palm trees out of South Texas and Mexico. Then I went to work for the California Division of Forestry in San Bernardino County.

I didn't have much time for camping during those times, but I guess you could say the Forestry job was like camping. I spent a lot of time in the forest and stayed out overnight a lot of the time. I don't think sleeping on the fire hose in the back of a fire truck could be considered camping, but I did enjoy being out in the forest, and I really liked the job. It was the 120-hour-per-week work schedule that I didn't like. If it hadn't been for the hours, I probably would have retired from the Forestry.

I met my wife and we got married while I worked for the

Forestry, but I left them and joined the Riverside City Fire Department not long after getting married, to allow more time with my family. It was while I was in the fire department that we began to spend more time camping.

My wife and I loaded up a tent and camping supplies in my Cadillac in May of 1962 and headed to the High Sierras on our first camping trip together. Our first child—a daughter—was born three months after the High Sierra trip, and that curtailed our camping for a while.

We did make a lot of one-day drives to the mountains while our daughter was an infant. We would just drive around, then park and look at the scenery and smell the fresh, pine-scented air. Eventually, we moved to the mountains and raised our children there.

By the way, I know some people think motion sickness is psychological, but I can attest to the fact that it is not. Our poor daughter would throw up darn near every trip up to the mountains. There is no way that a six-month old baby could have a psychological hang up.

By 1966, we had three children, and our 1958 T-Bird was so small that we couldn't get everybody into it, so I ended up trading it for a 1960 Ford station wagon. I built a box to put on top of it to hold all of our camping supplies. It took a lot of stuff to take that many people camping. I was still working for the fire department at that time, and I would get two, 2-week vacations a year. If I traded shifts with a couple of guys, I could stretch it out to three weeks.

We used that time off to go to the beach and the mountains. We drove up the coastal California Highway 1 all the way to Concord to stay with my wife's classmates John and Lois at their residence. We toured San Francisco, took the kids to the zoo, and took the bay tour.

On that tour, my wife's little sister insisted on standing on the bow of the boat, even though the boat captain kept warning everybody to come inside and watch through the glass-enclosed observation deck. Just as we went under the Golden Gate, a large wave came over the bow of the boat, thoroughly drenching my wife's little sister. The spectators in the observation deck got quite a kick out of it. My sister-in-law spent the remainder of the day wet and obviously very cold. But to her credit she never complained. We spent a week with John and Lois and then headed to the Yosemite Valley and camped there for a week before heading home.

I decided to set the station wagon up to tow. I reinforced the rear springs and had my friend Ron help me change the rear end ratio to 4.11 to one. I removed the automatic transmission and put in a standard, floor-shift transmission. I put a heavy-duty trailer hitch on it, and I was ready to tow.

We headed north to meet up with our friends John and Lois and a group of their friends for a camping excursion. We rented a 14-foot Scotty trailer while we were up north and headed out to the Trinity Lake area for a week of fishing and beer drinking.

My son Gerry was just an infant during that trip, and I have pictures of him being bathed in a washtub. We had a great time. There were plenty of small children for our kids to play with and they really enjoyed themselves playing in the lake and on the beach.

My wife almost drove us nuts trying to keep the trailer clean. She was so afraid we would lose our deposit when we retuned it that she was sweeping and cleaning right behind us as we went in and out of the trailer. That trailer was so clean when I took it back that I thought the guys were going to kiss me when they inspected it. Obviously, we got the deposit back.

I left the fire department in 1968 and went on to pursue a career in electronics. That curtailed our camping for a while. We were still using the station wagon and would take short trips in it, mostly to the beaches, and when vacation time came we would head for Lake Tahoe.

I started Layton Electronics in 1971 and then took another

hiatus from camping. Around 1974 I was able to take some time off, and I cleaned out one of my Chevy service vans. I pulled all the inventory, tools, and equipment out of it, removed the workbench, and took the queen-sized mattress off our bed and put it in the back of the van. I loaded all of the gear onto the roof-top carrier, and we took off to Lake Tahoe. We set the tent up for the kids to sleep in, and my wife and I slept in the van on the mattress. I can honestly say that is the first time in years that I woke up fully rested while camping. I decided it was time for a real camper.

We started looking for a camper and found out that my wife's cousin Kaye and her husband, Gary, were trying to sell theirs. It was a 12 ½-foot Eldorado with a full bath, sitting on top of a 1970 Chevy ¾-ton pickup. It was a really nice rig, and I gave them $3,000 for it. Our older daughter was old enough by then that she didn't want to go anywhere with us, and I think our older son only went with us a few times, but our younger daughter and our younger son went everywhere with us.

We made many trips to the beach, staying at Campland on the Bay in San Diego. We would tour San Diego and go to the Zoo. We stayed at state parks up and down the coast in the camper, and, over the years, went all the way into Oregon, Washington, Canada, and down into Colorado in the camper. We toured the Mesa Verde Cliff Dwellings in Colorado and the petrified forests in Arizona. We put a lot of miles on that camper in the 11 years we had it and had a great time and made a lot of memories.

I sold my electronics business in 1985 and bought a 1977 Ford F250 pickup—which I still own today—and a 31-foot Coachman fifth-wheel trailer from a neighbor. We sold the camper to my wife's niece and nephew, Steve and Tammy, loaded up the fifth-wheel, and headed out. I thought I was retiring and was going to travel full time.

We went back to Campland and spent a lot of time there. We went to Oregon and camped on the coast. We spent a lot of time around the Lake Tahoe area. It was great riding our bicycles on the trails around the Lake. We made quite a few five-day trips to Las Vegas, usually staying at the Circus Circus RV Park.

Eventually, we grew tired of traveling and returned home. I went back to school, earned a degree in business, and went back to the company that bought me out and became a branch manager. That lasted for about a year. I left in disgust over how they wanted their shops run, and I went to work for the County of Los Angeles Internal Services Division. That limited our travel to days off and vacation time. Mostly, during that time, we would take the fifth wheel up to the Kern River for fishing trips.

By 1996 I had built up six weeks of vacation with the county and was ordered to take it. I planned out a trip to Calgary, Alberta, Canada, to see the Calgary Stampede. We planned the trip in conjunction with our younger daughter and her family. We took the fifth wheel and they drove their car. We headed out to Las Vegas and then to Bryce Canyon in Utah. We stopped at Layton, Utah, and toured the Layton Hills Mall. We went on to Salt Lake City to tour the Mormon Tabernacle and then headed out to Yellowstone National Park. We sat in the freezing cold in Yellowstone, waiting for Old Faithful to spout off. It finally did—it was just a disappointing fizzle. We had made several stops along the way to Yellowstone so my son-in-law and I could do some fishing on some side trips. The fishing was not good and turned out to be disappointing, but we had a good time trying.

We headed out of Yellowstone in a snowstorm and headed for our old friends Jim and Ellen's home in Absarokee, Montana. We spent several days visiting with them, fishing on the Stillwater River that ran through their property.

We bid farewell to Jim and Ellen and headed north to Calgary, Alberta, Canada, where we attended the famous Calgary Stampede Rodeo and spent a couple of days touring Calgary. Our younger daughter, Christine, her husband, Eric, and their girls had reached the end of their vacation time, so they packed up their car, said their goodbyes, and headed home. We had had such a good time traveling with them, especially, traveling with our granddaughters. We always had one of the granddaughters sitting in the center seat of our truck with us on our journey. It was such a delight and we were severely depressed when they left.

Christine and Eric were unable to haul the girl's bicycles home, so they left them behind for us to take back. We got so depressed, looking out in our camp space and seeing those little bicycles, that I finally wrapped them up in a tarp and tied them down on the luggage carrier on the roof of the fifth wheel.

We spent a couple more days in Calgary, toured the Olympic Park, and then headed west toward the Puget Sound. We eventually worked our way south to Modesto, California, where we dropped the girl's bicycles off at their house.

We made our way home and parked our fifth wheel in the secure, RV-storage area where we kept it when not in use. Not long after that, a couple of 11- and 12-year-old boys broke into the RV-storage area and torched several trailers and motor homes, including ours.

I bought a small, fifth-wheel trailer that we used until 2002, when I retired from Los Angeles County. We made numerous trips back to Campland and our favorite fishing hole on the Kern River with that little trailer. We sold it right after our retirement and bought a larger, fifth-wheel that we have to this day.

We followed our daughter Christine and her husband and their girls on their vacation to Steamboat Springs, Colorado, and we set out on our own when they headed home. We stayed on the road for a couple of months, visiting many of the national landmarks through Colorado, Wyoming, Nebraska, Montana, Idaho, Washington, Oregon, Nevada, and California. We visited several friends during the course of that trip.

That was the last big trip we made in the RV. All of the trips since that time have been short ones to local rallies and winter trips to spend time in Yuma, Arizona, to get away from the cold winter months at home. We are not going much anymore, due to my wife's illness, but we still enjoy getting away. We are blessed with many wonderful memories.

P.S.: In the three years since my wife's passing, I continue to travel with my fifth wheel, exploring nature and visiting with family and friends. Once a nature lover, always a nature lover.

Gay & Larry's

Gay and Larry's was a Mexican restaurant located on what is now Mission Blvd. in Rubidoux, California. Gay and Larry's was noted for their unusual and delicious chile rellenos. Those rellenos were famous the world over, and you can still find them mentioned in chat rooms all over the Internet.

After many years of being in business, Gay and Larry's closed their doors. I have no idea why—maybe it was just old age or sickness—but they shut down and never divulged the recipe for their rellenos. I would have thought they would have found someone to sell that recipe to. It probably would have brought a pretty good price.

Many people are still searching for the perfect imitation of those rellenos. We followed several Internet chat rooms in the hopes of finding other rellenos like the famous Gay and Larry's ones. We had even sought out restaurants that were, supposedly, producing Gay and Larry's rellenos, but we were always disappointed to find they were just the plain old rellenos you can get at any Mexican restaurant. We decided the owners of these restaurants were probably posting the lies themselves to draw in business.

I discovered Gay and Larry's early in my dating career and would impress my dates with my culinary sophistication by taking them there for dinner dates. I took my wife there, and she immediately fell in love with the place. We spent many a night dining there. We spent so much time there that we ended up knowing everyone employed there and we became like family.

My children literally grew up celebrating every special event in their lives in Gay and Larry's party room. Later, their spouses spent special occasions there as well with our entire family. They all talk about it to this day.

Gay and Larry's was quite an institution. I doubt the owners had any idea of the impact they had on people's lives. It was with great sadness we received the news of their closure.

We used to babysit a friend's daughter. The little girl was a pretty little thing and just as sweet as she could be. We all adored her and treated her like one of our own. One night we decided to take our entire family, including the little girl, to Gay and Larry's for dinner. Here we came walking in, our children in tow. I was leading with them in tack like a duck with all the little ducklings following behind. My wife was a petite thing and was about seven months pregnant with our younger son. She really showed when she was pregnant, and she looked like she was about to have an elephant. Being so petite, my wife looked like she was 15 until her late thirties or even early forties, so God only knows what those people in the restaurant were thinking. But by the looks they gave us, I can imagine.

We walked in and waited to be seated. My wife was right behind me, all pooched out from her pregnancy, followed by our friends' daughter, our older daughter, older son, and younger daughter all on her tail. The stares were like knives in my back. I could just imagine what they were thinking. "Who is that creep with that pregnant sixteen-year-old girl with all those babies. He must be from the south and married her when she was twelve."

They didn't have any idea that my wife was 25 years old. I just smiled as we walked in and sat down to a great dinner and a wonderful evening.

I have never forgotten those stares. If a stare could kill I would have been dead a long time ago.

My Cadillac

I always had this love for the 1952 Cadillac Coupe DeVille. Financing and credit cards back in the '50s were unheard of except for housing, so you just saved up your money to purchase appliances, clothing, tools, automobiles, etc. I finally saved up $1,400 in cash, and in 1958 I bought myself a 1952 Coupe DeVille.

The first thing I did with that car was lower the front end two inches. (Which was the fad in those days.) I removed the bumpers, all the chrome trim, and the emblems. I wet sanded the entire car and took it to the local automotive paint shop just north of the underpass on North Main Street in Riverside and had it painted 1958 Chevy Impala Cashmere Blue. It is possibly one of the prettiest blues I have ever seen. I saw an Impala on the showroom floor when they first came out and fell in love with the color.

It cost me $10 to have the car painted, and that included the paint. Can you imagine what it would be like to have lived back then on the salary you're making today? You could have lived in absolute luxury.

I brought the Cadillac back to my sister's house in Arlanza after it was painted and let it sit in her garage for a week before I started putting all the chrome, bumpers, trim, lights, emblems, etc. back on. The Cadillac looked like a brand new car when I was finished.

The Impala with that color never was seen on the street. I don't know why, because the color was beautiful. But it did afford me the opportunity to have the only car in the area of that color. The Cadillac was a real eye turner. Every time I parked, someone would notice and come over and comment on how beautiful the car was and ask what color it was.

If someone in those days saw a color they liked on a car, they would run down and get their car repainted, and pretty soon there would be a dozen cars running around with that color on them. Not wanting that to happen, I always answered their question about the color with, "It's just a powder blue." I never told anyone what the color was, not even my close friends.

About a month after I had it painted, one of my close friends, Jerry, borrowed the Cadillac to go pick up his future wife, Earlene, from work at the Golden State Theater in Riverside. When he got back there was a two-foot long gouge in the right rear quarter panel. The car was big and long, and I guess he misjudged, pulling into a parking space. I never had that gouge repaired, and it was the only dent that car ever had in it for the entire five years I owned it.

The most amazing thing about that car was the gas mileage. It averaged 20 miles per gallon, which was unheard of in those days. This was a 6,000-pound car that was over 20 feet long. It had a fair amount of power.

The only problem was the brakes. Pushing on the brake pedal at over 55 miles per hour felt like pushing on the floorboard. There was just no reaction. The brakes were simply inadequate for a car that heavy. You had to slow it down before it would start to stop. Fortunately, the engine had enough compression that it would start slowing down quickly when you let off on the accelerator.

I went everywhere in that Cadillac. It made numerous trips to the beach and mountains. That Cadillac was so comfortable to drive that a 300-mile trip in it felt like a drive across town. Sitting in the seats in that car was like sitting on a comfortable sofa in your living room. That car was so classy looking that the girls just loved it, and it spent many a night at the drive-in theater or the drive-in burger joints with me and a girl by my side.

I made several trips to Las Vegas with my friends in that Cadillac. We even made trips to Colorado and Utah. The car was so dependable that I could take off anytime with the confidence there would be no problems. I dated my beautiful wife in that Cadillac. I even proposed to her in the Cadillac. We took the Cadillac to Las Vegas together to attend her best friend Pat's wedding to Ed. (My future wife stayed in Pat's room, and I stayed in Ed's room, if you're curious.)

Doyalene and I took the Cadillac to Las Vegas to get married. We spent the first three years of marriage with that car. We would put a tent in the trunk, along with sleeping bags and an ice chest, and take off on camping trips. We would go to the High Sierras and the beach. That Cadillac was part of our family. I always get my granddaughter's goat by telling her that her mother was conceived in that Cadillac.

I don't know why, I guess I just got tired of the Cadillac, but one day I sold it to my friend Jerry. He pulled the engine and transmission to put in a hot rod he was building and hauled the body off to a scrap yard. It was years later before I realized what an integral part of our lives that Cadillac had been and started regretting getting rid of it.

I actually had dreams about the Cadillac. In one dream the Cadillac was parked in someone's garage on Beechwood Place in Riverside. The dream was so vivid that I went to the guy's house and asked him if I could look in his garage. To my disappointment the Cadillac wasn't there.

(Photographs on pages 222 and 223.)

Skating

Our family moved from Highgrove to Riverside in 1946, soon after my brother died. Shortly after that, I met my lifelong friend Doug. Doug and I were both from poor families, and having everyday necessities was difficult. Doug and I spent every day from dawn to dark together. Doug was as high spirited and adventurous as I was, and we explored every nook and cranny in Riverside and the surrounding area. I believe, now that we are grown, that back then we gave each other balance and a sense of normalcy, and that was the glue that solidified our relationship. Doug was with me for virtually all the exploring and adventures I have written about in my essays.

Doug is a very charismatic person, and I have joked that he could sell an icebox to an Eskimo. His abilities provided us with the funds to entertain ourselves. I would come up with the ideas and implement them, and he would use his charm to sell them and make money. We were entrepreneurs by the time we were 11 years old. We sold salve, ice cream bars, snow cones, lemonade, scrap metal, and just about anything we could come up with. Our parents didn't have any money, so we had to make it ourselves if we wanted to go to the show, the plunge, the fair, skating, or any other activities we wanted to be involved in.

I got a paper route with the Los Angeles *Herald Examiner* and Doug got one with the local *Press Enterprise*. We both delivered papers and collected with each other and shared the proceeds.

We used to go skating every Friday night with the idea of picking up girls. I can't remember ever picking up a girl, but we sure learned to skate. We used to get out there on the boys-only skate and go as fast as we could. I was a foot taller than Doug at that time, and with those little legs of his, he just couldn't keep up. We would get going so fast that we were nearly prone going around the corners. We had to do crossover skating to get the back skate in front and over the front skate, or we would go into the wall. Once in a while we would get so low that the skates would just kick out from under us and we would slam into the wall. (Hopefully, rump first.) That was extremely exhilarating, and I can still remember feeling the thrill of cranking around those turns with my adrenaline spiking.

One day some girl told Doug that he looked like Bing Crosby, so he started singing Bing Crosby songs. Believe me, he was no Bing, and he was driving me nuts. Everywhere we went he would be singing those songs.

We always rode our bicycles out to the skating rink in Magnolia Center. It was a long ride from the north end of town to Magnolia Center, and listening to those songs all the way was unbearable. Fortunately, my legs were much longer than Doug's, so I would take off and leave him behind. I always rode just far enough in front of him so I didn't have to listen to his horrid singing.

About 60 years later Doug received a horrific diagnosis from his doctor, and the thought of losing my best friend was unbearable. Doug and I talked every day while he was going through the treatments, and we would talk about our childhood adventures. Reminiscing seemed to calm him. One day we were congratulating each other on our successes and our families, and Doug was talking about our wives. I congratulated him on marrying one beautiful woman, and he was returning the compliment when all of a sudden, he blurted out, "How did you marry such a beautiful woman? You never were much to look at."

I was taken aback but finally said, "Not everybody can be a Bing." There was a long pause, and I thought "Oh my God, he's forgotten."

After I married and brought my bride back to Riverside, we would go skating on Wednesday nights. We used to go to a rink around Tequesquite Avenue and Pine down in the hollow. As our children grew we would take them and put them on skates as soon as they could walk. They all learned to be excellent skaters.

We had great fun as a family on skate night. My wife and I

would waltz around the rink with our young children skating around us. It was a great time. My children have brought up their memories of those nights on the rink many times. My younger daughter often recalls how enthralled she was, watching us waltz around that rink floor.

After we moved to Crestline, we would go to Blue Jay and spend the evening ice skating together. In addition to being good skaters, the kids all went on to be excellent skiers and snowboarders. In later years I would pull our skates out of the closet and my wife and I would take our grandkids skating, which started the memories all over again.

After we quit skating, I used to pull the skates out of the closet once a year and oil and polish them. One year I pulled my wife's out and the leather was all rotted, so I had to discard them. Mine were ok, so I oiled and polished them and put them away.

I just don't bother anymore, but every time I get a pair of shoes out of the closet, I see those skates and think about putting them on and trying them out again. Then I remember my age, and the thought vanishes.

The Carny

I decided to go back to college, so I attended Riverside City College in 1957-58. I visited a local fair in Arlington at the end of the spring semester in 1958 to visit a friend who was running a fund-raising booth at the fair. I was talking with a couple of people at the fair and mentioned I was on summer break and looking for work. They took me over to the man in charge of the fair. He hired me on the spot to run one of the small children's rides. That set me up with some unusual friendships and experiences. The carny circuit is an altogether different world.

I cannot recall the name of the man who owned the carnival, but the name of the company was Ritter's United Shows. I still have the pay stubs and W-2 for my time of employment there. I assume the man's last name was Ritter. He was a tall, slender man of about six foot three inches, and he was the reason I learned to punch with my elbows.

We used to have problems at the fairs; some of the male customers would get drunk and cause trouble. The booths would always clear out, with the women and children staying behind to guard the booths, as the men all responded to the trouble spot when the alarm was sounded. Mr. Ritter would run up close and start knocking people down with his elbows. They would hardly ever get right back up once he popped them.

I was so impressed with that old man's ability to handle himself that I asked him how he did it. He showed me the proper way and emphasized that the main element was surprise. Most people think you are going to swing at them when you approach them, but the elbow is such a short, quick blow that it catches them completely off guard. Plus, if done right, there is no pain to yourself when compared to the bruised knuckles if you hit someone with your fist. I used my elbows from then on whenever a situation occurred. That bony old elbow would literally knock the snot out of my opponents, and there was little discomfort to me.

* * *

Part of the guys' jobs was to take a break every few hours and meet up with one of the girls whose parents ran one of the booths. We would grab a large stuffed animal and walk around the fair, pretending to be a couple. The suckers' girlfriends would see us, and they would insist that their boyfriends win one for them. (Which was nearly impossible.) We even had couples stop us and ask where we won our prize. We would always be cordial and escort them to the booth where, supposedly, we had won it.

We would all take turns during the day so that people wouldn't see the same couple walking around. Some of the girls I walked around with looked pretty nice, and it was kind of fun pretending we were a couple, but some girls were pretty gross, and it was really embarrassing to be seen with them. I always hoped that none of my friends would see me with them.

***

All of the booths where they did the coin tosses, hoops, bottles, goldfish, etc. were all owned by individual entrepreneurs who paid a space fee. We were only responsible for the rides owned by Ritter's United Shows.

Disassembling those rides and moving them gave me quite an insight into construction practices on that type of equipment. Everything was on hinge pins; we pulled the pins and everything folded down. It only took an experienced crew a few hours to pull down all the equipment and be on the road. We would usually pull the equipment down the night the fair closed and be on the road to the next fair at daybreak. Setting up was literally as easy. It was quite an experience.

We always had a lot of fun putting the rides up at the new locations. We would fire up the equipment and give it a test run. We would all pile on, and one of the guys would run the ride at full speed. I learned how to spin the octopus chair with body movements so fast I would almost lose consciousness. Over the years I have given the kids and grandkids quite a ride in the octopus with my ability to spin it so fast.

We got the giant swing spinning so fast one time that the chains were almost horizontal with the ground. We were so disoriented when we got off that we could barely function for the remainder of the day. We found out later that we had it rocking so severely on its sweeps that one of the arms bent. We probably wouldn't have survived if that thing had come down with us on it, but it was sure a blast.

***

The ride operators got their rides by seniority. The guy lowest on the totem got the little kiddies rides. They were the most boring to run. The top guy always got the hammer. The hammer was hard to run, but an experienced man could pause it at the top and jerk it back. That movement would empty the change out of the pockets of the guys riding it, and the operator could pick up the change and make several dollars a night extra running the hammer. The hammer operator never shared his bounty with the other guys.

***

Working as a carny was quite an experience. The hours were long and the work was hard. A 14-hour day was common, and we slept in the bed of the equipment trucks with no bedding or mattress padding available. There was no lodging available and the sanitation facilities were few and far between. We were always happy when we were at a fairground that had full restroom facilities with shower access. The carnys all emitted an odor because of the lack of sanitation facilities. I myself was quite pungent at times.

The food was another situation. There was no transportation available because we all had to drive the equipment to the fair sites, and the trucks were usually attached to the equipment. The only option was to eat at the booths at the fair, and as most people know, fair food is quite expensive. We made about $7.00 per day and spent around half of that for food, which didn't leave much spending money. By the end of the carny season, after all the gambling and drinking, we didn't have much left in our pockets.

***

The Ritter family was a strange breed. Mr. Ritter's family always traveled with him through the entire season. They had a daughter who was about 15, and she thought she was a queen. We were about the lowest of all human subculture in her mind—and in her mother's mind, too—and if we slipped and called Mr. Ritter "the old man," we were thoroughly chastised about it. I have never been ridiculed so much in my life and find it hard to believe the workers tolerated it.

We were expected to go over to the Ritters' trailer in the evenings to visit after the day's work ended. It was very uncomfortable being around those arrogant people. You could tell they had nothing but disdain for their help.

***

We cleaned and repainted all the equipment before putting it in storage at season's end, and then we had one final party. I said goodbye to all my new friends and never looked back.

I can't imagine living an entire life as a carny. Carnys are definitely a different breed of people.

The Tow Trucks

In the 1960s I was a fireman with the Riverside City Fire Department. One night I was on duty at Fire Station 1 and was standing on the apron in front of the station, enjoying the cool summer evening and talking with Captain Folkers. The bells went off announcing a call for Rescue 1 and Engine 6 to respond to La Cadena Drive and the freeway.

Captain Folkers was on the rescue truck that day, and we were standing there, wondering why the driver wasn't showing up. After a couple of minutes, Captain Folkers told me to jump in the driver's seat and respond to the incident.

We arrived at the scene and found a Hispanic gentleman had taken the La Cadena off ramp on the 91 Freeway, and apparently, the driver's-side door had flown open, causing him to lose control. Somehow, his left leg came out of the car and his vehicle was wedged into the guardrail with his leg sticking through the space between the curbing and the bottom of the guardrail.

The crew from Engine 6 was already on scene, trying to jack the car up to get the victim out of the vehicle. The poor guy let out a scream every time they caused the vehicle to move. I stuck my head through the window and tried to check on the condition of the man. He was just sitting there, puffing like crazy on a cigarette.

I asked him if he was in pain anywhere else besides the leg, but he didn't answer or even acknowledge that I was there. He just sat there, puffing on that cigarette. He had to be in a terrible amount of pain. I told him we would have him out in a minute and went to the back of the vehicle to survey the situation.

I lay down on the road and looked under the vehicle. I realized that his leg was sticking through the opening between the curb and the bottom of the guardrail and was in the clear, not touching anything. I called Captain Folkers over and asked him to lie down and look. I explained the situation and advised him that we could have the tow truck driver do a low snatch with the cable, hook it to the car, and pull the car straight away from the curb without doing any more damage to the driver's leg.

Captain Folkers asked, "Can he do that?"

I said, "Sure. Any good tow truck driver can make a straight pull from almost any angle."

Captain Folkers called the tow truck driver over and explained the situation. The tow truck driver agreed, hooked up to the car, and pulled it away from the guardrail. The guys opened the driver's door and lifted the man out, laid him on the gurney, and he was off to the hospital with a very painful and damaged leg. We returned to the station, and I was stuck on that rescue truck for the remainder of my time at Station 1.

***

The highs and the lows of working rescue were indescribable. The elation when you are able to resuscitate someone, especially a child, is an unbelievable feeling, as are the horrid, depressing lows when you lose one. There were many happy moments, as well as sad, and many funny things. It is amazing the situations human beings can get themselves into. Even today, many years later, I can still recall some of the more memorable rescues.

One day we responded to a call for a child with his finger caught in a bicycle sprocket. We arrived on scene, and there were already two police officers and three firemen there. The fireman count increased to five with our arrival, and sure enough, they were standing around this little boy of about five years of age whose finger was stuck between the chain and the sprocket.

The guys decided the best bet was to just cut the chain, so one of the guys went back to the fire truck to get the bolt cutters. You have to understand that in the days those guys were growing up, bicycle pedals would not go backwards. You pedaled forward to propel the bike, and pushed backward on the pedals to stop the bike, so in their paradigm, the only way to get the kid's finger loose was to cut the chain.

About this time the kid's little brother came walking up. The little guy appeared to be about two years old. He looked at his big brother, looked at his brother's finger, and pushed the pedal backwards—releasing big brother's finger. Big brother looked quizzically at his finger and just walked off. You should have seen the look on everybody's faces. It was priceless.

***

There were other late night calls, like calls to accidents on Victoria Avenue, that we dreaded because we always knew what we were in for before we arrived on the scene. Victoria Avenue was a horrid road. It was as deadly as it was beautiful. One night we arrived on the scene, and this guy had apparently hit a palm tree at high speed. The car must have bounced back at the same time that he was thrown through the windshield, because he was wedged between the tree and the car.

We had a heck of a time getting him out of there. We must have worked for an hour to extricate him. There was never a moan or groan from him, and we just figured we were recovering a body. We turned him over to the ambulance crew when we got him out and went back to the station.

I believe it was Captain Guzzeta who called the hospital the next morning to inquire about the status of the man. The captain came in with a shocked look on his face. He told us the hospital said the man was ok, and they had released him earlier.

***

Many calls did not have a happy ending. We had a family tragedy one night on Victoria Avenue. Thankfully, I was not on duty that night. The guys arrived at the scene and recognized one of the bodies as the son of one of the captains. They called on the radio, requesting the battalion chief to come to the scene immediately. We didn't have cell phones is those days, and the radios only had one frequency, so all the traffic was heard in the stations, as well as the scanners in everybody's home.

The battalion chief was advised of the situation as soon as he arrived on scene and quickly drove back to pick up the captain and bring him to the scene to identify his son. It was a bleak time for the fire department.

One night some kids hit one of the palm trees at high speed. They had put a bunch of heavy chunks of concrete in the trunk of their car in an apparent attempt to lower the car to make it look cool. I won't describe what those chunks of concrete did to them as they ripped through the back seat, but it wasn't pretty. Big lesson for everybody: "Don't put heavy objects in the trunk of your car. They can become missiles."

***

We also had a lot of calls involving Corvairs. The Chevrolet Corvair had just come out and was becoming very popular. A lot of the kids were getting them, and they turned out to be deadly. They were so bad that the CHP bought two of them and did high-speed tests on them. They discovered that making a lane change at high speed caused the car to lift just enough for the inside tire to tuck under, so when you turned back into the lane, the car would go out of control. There was an option for a stabilizer bar—known as a Camber Compensator—that prevented this from happening. The option only cost about $8.00, but some people wouldn't pay for it. Knowing that some Corvairs were equipped with this stabilizer solved the puzzle of why some of them were crashing and others weren't. I understand they all came with the stabilizing bar after the CHP report came out.

With the later model Corvairs, General Motors changed out the rear ends to the same style as the ones in the Corvette to stop the tire-tuck problem. General Motors did everything possible to cover up the stability problem with the Corvair, even vilifying some people who tried to bring the problem to light.

We could almost bet we would be responding to a Corvair accident on the freeway every Friday or Saturday night we were on duty. One night we responded to an incident on the 91 near Central Avenue. The CHP officer on scene walked up to us as we arrived and said, "Soon we won't have to go to the trouble of cutting them out, because next year's model will be coming out with three handles on each side." It just shows what an epidemic they were when people start making casket jokes about them.

***

Cars started coming from the factory with seatbelts in them in the '60s, and I noticed that the people who wore them seemed to sustain fewer injuries than people without them. That made me a real fan of seatbelts. I went out and bought seatbelt kits for both of my cars, and my kids all knew the car wasn't going to move until all the seatbelts were latched.

***

One night we were at the 14th Street underpass and cutting a guy out of a Corvair while the lookey-loos were driving by. We heard this tremendous crash and looked up just in time to see a guy rear end a '58 Cadillac. The guy in the Cadillac was probably going 45 miles per hour, and the other car about 65 miles per hour when they hit. They were probably both looking at the accident and didn't see each other.

When that Cadillac was rear ended, the gas tank came out and exploded in a ball of flames. The Cadillac took off from the impact like it had been shot out of a cannon, with that burning gas tank following it. It looked just like a rocket being launched, the poor driver with his head pinned back, hanging on for dear life. That's a memory I will never forget, and I can't tell the story without laughing. It was one of the funniest things I have ever seen.

The CHP instantly shut down the freeway. Since the Corvair driver was deceased, we dropped what we were doing and headed across the freeway to help the guys out. Fortunately, no one was injured—but the cars were totaled.

***

We didn't have the tools available in earlier years that are available today to extract people from cars. All we had was a sawzall and our ingenuity, so we utilized the tow truck drivers to give us the power to pull cars apart. Some of those drivers were brilliant in their ability to peel back the roof of a car or pull a door off with the winch and cable on the tow trucks. The tow truck was a valuable tool for us in earlier years.

***

Another call we responded to was a driver vs. a light pole. I wish I could remember the location, but I just can't recall it. Central Avenue came down the hill, made a slight turn, and the road was about ten feet higher than the terrain around it. One of the military guys from March Field was coming home from his shift on the base, and I believe he was just tired, fell asleep, and went off the road.

His car launched off the embankment and hit one of the city's light poles. I seem to recall that the light pole went through the windshield and came out through the rear window, or the car hit the pole and took it down. I do remember that the car was upside down with the roof completely collapsed, and the light pole was under it with the broken light fixture sticking out from the collapsed roof.

The city streetlights were high voltage connected in parallel throughout the city. They ran high voltage to the lights to keep the current low so there would be very little voltage drop on a long string of lights. The pole was still active, and the entire car was electrified. It would really sting when you tried to touch it.

There was no way of opening the crushed doors, so we got the idea of going through the trunk. Gas was pouring out of the tank, so we knew we had to get this guy out quickly. One of the guys took an axe and started chopping the trunk lid around the lock, and the lid dropped open.

Dan Torchia was one of those guys who wasn't afraid of

anything. He jumped into the trunk and started chopping the back seat down. As soon as that seat fell down, the driver shot out of the car like a bullet. We laughed later when Dan said all he saw were these eyeballs coming at him. The guy didn't even wait for Dan to get out of the way. He went right over Dan's back on the way out.

***

Just a quick note about Dan. Dan was a great guy with a good personality and was a lot of fun to be around. One day we got a call about a bomb on Terracina Drive near Riverside City College. When we arrived on scene, law enforcement was already there, evacuating the area and roping it off.

A car was sitting next to the curb with the trunk open and the supposed bomb sitting in the trunk. Dan climbed off the engine, sauntered over to the car, and looked in the trunk. Then he reached down, picked up the bomb, and raised it over his head. Everybody was ducking for cover as he turned around with a big grin on his face and shouted, "Highway Flares." We got quite a laugh out of that one.

***

My time as a firefighter ended when I had to move for my son's health. My father suffered terribly from asthma, and thankfully, I never inherited it, but I am afraid my older son, Gary Jr., did.

Riverside was really starting to have smog problems in the '60s, and it was getting progressively worse. My son started having convulsions when the smog rolled in, and the doctors attributed it to the asthma. I didn't want to leave the area, so I started doing research. I found that the inversion layer in Southern California hardly ever rises over 4,500 feet, so in 1969 I purchased a home on top of a 5,000-foot peak in Crestline.

***

I left the fire department after my move to Crestline and took a job with the Motorola service shop on North Main Street in Riverside. The tow truck drivers would come in to get their radios fixed, and it was great seeing them again. They were all like good friends, and we would talk shop while I was repairing their radios.

One day I was called into the office and told I had to quit talking with the tow truck drivers when they came in. I asked why and the boss told me I was making everybody sick, talking about the gory stories with the tow truck drivers. The boss asked me if I had noticed that everybody left the shop when a tow truck came in. I said, "No, I haven't paid any attention."

He said, "You have got to stop it. You're making everybody sick when you talk in detail about cutting all the bodies and pieces of bodies out of cars with the tow truck operators. Everybody leaves the shop, and it's cutting into our productivity."

It seems my storytelling days were over.

Fire Department Humor

The firemen I worked with were a bunch of characters. They did a lot of teasing and pulled pranks all the time. I think it was a way of relieving the stress of the job, or possibly, it is a personality trait of the type of individual who becomes a fireman.

There was a guy when I was at Station 5 who had a cigarette lighter that he could turn the flame up on. He thought it was really funny whenever he became flatulent to pass the lighter near his posterior as he was doing so and increase the flame to simulate an explosion. He always beamed with pride when he performed his act. I believe he was the only one enjoying the entertainment.

One day he let out a gnarly one and had what we could say was a backfire. It was a methane explosion of great magnitude. We extinguished him, but he was in a fair amount of pain. He had burned his tushy-wushy pretty badly. His wife had to come and get him and take him home. He was off for several shifts. I believe that stopped his exhibitions.

***

There was an engineer named Roby at Station 3 who was getting up in years and was starting to have health problems. The engineer's duty, besides getting the fire truck to the fire, was to maintain it. We had these sponges that we would use to wipe down the fire trucks every morning to keep them clean. Poor Roby dropped the sponge on the floor one day, and his back went out as he bent over to pick it up.

We heard the scream, and we went running out to see what was happening. There was poor Roby, bent over in the middle of the apparatus floor, white as a sheet and moaning. We got him straightened up, laid him down, and called an ambulance. Roby had trouble with that back from then on.

The ridiculous part of Roby's story was the Workers Compensation claim. The captain filed a report on the incident but the Workers Compensation Board denied the claim, stating that you couldn't hurt your back picking up a sponge. The captain refiled the claim, stating Roby had to pick up the fire truck to get the sponge. Workers Compensation approved the claim after receiving the second filing.

***

After some time, Roby started having trouble with his right knee. (Knee problems are always plaguing firemen.) The captain had filed a Workers Compensation claim on Roby's knee and they had done the prelim on the knee. He had all the x-rays and scans, but they couldn't find anything wrong, so they had him scheduled for explorative surgery.

We were watching a football game one Sunday at the station when Roby felt a bump on the top of his knee. He pulled his pants down to expose the knee, and sure enough, there was a protrusion sticking up above the kneecap. Roby started massaging it, and it moved up a little. One of the guys grabbed onto it with his clamps and it pulled straight out.

We couldn't figure out what the heck it was. It was about an inch long and covered with cartilage. We thought it must be a piece of bone. One of the guys started scraping the cartilage off with a razor blade and exposed a finishing nail about 3/4"–1" long. Roby remembered getting hit hard just under the kneecap a couple of years previously while mowing the lawn. He just thought it was a rock, but it must have been that finishing nail, and it slowly worked its way through the kneecap and finally came out the top. Roby never had a problem with his knee after that.

***

Fire Station 3 had a fairly large crew, and we all shared cooking duties. Nobody wanted to cook, but I hated doing the dishes more than cooking, so I did all the cooking. I would usually bake a couple of pies for desert and make some pretty good meals. Everybody was happy to do the dishes in return for the enjoyment my dinners provided. We would make up a menu and then go to the store and pick up the groceries for the evening meal.

One evening the captain came in and said he wanted tacos for dinner. I explained I had already bought all the supplies for dinner, and I didn't have anything for tacos. I asked if it would be all right to proceed with what I was making, and I said I would make tacos on the next shift. He didn't say anything, just walked out and went back to his office.

The captain informed me on the morning of the next shift that Slim would be doing the cooking from now on. I said, "Ok," and went on about my business.

That night we had tacos, the next shift we had tacos, and the next and so on and so on. It turned out that all Slim knew how to cook was tacos. The guys got so sick of tacos after a month that they started having their wives bring them their dinners. The communal dinners at the station pretty much came to a halt. There was a lot of grumbling and complaining, but that captain wasn't about to let me cook ever again after I ignored his request.

***

Fire Station 3 had this huge parking area behind the station. One of the guys decided to buy one of those new-fangled skateboards that were the craze for his daughter's birthday. Before giving it to her, he decided to try it out in the parking lot behind the station.

He took off on that skateboard, going downhill in the parking lot, and went down "big time," right in front of the whole crew. He took the hide off his knees and elbows on the asphalt and tore the heck out of his pants. He picked up skateboard and went over and chucked it in the dumpster. He commented as he was dumping it that there was no way his daughter was going to hurt herself with one of those things.

***

There was a pool table in the recreation room at Fire Station 1, and the guys played pool in their off hours. We weren't allowed to gamble at the station, so the guys started playing for dinners. (The crew at Fire Station 1 was quite large, so we had communal dinners, and we would each put in a dollar to help pay for groceries.) I wasn't much of a pool player, but I remember I hardly ever paid for my own dinner. That's kind of a testimonial to the skill of the other firemen.

There was a new recruit name Fisher who would just slam the cue ball when he broke. He would hit that cue ball, holler, "Fish," and several balls would fly off the table when the cue ball hit the rack of balls. I can't remember him ever doing much winning.

***

There was an engineer at Fire Station 1 whom I shall call Shultz. Shultz was a brilliant man of, I believe, German descent. We would often have these small drills during our off hours to hone our skills. If we queried Shultz, he always had the correct answer. If we asked him how he would respond to a structure fire at 2560 Lime Street, he would say, "You take Holding to Lime, turn south onto Lime, and pick up the hydrant on the west side of the corner of Lime and Holding, then proceed south on Lime Street to the third house on the east side at the scene of the fire."

Schultz was always right. The only problem was that when the alarm bells went off, he got so excited he couldn't even find the fire truck.

Driving the Tiller

I had been driving fire engines and the rescue truck at the Riverside Fire Department for quite some time, and they decided it was time for me to learn the tiller on the ladder truck, so I went into training to learn to steer the back of that darn thing. We went out and did some low speed maneuvers and drove around for a while.

Now, in case you don't know, the tiller position is a little tricky. To turn left you steer right, and to turn right you steer left. It is the opposite if you're backing up. So, there I was, a guy who can't chew gum and walk at the same time, sitting up there in that darn seat.

Before long they decided I had had enough training and was ready for action. I adamantly protested without success. The next shift I was assigned the tiller position. I again protested without success. The guys assured me they would only use wide streets and go slow if we had to answer a call. It was my misfortune that we soon had a response.

As I have said, the guys on my shift were all a little wild and just slightly touched. They took off like a bat out of you know where. You could see them up in the cab, laughing their rears off. Then they turned at high speed onto Main Street, one of the narrowest streets in Riverside, with cars parallel parked on both sides of the street. They had to be going over 473 miles per hour and swinging in and out of traffic. There I sat, white knuckled, without an ounce of blood in my head, hanging on for dear life. I knew my career would be over just as soon as I wiped out 35 parked cars and two department stores with that darn tiller.

The tiller has a steering lock out that holds the wheels in the straight-ahead position for transporting the truck when only one driver is available. I hit that button, locked that steering down, and raised my hands so they would know. They slowed the darn thing because they knew they would be in trouble if they damaged the truck. That was my last shift as a tiller.

Fire Department Turnouts

For those of you who don't understand the meaning of turnouts in fire department terminology, I will give a brief explanation. The turnouts consist of a pair of boots, trousers, and a coat. The trousers are placed on the right side of the bed at night. The trousers are folded down over the boots, with the boots sticking up over the top of the trousers. If an alarm comes in, we simply jumped out of bed into the boots, grabbed the suspenders and pulled up, and the trousers came up with them. We put the suspenders over our shoulders and we were dressed. It only took a matter of seconds to be up and dressed.

We would then run out to the apparatus floor and grab our helmets and turnout coats. We would put on the coats and helmets, jump into the truck, and we would be on our way to the emergency. This whole procedure generally took less than a couple of minutes.

During the time I was at the Riverside Fire Department, we only used our turnouts at night. We wore our regular fatigues during daylight hours.

I was stationed at Riverside Fire Department Station 6, located on North Main Street near Russell Street, for about a year. Our captain's name was Scoop. Now, Scoop was a pretty good-sized man. He stood about six feet four and was slender but husky. Bob was a fireman like me and was about five foot eight and rather thin. Buzz was the engineer and was a rather nervous guy. We were a pretty good crew, and all got along well.

One night we got an alarm. I usually slept through them, so the other guys would always come over and shake me to get up. This time something woke me up before they started shaking me. Bob was crawling around the floor, waving his hand around like someone who had been blindfolded. He was hollering, "Where's my boots? Where's my boots?"

About that time I heard some noise coming from the hallway, I looked over and there was Scoop, pulling and tugging on his suspenders, cussing as he tried to figure out why he couldn't get his pants up. It dawned on me that he had jumped out of the wrong side of the bed and stepped into Bob's turnouts. You have to realize that Scoop's feet were probably four sizes larger than Bob's. How the heck he got his feet into those boots I haven't a clue, but there was no way he was going to get those small trousers up.

I got so tickled I could hardly get into mine. I finally made it over to Scoop, and he was still confused and half asleep. Bob and I finally got him calmed down and convinced him that he was in Bob's turnouts.

We had a heck of a time getting Bob's boots off him. He had really jammed his feet into them. We finally got everybody into the right turnouts and were on our way. That was one night we didn't make it out of the station in two minutes. I still laugh whenever I think about Scoop standing in that hallway trying to pull those little trousers up.

Riverside Fire Station 5

I was stationed at Station 5 for about a year. We had a captain at the fire station whom I'll call Captain Pat. Firemen have a propensity for having short lifespans due to heart attacks. One of the chiefs died within weeks of retiring. I think four or five guys died from heart attacks in the short time I was in the department, and the thought just plagued Captain Pat.

Captain Pat was past retirement age but refused to retire. He told me after the chief's death that he was going to die if he retired, and it scared the heck out of him. They forced him to retire after I left the department, and the last I heard of Captain Pat, he was nearing 90 years of age. All that worrying for nothing.

***

Early one morning we got an alarm to respond to a house fire. We rolled out of the station, and we could see the smoke plumes billowing hundreds of feet in the air. There was always a concern about people safely getting out of a house that early in the morning. It was no fun going through rubble, looking for remains.

As we pulled near the house, Captain Pat stood up in the seat, turned around, and looked at us with this look of excitement on his face. He was looking for confirmation that we were ready. He got on the radio and shouted, "Fully involved," to call out the troops. We knew it was going to be a long morning.

From our vantage point we could see the flames were shooting well over the top of the house, maybe as much as 30 feet. The house was one of those beautiful, old, multi-story, Victorian-type mansions that were prevalent in Riverside in those days. As we turned the corner, the house and property came into view.

There was a large pile of orange trees piled up and burning about 50 yards behind the house. There was even a 1,000-gallon water tanker sitting between the house and the fire, with men standing there, ready with fire hoses. They were taking down an orange grove around the mansion and had failed to notify the fire department they were going to be burning that morning.

From the first, straight-on view we had of the house earlier, it had looked like the flames were coming from the house. Were we relieved to see the house wasn't burning! We checked the guys' permits, called off our troops, and headed home.

***

We would sit around the station and school ourselves during idle time. One day Captain Pat was giving us addresses and asking how we would respond. He gave an address for a car fire on a street that nobody could recall. The address was near Streeter, and Fire Station 5 was located on the corner of El Molino and Streeter, so we figured it was close, but we were all stumped.

I happened to look out the window and saw the street sign on the corner. There it was. I started chuckling and pointed it out to the guys. Everybody got a laugh out of that. We turned on that street every day as we arrived at or left the station, but nobody had ever noticed the name. Nobody ever forgot the name of that street after that.

***

The fire department had a Gamewell system in those days and had fire alarm boxes located all over the city. Each station had a receiving station for the fire alarm boxes. The receiving station was a large cabinet about five feet wide and four feet high. It had a reel of paper tape on top. The only way I can describe it is to liken it to a movie-film reel on a projector, sitting there loaded with a roll of paper about 1/2-inch wide. The paper went into a feeder roller that would pull the tape through when an alarm came in and punch holes that corresponded to the four-digit code of the reporting alarm box in the tape.

When someone opened the glass door on the front of one of the alarm boxes and pulled the lever down, the bells would start clanging in the fire station. The bells would sound out a number of clangs, the paper tape would start running, and the machine would start punching holes in the tape that corresponded to the number of clangs of the bells. We would read the punches in the tape to get the four-number sequence of the alarm box and then look at a chart to see where the box was located. We ignored it if it was out of our area and responded to the location of the box if it was in our area.

We had trouble with kids pulling those alarm boxes all the time. They liked to watch the fire trucks come. A large crowd would always form whenever we responded to the alarm to see what was going on, and we would walk through the crowd, asking who the culprit was who tripped the alarm. Of course, nobody knew anything. What the kids didn't know was that the levers on those boxes were painted with a luminous paint, and we would walk around in the crowd with ultraviolet flashlights, looking for the kid with the blue finger. I don't think the kids ever did figure out how we knew who did it.

***

Late one evening we were sitting around watching TV when the power went off and the Gamewell started going nuts. The bells were clanging erratically and the tape punches weren't making sense. We messed around for several minutes, trying to figure out what was wrong with the Gamewell. We had no communications by radio or phone because of the power outage, so one of the guys decided to get in the truck and call headquarters on the radio. Headquarters flipped when they found out we weren't responding to the plane crash. We asked what plane crash? We got the address and responded.

I don't remember the street, but it was somewhere near the runway of Riverside Airport around Wayman Street. There was a high voltage power line running north and south in the area at that time.

A man had purchased a surplus WWII military aircraft at

auction in Long Beach and was attempting to fly it to Phoenix. It was a double-cockpit dive bomber of the A series. It was possibly an A-31 Vengeance. The pilot had patched holes in the thing with duct tape and even put the registration numbers on the plane with duct tape.

I have no idea how he got it to pass inspection, got it licensed, and got permission to take off in the thing, but the plane blew an oil line over Riverside, and he was trying to make it to the airport. The plane lost power, came in too low, and clipped the high-voltage power lines, knocking out power to half the city.

The power lines threw the plane onto the roof of a house, totally tearing the roof off the house. There were rafters and shingles from that roof scattered for a block. The plane then continued across the street, right into another house and through the front room. The propeller ended up on the patio.

Due to our late response, everybody was already there except for us. The press was there, frantically snapping pictures. Percy and I bailed off the back of the truck and started running toward the plane to check on the pilot. We stopped when we realized there was about two inches of gas on the lawn.

The press was using the old cameras with flashbulbs that you see in the movies. Every time they took a picture, they would pop those hot flashbulbs out to put in new ones, and we could hear the ejected bulbs sizzling when they hit the gas. We hollered at the police to get them out of there. It could have been a disaster if one of those flashbulbs had broken open when it hit that gasoline!

Percy and I made it to the plane, and I scrambled up the wing to check on the pilot. The front and back seats were empty. I turned around, still standing on the wing, and asked where the pilot was. This guy answered and said he was the pilot. The guy had just wiped out a high-voltage power line and two houses, and he was standing there with one, 1/4" wide by 1 1/2" long Band-Aid on his eyebrow. I think that guy had just used up eight of his nine lives.

It was near daybreak by the time we got the area secured and the plane removed from the house. Airport workers removed the wings on the airplane, hooked the body to a tow truck, and we escorted the plane back to the airport.

It turned out to be a long night but could have been much worse. Not one injury was reported except for a scraped eyebrow.

Lightning

I have written other essays about firemen teasing and razzing each other. This essay relates to that subject.

I sleep very soundly, and I think a freight train driving over me wouldn't wake me up. I always missed the alarms and the guys would shake and kick the bed to wake me up. I was always the last man to get to the engine on night responses. This became a problem when I started driving the fire engine. When I climbed into in the fire truck, I didn't have a clue where we were going on half the responses, so I had to rely on the captain for directions. I soon earned the nickname "Lightning" for my rapid responses.

I was stationed at the old Station 3 on Magnolia Avenue when one morning I woke to the sound of loud car horns. I thought, *What the heck is happening?* I looked around. I was still in my bed, but it was sitting on the lawn between the sidewalk and the curb. Everybody driving by was laughing, waving, and blowing their horns. I was the laughing stock of Arlington that morning.

There I was, in my tighty-whities, cars coming in both directions with no let up. I had no choice but to wrap up in a blanket and run for the door of the station. The door was locked: they had locked me out! I had to run all the way around the station to the back door.

Some of the "A" shift guys had already arrived, and they were all sitting around, drinking coffee. No one paid any attention to me or said a word when I walked in. I went in and showered and dressed for the shift change. I heard some laughing and snickering while I was dressing; I'm quite sure they were having a lot of laughs at my expense. We did the shift change, and as I pulled out of the driveway, heading home, I could see my bed still sitting next to the street.

My bed was back in its place when I returned to the station for the shift the following day. To my knowledge, nothing was ever said about the incident. It was like it never happened.

I solved the problem of over-sleeping by bringing an alarm clock to work with me and setting it to go off three minutes before the morning bells. This turned out to be a problem as well. I learned very quickly to always recheck the alarm and time settings and make sure the alarm was on before going to bed. Somehow, the settings seemed to be resetting themselves. I also had to put the alarm clock inside my pillowcase while sleeping to keep the darn thing from running off.

We moved to the new Station 3, and I believe we were the first shift to occupy it. Late one night we got an alarm. The guys started kicking my bunk as they ran by. I jumped into my turnouts, climbed up into the engine, and asked where we were going. Lou just said, "Get on the freeway south."

I pulled up on the freeway and headed south. The old Generals had a drone to the engine. The truck just pulsed, and it was really soothing. The only thing I can compare it to is it's like riding a horse stretched out at full gallop. The rhythm of a horse is soothing like that of the General fire truck.

We had gone quite a ways and were nearing Adams, which is the end of our first response area. I looked ahead and could see red lights coming north from the other side of the freeway. Pretty soon Engine 2 passed us, heading the other way. I was looking at them as they went by, and they were all looking at us, wondering where the heck we were going.

I asked Lou, "Where are we going?" I didn't get a response so I looked over—Lou was dozing off. I started hollering and asking Lou where we were going.

Lou snapped awake and said, "Get off at Arlington Avenue."

Too late. We were two exits past Arlington. I jumped off at Adams and headed back north on the freeway. Needless to say, we were the second engine in when we should have been the first. I guess nobody checked the response log, because nothing was ever said about the incident.

More Fire Department Stories

I don't know if it's a fireman's personality or a trait that is picked up by becoming a fireman, but firemen are a peculiar breed. Most firemen never take anything seriously and are a bunch of jokesters. I think all the teasing and joking is an attempt to relieve the stress of the environment. If you don't have thick skin, you would never survive as a fireman. You come to work in the morning in your dress blues, stand at attention, and execute the change of shifts. You put on your work fatigues and start your day. You never know what's in store for you. You might have a quiet day, or your quiet day could suddenly turn into the most horrific situation you've ever had to endure. I think we all razzed each other in order to keep our sanity.

***

Riverside was full of old mansion-type homes, and they were beautiful but they were firetraps. There was one located near First and Market streets, and a lady with young children lived there. A college student living there as well. I assume she was renting a room while attending college. This girl was in her late teens or early twenties and was gorgeous.

The lady who owned the house had a young boy about five or six who loved playing with matches. He had already started a few fires, and fortunately, the lady had always caught the little tyke before the fire got out of control and was able to call for help. Luckily, we had always been able to put them out with little or no damage.

One morning about 5:00 a.m. the kid got up before everybody, and this time he did a number. The fire was going through the roof when we arrived on scene. Fortunately, everybody got out of the house, but just barely. The poor college student must have slept in the buff, because the girl was standing out in the street in her birthday suit.

The ladder truck's purpose is to provide ladders—including

the aerial ladder—at scenes. The truck only carries ladders and tools, making it considerably lighter than an engine that carries hose and water, so the ladder truck responds much faster than the engine and usually gets to the scene first.

As usual this day, the ladder truck pulled up ahead of the engines, and the guys saw the freezing, naked girl standing there, trying to cover up. So Jim jumped off the truck, grabbed a blanket, and covered the poor girl up.

When we showed up, all we got to see was the family standing in the street, watching the house burn to the ground. Not even a peek at the gorgeous girl was possible, thanks to Jim. We extinguished the blaze and secured the scene. The house was totaled and nothing was salvageable.

Jim took a major razzing, and we made a new rule that morning. "The last engine in gives the girl the blanket."

***

One of the firemen's mothers lived in Montana, and every vacation Bob would go to Montana and spend his vacation with his mother. The guys would always start ragging on Bob close to vacation time about his trip to Montana. "Hey, Bob, are you going to look up your favorite sheep when you get to Montana? Think she still remembers you, Bob? Think she still loves you, Bob?" The teasing was relentless.

My wife and I were living in a duplex on Russell Street when Bob showed up after his vacation one year to do some work on the duplex for our landlord. Bob came in and we had some coffee and were visiting. My wife was in the kitchen, preparing a snack for us while engaging in a conversation with Bob. She asked Bob about his trip to Montana. Bob was telling her about the trip when my wife all of a sudden asked, "So, Bob, did you see any sheep?"

Bob was stunned. He just sat there with this "You @#*&$" look on his face. I was shocked myself because I had never said anything to my wife about the teasing.

I asked her later why she made the sheep remark. She said, “I don’t know. I just heard there were a lot of sheep in Montana.”

House Burning

The landscape of Riverside was rapidly changing in the '60s. The developers were coming in and razing the orange groves and building housing. Riverside was fast becoming a bedroom community for the industrial complex of the Greater Los Angeles Area. The groves were coming down, and the beautiful mansions that once covered the landscape were being bulldozed. Some of these beautiful homes were being donated to the fire department to use as training fires.

The fire chiefs would go into these houses and set fires to simulate certain scenarios. We would rush in when the signal was given and extinguish the fire. Then we would be critiqued on our performance. These training exercises always attracted a large crowd of off-duty personnel, the press, fireman from neighboring communities, and just curious onlookers coming to watch.

My friend Jerry from the Forestry brought my wife to one of the burns with my 8-mm movie camera to film the action. It turned out to be a mistake, having my worrywart wife watching me at the scene of a fire.

We went inside to extinguish a fire in the living room in one scenario. We put out the fire and were bringing the smoldering couch outside when my wife noticed that my jacket was on fire. (Which was a common occurrence.) My wife started screaming that I was on fire. The guys just hit it with a little water and it was out. That was humiliating, having my wife screaming her head off in front of the entire crowd.

Later, I was on the roof of the house, getting ready to ventilate it. (Ventilating is the process of cutting a hole in the roof to let the hot gasses escape.) I had put a roof ladder over the peak of the house to secure it, and one of the legs was hanging out over the edge of the roof in mid-air. My wife didn't know that a roof ladder is secured to the peak of the roof with hooks to hold it in place. I started climbing the ladder, and she started screaming in front of the spectators and firemen again.

My wife was forbidden to ever attend another house burning.

***

On a different day our fire training chief had procured a fireproof suit from a supplier and wanted to try it out in a real case scenario. We were burning a house near 14th and Kansas streets, and he decided this was the time to test the suit. The house had a big bay window, about 6 feet high and 8 feet long, in the living room. We set the house on fire, and it was going pretty good. The red and white flames were rolling, so the house was quite hot.

The chief entered the back door and walked through the house into the living room into view of the crowd. We were standing there in the yard in front of the bay window, watching, two 1 1/2" hoses with fog nozzles at the ready.

The suit was quite impressive. The chief was feeling no heat from the fire and was quite comfortable in it. The press were all standing there, taking pictures of the great event, while the chief stood there, smiling and waving at the cameras.

After a couple of minutes, we noticed that the aluminized look of the suit was starting to darken. All of a sudden, flames started coming off the fabric of the suit. We all started frantically waving at him to get out. He must have thought we were just waving to say hi, because he just stood there looking like a human torch, smiling and waving back at us.

We turned on the fire hoses and started drenching him, and he finally realized something must be wrong. He bailed out through the window to get out of the house. Fortunately, he was fine, but that suit was sure messed up. It looked like a roasted marshmallow.

***

Some of the houses we were given to burn were unbelievably beautiful. They had beautiful windows, fireplace mantles, woodwork, doors, and loads of red brick. The firemen were given a couple of days before the burn to make bids on items they wanted. The money from the accepted bids was given to the Firemen's Association Fund. We had a couple of days to remove the items before the house was burned.

Chuck was one of the guys who purchased most of the items, especially the brick. Chuck had purchased some property up on the side of Box Springs Mountain and built a home on the land.

The house was very unusual. There was a huge rock on the property, and most people would have had it blasted out, but not Chuck. And when I say a huge rock, I mean huge. That rock had to be at least 7 feet high and 8 feet in diameter. Chuck didn't even try to remove the rock—he just built the living room around it.

It was strange, walking into someone's living room and seeing a huge boulder. Also, the property had not been leveled. Each room just followed the lay of the land. If the land went up, the room was higher than the adjoining room, and if the land went down, the room was lower than the adjoining room. It was ingenious, and the house was intriguing and beautiful.

Chuck put in a nice pool and did the entire surrounding patio with the red brick taken from the house burns. It was just beautiful, sitting on that patio, watching the kids enjoying the pool.

My last remembrance of Chuck was playing handball with him at Fire Station 3. I lost track of him after I left the department.

The Burnt Potato

We used to have repetitive humorous events when I worked for the Riverside Fire Department. One night, out of Station 5, we responded to a house fire. We found the source of the fire and smoke. It turned out the lady was getting ready to prepare dinner and had warmed up the oven. Unfortunately, there was an old potato on the shelf at the back of the oven, and it caught on fire and filled the house with smoke. We extinguished the potato and put the evac fans up to suck the smoke out of the house.

We noticed the woman had paintings of nudes hanging in the house. She commented that they were all self-portraits. She wasn't a bad-looking lady, possibly in her late forties.

She latched onto the battalion chief and kept a good arm lock on him as she escorted him around the house, explaining the history of each painting. You could tell she was really putting the charm on him.

We finally cleaned up the scene and were getting ready to leave, and you could tell she was trying to get the battalion chief to stick around. She finally asked our hours and we knew there was going to be a repeat call.

Sure enough, on the next shift we got an evening call to the same location. The lady was standing at the door, waiting for us, dressed to the nines. She kept inquiring where the battalion chief was. She was really let down when we told her he was on another call.

The Electrocution

In the '60s while I was serving as a fireman with the Riverside City Fire Department, we received an emergency dispatch to the Canyon Crest area of Riverside for an electrocution. Upon arriving at the scene, we found a man wedged in a 5-foot alcove at the rear of his house. This was during the era of the citizen band radio craze, and we later learned he had been attempting to put up a huge antenna. The man had attached an antenna mount to the eaves of the house in the alcove and had attached a 40-foot telescoping mast to the mount. He had a huge, beam-type antenna attached to the top of the telescoping mast.

There were high-tension electrical utility lines about 20 feet away from the opposite side of the house, and the telescoping mast and antenna had been sucked into these high-tension lines while he was trying to raise them.

There was a gas meter and piping located next to the opposite wall of the alcove, and due to his injuries, it appeared that he had completed continuity through the high-tension lines and mast and grounded it through his body into the gas meter.

We assumed the man could not have survived those high voltages, and due to the fact that the antenna and mast were still energized by the high-tension lines, we decided to wait for the electrical utility personnel to show up and turn off the power to the lines before retrieving the body.

We were standing around, making idle talk while we waited for the electrical utility personnel to arrive, when we heard strange sounds coming from the victim. The human body will sometimes make noises even after death as air is released from collapsing lungs. We just assumed that was what it was until we heard a noise that sounded like an inhale moan instead of an exhale noise. We decided we had to get him out of there fast.

I went to the truck to retrieve a pike pole. (A pike pole is a long, wooden pole with a sharp, metal, spear-like end and a hook that is a couple of inches down from the spear. It is used to plunge into ceilings of burning buildings and for ripping the ceilings down to gain access to the burning rafters of the building.)

I returned to the alcove and very carefully laid the hook end of the pike pole on the ground. I held the handle of the pike pole as close to the opposite end as I could and still maintain control of the handle. Then I carefully pushed the pole toward the body, with the idea that the pole was going to be immediately dropped if I felt even the slightest tingle. I was finally able to grab his belt with the hook and very carefully drag the man to a safe area.

We checked his vitals and administered resuscitation. He was very badly injured: substantial damage to both legs around the calf area and to his hands and several fingers destroyed. We had him transported to the hospital and headed back to the station.

Now this is the strange part of the story.

The fire department annually published a book called the *Street Guide & Shopping Directory*. This book listed all the fire department personnel and had small, section maps of the City of Riverside. These maps were hand drawn by fire department personnel and showed their respective areas of response. Throughout the book we also had ads from local businesses. The ads were essentially worthless and were actually just a donation from the local businesses to support our firemen's association.

One year I had the duty to go out and canvas the area and sell ads in this street guide and shopping directory. I walked into a business in an industrial complex that wasn't listed as an advertiser. I introduced myself and addressed my intentions to try to sell them an ad. The lady was very responsive and said she would definitely buy an ad. She then related that the fire department had responded to her home when her husband had electrocuted himself trying to put up a CB radio antenna.

I told her I remembered the incident and that I was the one who pulled him out from the alcove. We talked for a minute, and I was about to give my condolences for her loss, when a man stepped through a set of café-type swinging doors that led to a rear room in the building. The lady looked at the man who had just entered the room and said, “Honey, this is the fireman who pulled you out from behind the house when you were trying to put that stupid antenna up.”

I was absolutely dumbfounded. I had no idea a man could survive an incident like he had endured. I was glad he had come out before I offered my condolences. It would have been embarrassing to have her know that I didn’t know the outcome of the incident and had just assumed he had died.

We talked for a few minutes and discussed the damage to his body. He lost his right leg below the knee but was doing well with the prosthesis. His left leg had been damaged too, but they had been able to restore it back to normal. He lost some fingers on his left hand, but they managed to save all the fingers on his right hand. Other than that, he was doing fine.

I didn’t have the nerve to ask if he ever finished putting up the antenna. I was afraid his wife would go ballistic if I brought it up.

Needless to say, they bought an ad from me. (A very big ad.)

UCR

One night when I was stationed at the Riverside Fire Department Station 6, we got a call to the women's dorm at the University of California, Riverside (UCR) campus. When we arrived, everybody was milling around while smoke poured out of the windows of the women's dorm. Most of the girls had been forced to get out quickly and were scantily dressed it their negligees. The guys were really enjoying it.

You have to understand that firemen are a strange bunch. You have to be strange to run into a burning building with the roof falling in. But the guys on our shift were just a little wilder than some. We partied constantly. We closed down many a bar and dancehall in our day, dancing all night and consuming mass quantities of beer, so we fit right in with the college crowd.

We spent some time locating the source of the fire. It turned out a girl had thrown a cigarette into a trashcan and caught the contents of the trashcan and some curtains on fire. It took us a while to get all the smoke out of the building, so we did a lot of standing around with the students, talking with them.

Before long the students had a piano in the street and were doing sing-a-longs with the girls. Beer was being consumed as well, and everybody was really enjoying themselves. Of course, we were joining in. (Except for the beer.)

We finally got the scene secured and were ready to go home. The kids commented that we were really a cool bunch and asked when we were on shift again. We told them and said goodbye to all our new friends. We knew what was coming.

Sure enough, at 9:00 p.m. the night of our next shift, the bells went off and the speakers came on: "Engines 231, 241, 234, 236, and Truck 251, respond to the women's dormitory at UCR." When we arrived, the guys and girls were lining the street, cheering and raising their cups to toast us as we drove up. The piano was already on the street, and the beer kegs were chilling in washtubs. The party had begun. This time they had secured the trash can so all it would do was put out smoke, and there was enough clearance around it that it wasn't a hazard.

Well, the chancellor didn't take the stunt too lightly. He had the cops there before we even had everything secured. The administration made us leave as soon as we secured the scene, so we missed the party. I'm sure some of the students missed the party as well.

The Day the Pirsch Wouldn't Start

I drove the engines exclusively while stationed at Fire Station 3. I usually drove "The General." I loved that old truck. It was built during the war when steel was scarce, so a lot of it was actually made out of wood. It had an 800-cubic-inch, Hall Scott engine in it, and it would haul. It would even accelerate going up the Central Avenue hill, and I would keep it floored all the way up. I loved going fast, and that was the truck for me.

It had a strange rhythm when I was getting hard on it. It is hard to explain, but it seemed to oscillate. It felt really good and was almost like running a horse at a full gallop. I had a half-thoroughbred, half-American-saddle-breed horse that just loved to run, and he was fast. I just loved to kick him out. That truck reminded me of being on the back of that horse, going full out through the brush in the riverbottom in San Bernardino.

We had a couple of kids fresh out of the fire academy assigned to us at Fire Station 3. Gary and Vance were pretty good friends. Gary would later go on to become a chief. I have no knowledge where Vance's career went. They were both chomping at the bit to respond to a fire. Station 3 was usually an active station, but we were in a long null, and they were going crazy, waiting for some excitement.

One day we finally got a call, and they were excitedly high fiving each other, hollering and carrying on. For some reason I was assigned to the Pirsch on that day, and Gary was riding tail with me. Vance was on The General. We hopped on the trucks, and The General fired up and was headed out the door. I was cranking the starter on that darn Pirsch, but it just wouldn't fire. Gary was standing on the tailgate, begging me to get the darn thing started, but it just wouldn't turn over. We finally had to make the call to go out of service. Gary was certain that I did it on purpose. It didn't help when Vance got back and told him about his experience.

They called the fire department mechanic and Don came

out and that truck started right up. Now Gary was convinced for sure that I had done it on purpose. They put the truck back in service and we went on with our day. The other shift got a call the next day and the Pirsch wouldn't start again. They finally found out the ignition switch was intermittent. So I was absolved.

The Station Wagon

I was driving down Market Street in Riverside one day. I passed a used car lot and saw a 1965 Chevrolet station wagon with a price sticker on it for $275.00. That immediately caught my attention. I drove in, parked, and went over and checked out the vehicle.

I noticed the body was in pretty good shape with no body damage of any kind, and the upholstery was in excellent condition. About that time here came the salesman with the sales pitch. We talked while I was checking out the car. The salesman told me the engine had a blown cylinder and would need rebuilding, and that was the reason for the reduced price. We started it up, and sure enough, there was a definite stumble from the bad cylinder.

The phone rang and the salesman excused himself and went to answer the phone. I immediately started pulling plug wires until I found the bad cylinder. I shut the engine off and quickly swapped the plug wire with one from another cylinder. I started it back up, and the stumble went to the other cylinder. The only problem with that engine was a $2.00 plug wire.

I offered the salesman $225.00 for the car, and he accepted. We signed the paperwork, I gave him the cash, and went home and picked up my wife. We came back and she dropped me off at the used car lot. I picked up the car and drove straight to Pep Boys, where I bought a new set of plug wires. I replaced the bad one right there in the Pep Boys parking lot and drove the station wagon home to replace the rest of the ignition wires.

That station wagon was equipped with the 327 Turbo Fire, 275-horsepower V-8 engine with the power glide transmission, and it would scoot. We nicknamed it "the racecar," not because of how fast it would go, but because we drove it to the races at the Orange Show Speedway every Saturday night.

The Orange Show parking lot was a money pit for thieves. I don't know why the speedway didn't hire security to patrol the parking lot. I knew of a lot of people who quit going to the races because they just got tired of losing the stereos out of their cars. One guy who owned a Ford Bronco got so sick of it that he welded the radio in so it couldn't be removed. He came out one night after the races and found the entire dashboard missing.

The station wagon had a stock radio in it, which was of no value to the thieves. We always made sure nothing was left in the station wagon, not even a jacket. You could see through the windows and tell there was nothing of any value inside. We never had a problem after that with break-ins at the Orange Show Speedway.

One day my wife stopped for lunch at the McDonalds on Mill Street in San Bernardino after a shopping trip. After lunch she went out to the car to come home and couldn't get the key in the ignition. She called me, and I had one of the guys stop by to see what the problem was. Some guy apparently tried to steal the car, because there was a broken-off screw from a slide hammer stuck in the ignition lock.

I don't know what he wanted with the station wagon, except possibly, the engine. If he wanted the car, he had bad taste.

I ended up selling that car many years later to a tow truck driver for $75.00.

The Rattlesnake

If you look east of Riverside, you will see Box Springs Mountain, with antenna towers on top of the ridges. In the late '60s I worked part time as a technician for the Motorola service shop on North Main Street in Riverside, in conjunction with my job as a fireman with the Riverside City Fire Department. One of my duties was the repair and maintenance of the radio equipment on the southern peak of Box Springs Mountain.

There was a small building there that housed all the military and government repeaters. The civilian repeaters and base station equipment were all mounted on telephone poles that were located at the edge of the ridge and hung over the side of the mountain. I serviced both the government and civilian equipment on the south end of the mountain.

If you don't understand the term repeater, it is a radio that receives a signal at a higher frequency and repeats it back at a lower frequency. The radios in the vehicles and base stations receive this lower frequency and transmit at the higher frequency; hence, the radio that is talking sends the signal to the mountaintop, and it is repeated back to all the other radios, giving all the radios the same range as if they were sitting on top of the mountain. This greatly increases the range of the area in which the guys in the radio-equipped vehicles can talk to each other.

A base station simply talks and receives on the same frequency. It is usually controlled by a telephone line or a microwave radio that send signals back and forth between the base station on the mountain top and the central office located in the city, thus extending the range of the radio at the office.

The civilian base stations and repeaters on the mountain top were mounted in outdoor cabinets that were bolted directly to the telephone pole, with the bottom of the cabinets about three feet off the ground. The cabinets were about 4 feet tall, 2 feet wide and 16 inches deep. The antennas for the repeaters and base stations were on top of the telephone poles, and the coaxial lines to the antennas ran out of the cabinets and up the poles to the antennas. The electrical power ran underground to each pole and came up through the bottom of each cabinet. Each repeater or base station and its associated equipment was mounted on its own pole.

Some of the guys would have to use a small ladder to reach the equipment to service it. Since I was over six feet tall at the time, I could access the equipment without the use of a ladder. One day we had an outage with one of the repeaters, so I responded to the mountaintop to repair it. I arrived on site, went over to the cabinet, and unlocked it. When I opened the door, I was face to face with a rattlesnake, its mouth wide open and fangs extended. It scared the woohoohoo out of me, and I went stumbling backwards and over the cliff, tumbling down about ten feet. I got up, composed myself, went back up the cliff, and carefully approached the cabinet.

The rattlesnake was still there in the same position. I checked the rattlesnake and it was dead. The poor thing must have been cold and climbed up the pole and gone into the cabinet to stay warm. Those old repeaters were tube equipment, and the voltage, when receiving, was about 200 volts, but when the radio transmitted, the voltage went up to around 1,000 volts. The rattlesnake had wrapped itself around the high voltage section of the power supply, and when someone keyed the repeater, it blew the poor snake in half.

I pried the rattlesnake out of the power supply, got a shovel, and buried the head. The snake had shorted out the power supply, and it blew all the fuses. I replaced the blown fuses, tested the radio, and headed back to the shop.

That was a day to remember. I can still see that rattlesnake head as clear as the day it happened.

The Sage's Store in Riverside

Everybody is always talking about the Sage's store in Riverside. In 2014 the *Press Enterprise* published an article about the store titled, "What made Sage's so special?"

Mr. Sage was the first to incorporate many trades into one "super" market. Before then, people would buy canned and dry goods at a grocery store, meat from a butcher, bread and cakes from a baker, and have their milk and dairy products delivered. Sage gradually incorporated these into his larger store in San Bernardino, and when the Riverside store on Magnolia opened, it had all of those plus a pharmacy, garden center, and liquor outlet. It was called "complete shopping" because it was a one-stop shopping location.

My wife started shopping exclusively at the Magnolia Avenue store after we bought our first home on Emerson Street. They had a silverware giveaway program that was very popular. You had your choice of a piece of silverware—either a knife, fork, or a spoon—with each grocery purchase. You could choose a regular fork, a dessert fork, a tablespoon, or a teaspoon.

My wife amassed enough of this silverware through her grocery shopping to have a service for ten, along with some extra pieces. They are of the Versailles series and are quite nice. If you look them up on Ebay, you will find they have become collectors' items and are becoming valuable. Not bad, considering she got them all for free.

One time the store advertised some really nice dining table chairs for a very inexpensive price. Our chairs were hand-me-downs and were really trashy, so we discussed it and she went to the store to purchase them. They were out of stock, so she insisted on a raincheck, but they were reluctant to give her one. I think the ad was a mistake, and they were trying to discourage everybody, hoping they would go away. My wife was like a pit bull, and she got her raincheck.

She kept going back to the store, insisting that she wanted

her chairs. She went back for those chairs so many times that they finally gave up and ordered them for her. I noticed a feeling of animosity when I went over to the store to pick them up. They were nice chairs and served us well.

You could pretty much do all your shopping at Sage's. It was definitely a one-stop store.

(Photograph on page 224.)

The Espresso House

Back in the '60s the beatniks morphed into the hippie movement and went into full swing. All the kids were running around in flowered Volkswagen busses, and by the mid-1960s, the Haight-Ashbury neighborhood in San Francisco was the home base for this new counterculture.

The kids wore multi-colored bell-bottom pants, loose shirts and blouses, and gypsy style skirts. Homemade jewelry and beads abounded. The girls all had flowers in their hair and threw away or burned their bras. (To them the bra was the symbol of the establishment's control over the individual.) There were drugs and free love everywhere. Music started to represent this new counterculture, and some of the music was pretty darn good.

Coffee or espresso houses started springing up everywhere. These establishments had beads hanging down from the doorways, and psychedelic lighting as the source of illumination. The smell of burning incense permeated the air. There usually was a small stage where patrons could perform their talents. This was generally poetic prose, with some people actually playing a guitar and singing self-written songs. Some really great art came out of that period. It was definitely a fun time in our history.

Just for fun, one night my wife and I dressed up as hippies and went to one of the local espresso houses in Riverside. We sat at one of the little round tables and sipped our espressos, which tasted terrible, and listened to the entertainment. The poetry was just awful, but we applauded just like everybody else and picked up the language, phrases like, "Man, that was cool," or "Man, I dig it." There were many more expressions that I have long since forgotten.

We were having a great time watching this behavior and laughing our rears off at the situation. I believe the other patrons thought we were just stoned and having a great time. My wife and I both looked a lot younger than our actual ages, so I don't think they thought we were that much older than they were.

I did have a chance to strike up a conversation with some of the kids, and my opinion was that they were just as confused as I was when I was a teenager, and they were just going through the motions, trying to find their own identity.

It was getting late, and we had to get the babysitter home, so we headed out, laughing at what we had just witnessed. It really was a fun evening, and we laughed about our experience for years. “Man, that was cool,” and “Man, we dug it.”

In case you didn’t know, the first “hippie” movement in this country occurred in the Merrymount Colony—near what is now Quincy, Massachusetts—in 1625.

Newport Beach

We rented an apartment in Newport Beach for a week when our first son was an infant. We had my wife's cousin and our first daughter with us as well. An older Portuguese couple owned the apartment building, and they took a liking to us. The man took me out and taught me how to surf fish.

The process was simple. We used sand crabs for bait, and we would stand out in about a foot of water. We would wait for the waves to come in, and as they started back out, we would dig our feet into the sand and move them around. This would cause all of the sand crabs buried in the sand around our feet to be released, and they would go out with the waves. We were effectively chumming, and all the fish would come in to eat the sand crabs, and hopefully, one would get our sand crabs.

I went out every evening that week and always came in with a couple of nice-sized ocean perch for dinner. My wife's cousin refused to eat fish, so we would give her a dollar to go to the pier and get a hamburger for her dinner.

That Portuguese couple wanted to retire, and they offered us that apartment building for $45,000.00, with a minimal down payment. We turned it down, and I still think about it to this day. This apartment building was right on the beach at 47th Place in Newport Beach and has to be worth millions today.

Our First Trailer

In the 1960s we bought a ’58 Ford Thunderbird. This was the first year they made the T-Bird with a rear seat, and it made it more practical for a family car. Our T-Bird was black with a white interior, and it was a beautiful, stylish car, which we loved driving. My wife kept having babies for some reason, and after the third child, the car became impractical for our family.

I was a fireman with the City of Riverside Fire Department, stationed at Fire Station 3 in Magnolia Center at the time, and one of the captains had a 1960 Ford station wagon. We decided to do a straight-across trade. My wife and I were both unhappy about giving up our T-bird, but practicality took over and we made the trade. I soothed my wife’s concerns by promising her that, after the kids were grown, I would buy her another one. I didn’t realize at the time that the ‘58 T-Bird wasn’t very popular because of the rear seat, and only 8,500 were sold that year. That made the cost of purchasing another one after the kids were grown prohibitive.

I made a wooden box and mounted it to the roof of the station wagon. We would load the box with camping gear and head to the mountains and beaches whenever the fire department gave me days off. I decided to fix the station wagon up for towing, so I removed the automatic transmission and put a manual transmission in its place. I disassembled the rear end and geared it down to a 4.33:1 ratio to facilitate towing larger trailers. I really turned it into a towing beast.

Two of my wife’s high school classmates, John and Lois, called and invited us on a camping/fishing trip up to the Trinity Lake region. I made arrangements to lease a trailer near Sacramento, and we left Riverside and headed north for a two-week excursion to the Trinity area.

We arrived at John and Lois’s home in Pleasanton, spent the night, and headed for Sacramento the next morning to pick up the trailer and head off on our first trailer camping trip. We picked up the trailer at the rental yard, loaded the supplies from the station wagon into the trailer, and headed north for our first RV experience.

We arrived at a campground on the Trinity River in Northern California with our group and settled into our campsite. Our group consisted of my family, John and Lois, and four other families. They had a bunch of children with whom our children instantly became friends, and they spent the next two weeks frolicking through the woods and swimming in the lake.

These families were all friends of John and Lois, and we soon became friends with them as well. The guys said they would buy all the beer before we left for the outing, so I left them in charge of the refreshments. I didn't realize that meant going to the local discount store and buying cases of Brown Derby beer. Now, I am not much of a drinker, but I am very particular about the taste of beer, and that stuff was awful. I could maybe get three sips down while it was real cold, but after that it was disgusting.

My wife commented one day about someone leaving full cans of beer around the campsite. I had the problem of these guys being really friendly, and every time one of them saw see me without a beer in my hand, he would immediately open a can and hand it to me. Being polite I would thank him, take a couple of sips, and put it down. Then the routine would start all over again.

I explained the situation to my wife and asked her not to say anything. My wife, being much smarter than I am, suggested that I pour about half the beer out of a can and walk around with it. Every time someone asked if I needed another beer, I could just swish the can around, pretend to take a drink, and say, "No, I'm good." That was my routine for the next two weeks, and it worked just fine.

My wife, being a very thoughtful person, suggested we needed to go into town for supplies. We headed into town and she bought me a six-pack of Coors beer. We came back and she snuck into the trailer and put the six-pack in the refrigerator. I would sneak into the trailer every afternoon and open one of those beers and savor the taste. Oh, how I enjoyed those afternoon breaks.

***

John and I would go out early every morning fishing. The fishing was terrible—they just were not biting. We weren't even getting nibbles, but we didn't let that discourage us. We kept moving locations, trying different baits and lures, but nothing worked. We would come back into camp every day to women expecting their men to provide for them, only to be disappointed at the sight of an empty creel. Their taste buds were crying for fresh trout.

One day I got lucky and landed a fish. It was a pitiful thing, a rainbow trout barely nine inches in length. We came back to camp with that fish, and my wife and Lois fried up a big pan of potatoes, and I cooked that fish. We divided that fish up into four portions, which gave each one of us about half a mouthful. We all commented for years how delicious that fish was.

John and I would take the boat out every morning just before daybreak to try to find a new fishing spot. Trinity was a large body of water with hundreds of miles of shoreline. We would go out into the center of the lake, punch the boat wide open, and haul down the lake, looking for a fresh cove to fish in.

I was always amazed at the amount of wildlife that came down out of the protection of the trees to the shoreline to get a drink of water. The deer and the smaller animals didn't seem to be disturbed by the noise of the speeding boat. They would look up at us and continue drinking, but the bears would scamper back up to the tree line when they heard us coming. You would think as big and powerful as a bear is that they wouldn't be frightened of anything.

***

My son Gerry was an infant at the time, so this had to be the summer of 1969, and the beauty of the pristine area left me in awe. The blue, clear water, the green of the forest around us, and the beauty of the blue sky with all the reflections on the lake have left a lasting impression in my mind. I haven't been back to that area since that trip so long ago. I hope it is still as unspoiled now as it was then.

***

My wife just about drove us crazy over the trailer. We had to wipe our feet whenever we came in. She was constantly sweeping and wiping up every time we entered the trailer. She was so concerned that we wouldn't get our deposit back that she obsessed about keeping it clean.

The two weeks passed quickly, and soon it was time to say goodbye to our new friends. We packed up and headed home, stopping in Sacramento to drop off the trailer. The people from the trailer rental came out with their clipboards to inspect all the damage to their trailer inflicted by us during our trip. I thought they were going to kiss me when they walked inside. They commented that the trailer was cleaner and in better shape than when they released it to us. (They obviously didn't know my wife.) They immediately returned our deposit, thanked us for taking good care of it, and put it back in the line to be rented out again.

We headed home after a great summer vacation with friends.

Our Picnic on Box Springs Mountain

As I mentioned previously, I serviced the radio equipment located in the repeater sites on Box Springs Mountain when I worked for the Motorola service shop on North Main Street in Riverside.

My wife was always curious about what was up on the top of Box Springs Mountain, so one Saturday morning we decided to drive up there and have a picnic. I planned to show her around while we were there. We loaded the kids into the Ford station wagon and headed up the mountain. The road was all dirt once it started up the base of the mountain, and it was the first time I had ever been up there on a weekend. I had no idea how much traffic went up and down that road on weekends.

The traffic was really scary. Some of the people were driving way too fast for a dirt road, and a lot of them were driving in the middle of the road. Driving on a dirt road can be similar to driving on an icy road, but most people don't realize this. You can tell an inexperienced driver on a narrow road because they have a tendency to take the center of the road. We were about halfway up the road when I saw this Triumph TR2 sports car coming down a few turns ahead of us, and he was coming way too fast. I got a little nervous and pulled off to the side of the road as far as I could and parked to wait until the car passed us.

The Triumph came around the turn and the driver saw us. The driver was a young man, and being an inexperienced driver, he panicked, locked up his brakes, went into a skid, and plowed right into the driver's-side front fender of our station wagon. Locking up your brakes on a dirt road has the same effect as on an icy road: once those brakes come you, you are in an uncontrollable slide. That 1960 Ford station wagon was a tank, and it ate that Triumph. Fortunately, nobody was hurt.

I got on my amateur radio in the car and reported the accident. We waited and waited for the law to arrive. People would come by and ask if we needed help, and we would tell them no, that the accident had been reported and help was coming. It was a good thing we brought a picnic basket with us because, after four hours, no one had shown up yet. The kids were entertaining themselves by running around, exploring the mountain. We just sat there twiddling our thumbs.

It was getting late, and there was no more traffic coming down the road, so I got back on the radio and asked if help was coming. The CHP said they had already responded and cleared the scene. I said, We're still here. It has been over six hours, and it will be dark soon."

It turned out that there had been another accident below us, and they had responded to that one, thinking it was us. About 30 minutes later they arrived and investigated the accident. They cited the other driver for unsafe speed for conditions and had a wrecker haul the little mangled sports car away.

The poor kid was really distressed, so I drove him and his companion home. He was really scared and didn't know how he was going to face his parents, so I tried to give him some advice. I told him that they would be so grateful that he wasn't hurt, and he should just be truthful to them. I told him being truthful with your parents is always the best policy.

My wife never did get to see the top of Box Springs Mountain!

My Ranchero

Back in the late '60s I owned a 1957 Ford Ranchero. The engine was a 292 that I had reworked, and the built-up 292s would really perform. It had a 3-speed standard transmission with a column shift. It was a nice truck and was a great daily driver.

One night I got a call from my lifelong friend Doug. He was sitting on the Riverside Freeway, heading south between 14th Street and Central Avenue, with his badly broken 1949 Jaguar Mark IV. I quickly responded and found him safely off on the side of the freeway, with his car sitting in a pool of oil and engine innards scattered all around under the car. That Jaguar's engine had detonated.

We hooked a tow chain to the frame of the jaguar and to the bumper hitch of the Ranchero. I told him we would stay on the shoulder until we got up to highway speed, and then we would merge onto the freeway. I dropped the clutch on the Ranchero and merged onto the freeway in less than 300 feet. We towed the car over to Doug's house on California Street and got it parked. Doug was flabbergasted and commented that I almost snapped his neck when we took off. He said that the Jag was so heavy that he was amazed the Ranchero could accelerate that fast with it in tow. I don't think he realized how much torque that old 292 could produce.

We moved to Crestline in 1969 to get my eldest son out of the smog, and I sold the Ranchero to a friend of my wife's in Crestline. I sold it to her for $90.00 down and a promise of $90.00 per month until it was paid off. My wife's friend loaned it to her boyfriend the first month I sold it to her, and he drove it off of a cliff and destroyed it. That's the last I saw of the Ranchero, and it was the last payment I ever received.

My Most Unforgettable Character

As I have mentioned several times, I worked for a Motorola service shop in Riverside in the late '60s. They hired an additional field service technician whom I'll call Garry. Now, Garry was a friendly sort and we started hanging out. I would visit his home, and he would reciprocate with visits to my home as well. We became friends and our friendship lasted many years.

Garry decided we should spend a Saturday together, just as a guy thing. We drove into Los Angeles to check out the ham radio swap meets and to visit Ham Radio Outlet and then over to Bundy Drive to check out Henry Radio. We ended up the day by going to Henry Radio in Anaheim. (I would eventually purchase my Collins S-Line from Henry Radio in Anaheim.)

We had such a fun day, visiting all those stores and looking at ham radio equipment that we knew we would never be able to purchase. I decided we should end the day with a nice dinner at a nice restaurant while still in the Anaheim area. I picked out a restaurant that was a little higher class than most. Nothing black tie but a restaurant with a nice atmosphere, actual table linens, and nice dinnerware.

We ordered dinner and started out with coffee. They brought our salads, and I had the usual thousand island dressing while Garry had blue cheese dressing. That's when the trouble started. Garry didn't cut up the lettuce in his salad. He would just stab a big piece of it and literally shove it into his mouth. What wouldn't go in, he would take the fork and run it around the outside of the lettuce and shove it in. The end effect was blue cheese dressing all over his face, with him sitting there grinning at me. It was so gross I couldn't even stand to look at him.

There I was, sitting in a nice restaurant, trying to have a pleasant evening, and Garry was sitting there with blue cheese dressing all over his face. When he ran out of coffee, he started looking around and commenting in a loud voice, "Where's that waitress? We need some coffee." He started banging his cup on the table when he didn't get a response, and started shouting, "How about some coffee over here."

I believe everybody in the restaurant was staring at us, and it was so embarrassing. I was totally humiliated and just wanted to get out of there.

That was one of the worst evenings of my life. I learned a valuable lesson about knowing and understanding people before you commit yourself to situations with them. From that day on Garry and I would continue our little outings together, but prepared for his lack of etiquette, I always made sure we attended events that were geared to his style of living. It was nothing but Jack-in-the Box and taco stands from then on.

Lady Godiva

The original Lady Godiva was the Countess of Mercia, an English noblewoman who, according to legend, rode naked, covered only in her long hair, through the streets of Coventry. She reportedly was protesting high taxation by her husband on the people of Coventry. Her feat has been imitated many times over the centuries by, I imagine, ladies who were just exhibitionists. What follows is a story of Lady Godiva, 1980s style.

In the 1960s, Motorola Communications developed a hospital emergency alerting system called "HEAR." The HEAR equipment involved a two-way radio with a telephone dial and handset, similar to the standard telephone of that time. Each radio had a decoding system in it that would keep the radio muted until a specific, 4-digit number was dialed from another radio to send an alert signal to the emergency room of the particular hospital they were trying to connect to. The emergency room attendant would then pick up the handset and communicate with the calling station.

I believe that, over the next 15 years, we installed a HEAR radio system in every hospital in the Inland Empire and the High Desert.

In the late 1980s there was a rock concert at what is now known as Glen Helen Regional Park. I don't believe it was called Glen Helen at that time, but I cannot recall what it was called. The 1980s were right at the height of the drug culture, and there was grave concern over possible drug overdoses and heat strokes, so a large hospital tent was put up on site to treat anyone in need.

We were assigned the task of installing a HEAR station on site in the tent. Motorola was to ship the radio to our shop to prepare it for the installation. As usual the radio arrived the morning we were supposed to install it, and it was going to be a panic getting it ready and installing it on schedule. I sent the guys ahead with all of the antenna parts and equipment to install, so all I had to do was put the radio in place when I had it checked out and working.

I pinned the decoder for the correct 4-digit code assigned to the station, aligned it, and checked to make sure the radio was working properly. I loaded the radio in my van and started for Glen Helen. It was after 2:00 p.m., so I stopped for junk food to hold me until dinnertime. I called my wife and told her I was going to be a little late getting home and advised her of the task I was involved in.

It was about 3:00 p.m. when I finally arrived at Glen Helen, and the traffic was horrid. It was bumper to bumper and at a dead stop. I was getting concerned because the radio was supposed to be installed and operational for the 5:00 p.m. test. I was just sitting there with traffic stopped dead and no other way to get to the hospital tent. I heard all this commotion going on up the street but had no idea what was happening. I just sat there, hoping traffic was going to start moving.

This girl riding a horse slowly approached, and I didn't think much of it because we saw a lot of girls riding horses in those days. I did notice that the horse was a beautiful white color and was large, probably 16 or 17 hands high. The girl was riding very slowly as if to take in the scenery. As she got closer I thought, "What a strange bathing suit she has on."

When she came into full view, I realized she didn't have any clothes on. The only covering she had was her long, beautiful, blonde hair. She was smiling and riding very slowly so everybody could get a really good look at her. She smiled as she rode by me. I tried not to stare, but it was hard, so I just stared and smiled back at her. It was obvious that she wanted everybody to look.

The traffic finally started moving after she passed, and I was able to get to the tent and set up the radio. Needless to say, I was late getting home for supper. My wife started giving me heck about being late, so I told her it was Lady Godiva's fault. She gave me that stern look and said, "Sure! You stopped and had a beer with the guys, didn't you?"

Now, I can count on one hand all the times I stopped for a

beer on the way home. I just never did it. "No, it was Lady Godiva's fault!" was my retort. She just gave me that look, shook her head, and warmed up my supper.

The next day I saw a 3-inch-high headline in *The San Bernardino Sun* stating, "Lady Godiva Rides Again," with a picture of her on the horse. (Of course there were black stripes across the appropriate parts.) I bought the paper, took it home, handed it to my wife, and said, "See, I told you it was Lady Godiva." She looked at it for a second then just threw it on the table and accused me of having a dummy paper printed.

I just smiled and went on, because I knew that in my lifetime I had been able to see Lady Godiva!

The Mission Inn Bar

My wife is from Hesperia and loved Riverside because of the greenery and trees, so after our marriage, we moved to Riverside. I landed a job as a fireman with the City of Riverside Fire Department in 1962 and established our idyllic lifestyle in Riverside.

We dined out often, and after dinner you could often find us at the Mission Inn, sipping drinks, and listening to music. If you go in the Orange Street entrance to the Mission Inn and walk towards the registration booth, you will find a little bar and tables on the left just before the registration booth. I took my granddaughters through the Mission Inn to tour the lights a couple of years ago and noticed that the little cocktail bar was still there.

Back in the '60s, there was a little jazz trio that played some pretty good music there. My wife and I spent many a romantic night at the bar, listening to them. Even being forced to move to Crestline in 1969 to get our elder son out of the smog didn't deter us from enjoying the music. We would often sneak down the hill for a dinner date and end up back at the Mission Inn, enjoying drinks in the candlelight of that wonderful little bar.

I took a job with the County of Los Angeles in 1989, and we moved to Quartz hill and stayed there until my retirement in 2002. It was too far from Riverside to drive down for dinner dates, so the little bar was soon forgotten. We moved back to Hesperia in 2008, to a house less than two miles from where I proposed to my wife in 1961.

I have found that since my wife's passing I find music very soothing and relaxing. I listen to YouTube and have found some great music that wasn't previously available to me. I found a lady named Nora Jones who sings slow music and reminds me of those candlelight evenings at that little bar. I put my headphones on, turn on the music, and drift into dreamland, allowing all those memories to just fill my soul.

If you still live in Riverside and have the chance go into

that little bar, sip a cocktail and listen to some good music; it will fill your soul with a lifetime of great memories. I know it has for me!

Remembering Riverside

As I have said, we left Riverside in 1969 for the smog-free atmosphere of Crestline. I commuted back to Riverside for several years for my work at the Motorola service shop on North Main Street. It wasn't a bad commute from the mountain, especially in the warmer months. The winter drives were sometimes rough when the snow and ice made the drive tedious.

As time wore on I slowly tired of the commute, so I started my own electronics business in Crestline. It was nice having a short commute and being able to stay near family. The business became fairly successful, and several years later I opened a second shop in Hesperia to serve the ever-expanding High Desert area. I eventually ended up with 15 employees, and my shops had a pretty good reputation for doing good work at a fair price.

I developed a customer base in Riverside and was able to spend more time in the area. That allowed me to stop in on friends when there were breaks in my work schedule and spend time with them. There is something about Riverside that gets into your heart and soul. It leaves a feeling of happiness and contentment that lasts throughout your lifetime.

One of my suppliers was Electronic Supply Company on Third Street in Riverside. I would make excuses to drive down to pick up parts just to see the old neighborhood. One day I took one of my installers with me. I had a large order of different parts that I needed, and it required the parts counterman to do a lot of searching. He would, at times, be gone for several minutes, trying to find these items. During one of these breaks, I was looking out the front door of the supply house at a large trucking company across the street. They had hundreds of yards of asphalt and trucks and buildings everywhere.

My mind drifted back to an earlier era when I used to explore the area as a child. I started talking to my installer and describing the area of my youth. I talked about the golden fields of brush and grass that covered the area where the trucking company was now situated and of my hunting rabbits to bring home for dinner. I told him of the terraced ravine only a mile away that was filled with springs and beautiful vegetation, of how much cooler it was down in that ravine during the hot summer months, and the time I spent playing down there to escape the summer heat. I talked of the miles of orange groves that covered the area and how you could take your shotgun and walk into the groves and bag a pheasant to take home for dinner. I talked about Riverside being like a garden paradise in those days, with all the greenery and the smell of orange blossoms that permeated the air making it an unforgettable place to grow up.

I turned around and the counterman had apparently returned earlier and was listening to what I was saying. He was looking at me like I was nuts. He had no ability to fathom what I was saying. He could only see Riverside as he knew it and not as what it was or could have been.

I sold the business after 17 years, which afforded me enough money to retire early. Our children had grown up and moved away, so my wife and I climbed into our RV and traveled for a year. We got horribly bored and returned to our mountain home. We settled in to our daily living, and I decided to go back to school and get the education I had always regretted not having.

I visited one of the local colleges after I graduated in hopes of getting a teaching job, and I ran into an old friend. He told me that the County of Los Angeles needed someone to run the communications shop in the High Desert. I applied, and in 1989 I packed up the RV and headed west. I settled into my new job and my wife headed over to join me. I was fortunate that the county allowed me to buy back all my previous fire department time, and I was able to retire (again) with full benefits in the fall of 2002.

My wife and I purchased a winter home in Yuma, and we traveled back and forth between Quartz Hill, California, and Arizona. We also traveled around the western half of the United States and Canada and had a great retirement. My wife became ill, so we purchased a home on the mesa in Hesperia, near where I proposed to her in 1961. We sold both the Yuma and Quartz Hill properties, and due to her illness, our travels became short trips.

I lost my precious lady, but I have never stopped traveling. It helps me deal with my loss. I continue writing essays as I travel. (As I am now, writing this one sitting in a campsite in Nevada.) I hope someday my great grandchildren will read them and understand what it was like living in my era. One of my nieces read some of my essays about my youth and suggested I post them online. I posted one and got such a great response that I just kept on posting, now here I am, putting them in a book.

Reminiscing About Riverside

I had to make a trip to Fontana one morning, and after finishing my business there, I decided to make a leisurely drive into Riverside. It was to be an afternoon spent reminiscing.

I headed east on Interstate 10 from Sierra Avenue in Fontana then took the Cedar Avenue off ramp and headed south through the City of Bloomington. I cruised through the old mobile home park that my friend Doyle and I used to cruise through when we were teenagers. That brought back a lot of memories.

I drove past the old cement plant at the bottom of Crestmore Hill—where I had a contract servicing their communications system—and turned left onto Market Street. I proceeded towards Riverside, and as I passed over the river-bottom bridge, I glanced over at the riverbottom and reminisced about all the girls I had taken on dates to the riding stables at the edge of the river. It was there that we spent many a summer morning riding horses together across the river.

I turned off Market Street and headed into Fairmont Park. I stopped at the park, got out of the car, and walked around on the grass for a while. I sat on one of the benches, watched the people walking by, and reminisced about the times of my youth I had played and fished at the park. I thought of the times my friend Doug and I spent in that huge swimming pool, splashing around, trying to cool off on those hot summer days. I thought about the boathouse and the girls I took out for evening boat rides on the big lake. (The boathouse was on the little lake and you had to go under the Redwood Street bridge to get to the big lake.) The boats had electric motors in them, and all you could hear was a pleasant hum while you were in motion. It was so pleasant in the cool summer evenings, cruising on the lake with the radio playing our favorite music as we watched the sun go down.

I thought about the times we took the children to the park and spent the day playing with them. I remembered the evenings we sat as a family and listened to the summer concerts in front of the Bowl. I remembered enjoying the Fourth of July celebrations and watching the fireworks exploding over the lake. The reflection of the fireworks on the lake was spectacular. Oh, the many memories that park brings back!

I finally left the park and headed up Redwood Drive, heading for Indian Hill to look at the fancy homes that my wife and I had dreamed of being able to live in. We often drove up there when we were young to just cruise around and dream.

As I was driving up Redwood Drive, I looked up the hill at Houghton Avenue, and the memories of my first time with a girl on top of that mountain flashed back. What a magical night that was. She took me to places I had never been before. I can still see her beautiful face as clear as that night on the hill. I remember her name as well, but it will never pass my lips. That magical moment was for her and me alone. We dated for a while, and then I lost track of her. I hope she had a happy, long, healthy life.

I headed up Mt. Rubidoux Drive and looked at the houses my wife and I used to drive by. She loved riding with me and enjoyed looking at those gorgeous homes. I would take her up there every so often and wander up one street and down the next. It is such a beautiful area and is a delight to see. This day I did the drive in remembrance of her, and I like to think she was riding along with me.

I drove by the old Evergreen Cemetery and walked around and looked at the graves of four generations of my family. My father's headstone is missing, and I have made several attempts to find it, but to no avail. I know approximately where he was buried, but there is just an empty space where he would have been.

I drove up Fourteenth Street and stopped at Del Taco for a burrito and then drove downtown. I went down Almond Street to where my grandmother's house was. Now there is nothing but lawyers' offices at the spot where her beautiful Victorian home once stood. I drove downtown, stopped and took a few pictures of the downtown area, then hopped on the freeway and headed home, my head swirling with many beautiful memories.

Although I moved away from Riverside many years ago, Riverside is a part of who I am, and I am a part of Riverside. I should do the drive around Riverside more often. It was a wonderful way to spend an afternoon and was a day just for my memories and me.

(Photograph on page 225.)

Aunt Ginny

One of Grandmother Layton's younger sisters, Ginny, lived with her husband, Bill Bradney, in a nice home in Tustin, California. I assumed they were fairly well off financially because of their new car and the nice home, but you never know.

In the off-fire season of 1959, Bill said he could get me a job at his construction company in Santa Ana, so I loaded up and headed down there to find a job. I ended up staying a couple of weeks with them at their home in Tustin. Ginny was a good cook, and we always had nice meals with plenty of vegetables and salads. I enjoyed my visits with Ginny, sitting at the dining table, sharing tea and talking with her. She was a very interesting individual.

One Saturday morning they were going grocery shopping, and they asked me if I would like to go along. I said, "Sure," and we were off to the store.

We pulled up to one of the major grocery stores, and I expected them to park, but they continued on around to the back of the store and pulled up to the large row of dumpsters lined up behind the store. They got out of the car, and Bill proceeded to climb into the dumpsters and started handing items out to Ginny. He would say, "Look, here's a nice head of lettuce," or "Here's a good bunch of celery." He continued handing items out to Ginny, commenting on the conditions of said items.

Ginny was busy stuffing bags full of carrots, ears of corn, cabbage—we had just had boiled cabbage the day before—celery, radishes, bananas, and other various fruits and vegetables.

Bill and Ginny finished their "shopping," and we headed back to the house, with me sitting in the back seat in total disbelief. That evening we had a nice dinner of meatloaf with all the trimmings. I knew where the trimmings came from but was afraid to ask where the meatloaf came from. By early the next morning I had miraculously found job offers in Riverside and headed back to my sister's house in Arlanza.

Barbi Benton

It was a 102 outside with a hot wind blowing, so I decided to just stay inside and enjoy the air conditioning. As an old man I sometimes wander off into a dreamland of my youth, and at that moment Barbi Benton came to mind. In my youth I dated a girl named Barbara Johnson. Barbara was a beautiful woman. She stood five foot eight, had a slim, well-defined figure, and was striking.

We were stared at wherever we went. Eyes would follow us whenever we walked into a restaurant or a bar, all the way from the entrance to our seats, and I am sure they weren't staring at me. (Unless they were wondering what a plain john like me was doing with such a beautiful woman.)

We dated for a few months, and as with all my relationships—until I met my wife, of course—we slowly drifted apart. We parted ways, went off in different directions, and eventually lost track of each other. The last I heard, Barbara had moved to Northern California.

All of my relationships ended cordially, and we remained friends. I never believed in burning bridges. I often wonder how my girlfriends' lives turned out and hope they all had good, happy lives filled with love.

One day I was reading *Playboy* and there was Barbara, a playmate, a centerfold, and a confidant of Hugh Hefner. It appeared that she had changed her name to Barbi Benton and was doing well in life. I thought, *Good for you girl. You made it to the big time*. I was envious but extremely happy for her.

Over the years I often thought about writing Barbara and congratulating her on her success, but I am glad I didn't. She probably would have thought I was an idiot or a nut job, as I was about to find out how wrong I was.

Barbi Benton attended a fundraiser in Big Bear, and my niece Donna posted a picture on Facebook of them hugging. I couldn't believe it. Donna, who is about the same height as "my

Barbara," was towering over Barbi Benton. I Googled Barbi and found out she is five foot three and would have been about 11 years old at the time Barbara and I were dating.

Now I find myself wondering what happened to my Barbara. My only hope is that she had a happy, healthy life.

Does Anyone Remember Helms Bakery Trucks?

The Helms Bakery truck used to come by our home on Emerson Street every morning. I would run outside with my children and we would wait for the truck to pull up. My kids would get so excited waiting for the driver to stop his truck and step out and walk around to the back. He always greeted us with a smile as he opened the huge deep drawers, exposing those warm, creamy, sweet, soft-glazed doughnuts that melt in your mouth. He would pull out some tissues, wrap one around each doughnut, and hand one to each of the kids. They would run for the house, eating and giggling as they ran. I would get a loaf of fresh bread, pay the man, and head back to the house.

I remember the wonderful smell from those drawers in the back of the Helms trucks as if it were yesterday. My children are all in their fifties now, and they quite often bring up the memories of that Helms Bakery truck and how huge and delicious those doughnuts were.

Don't you wish, sometimes, you could just go back to the simpler times?

The '54 Mercury

In the early '50s my home life became intolerable, so I lived on the streets. One of my school friends, Doyle Miller, saw my plight and invited me to stay at his home. The Millers took me in as one of their own. Glenn and Idelle Miller were two of the most loving human beings I have ever known. I had never had the kind of love they offered, so I didn't understand or know how to deal with it. I just melted into the family and enjoyed the hot meals and a warm bed.

It was unusual and slightly uncomfortable, having someone caring about and looking after me. It took me several years to defeat my demons and be able to understand unconditional love. I am sure I caused them some disappointment at times, but they always exercised patience and understanding. I believe now that they understood what I was going through.

Charlotte, one of my newly adopted sisters, took me under her wing. She was much older than I was, so no hanky-panky was going on. It was strictly a brother-sister relationship. We would tease and play pranks on each other, and we did a lot of joking and laughing. She was quite a character, and we had a lot of fun together.

She was always sewing new shirts for me. I still have pictures of me wearing those shirts. I have many memories of just sitting around the Miller house, playing cards, doing jigsaw puzzles, and joking and teasing each other. It was great being with a big sister.

Doyle joined the Navy and went to San Diego for boot camp. We would head to San Diego every time Doyle had leave, arriving at the base early in the morning to pick him up. Doyle would usually have some of his new, Navy buddies come along, and in usual Miller fashion, they were always treated like family. We would spend the day, usually at the zoo, just being family and enjoying each other's company.

The zoo visits were always with the entire Miller family,

and that was a bunch. Idelle would pack a lunch, and we would eat and just tour around the zoo all day, visiting and talking. It was always disheartening to take Doyle and his friends back to the base and say goodbye for the time being.

Graduation Day came for Doyle, and a very proud family loaded up and headed to San Diego for the graduation ceremony. We attended the graduation, packed up Doyle, and brought him home for his two-week leave before deployment. Doyle commented that the first thing he was going to do when he got home was get out of his uniform and put some civvies on. But he was so proud of that uniform that we couldn't get him out of it for the entire two weeks he was home.

We took him back to the base at the end of the two weeks and, again disheartened, watched him walk through the gates of the base, knowing this time he would be deployed and it would be a while before we saw him again. Fortunately, we were in peacetime, and the fear of him going into action wasn't a concern.

My memory is a little vague here, but I think Doyle was assigned to a tin can (a destroyer) for his first deployment, made one trip to the Philippines and back, and then was transferred to the *Piedmont* for the rest of his time in the Navy. He would sail to Sasebo, Japan, and sit there for a while, and then come back to San Diego. He did this several times, but I can't recall how long each tour was. Charlotte and I would go down to pick him up when he got his three-day passes, and that was where the '54 Mercury came in.

We would have to leave at three in the morning to make it to the Broadway landing to pick up Doyle from the liberty boat at 7 a.m. The drive was long and hard, and there wasn't much traffic on that road in those days. It would be miles between any towns or signs of civilization. If you broke down around there, you were stranded, sometimes for hours.

About at this time, Charlotte decided it was time for a new car, and she settled for a brand new, 1954 Mercury Monterey. We took off at 3 a.m. and headed for San Diego in style. We made the hundred miles to the Broadway landing in an hour and a half, which was unheard of in those days. I think I had that Mercury at a hundred most of the way, but something was wrong. I kept watching the gas gauge and it wasn't moving. Most of the cars in those days got around 15 miles per gallon, and at the speed I was driving, it should have been down to no more than 12 mpg. I told Charlotte something was wrong with the gas gauge and that we had better get gas before heading back.

We picked up Doyle and a couple of his buddies and then we stopped and tried to fill that Mercury's gas tank, but we couldn't even get four gallons in it. I said, "Something's wrong. It has to take more gas than that." But it just wouldn't, so we headed home. We made a lot of those early morning runs to San Diego, picking up the sailors and returning them to their ships in that Mercury, all the time getting around 30 mpg.

I think that car might have been a test vehicle that slipped through and went on the retail market. I looked that carburetor over, and there was nothing unusual about it. I have always been a gearhead and know cars pretty well, and I would have spotted something. That car ran good and had plenty of power, so I don't understand why they couldn't have put that carburetor on all the cars. I can only assume it was a collaboration with the oil companies to keep their profits up.

A few years later I saw an article for a carburetor labeled a "Fish." They we using this carburetor on early Fords that were racing on the pampas in South America and they claimed they were getting 30 mpg on the things while racing.

I think the article on the Fish carburetor was in one of the Hot Rod magazines I used to subscribe to. It had an article and diagram of the carburetor. I looked at the diagram, and it looked from the outside to be a standard, Stromberg 97 that was used in those days. I told a friend of mine about the article and he went to the newsstand and got a copy of the magazine, but the article wasn't in his magazine. I went to get my magazine to show him the article and couldn't find the magazine anywhere, so all I have is my memory of the article. I wonder if the oil companies had the magazine pulled and I happened to get one before they had it removed. I don't have a clue what happened to mine.

In spite of the loving family that surrounded me, I made some bad choices that took me on a detour. I bought a motorcycle and got in with a bad crowd and drifted away from the Millers for a couple of years.

Charlotte kept up her runs to San Diego, and Doyle always brought his buddies home with him. With Charlotte's personality, she fit right in with all those sailors. They adored her and protected her with a passion.

One day the Mercury started running badly, and one of the good-hearted sailors took that carburetor off, took it to Pep Boys, and exchanged it for a rebuilt carburetor. The Mercury only got 14 mpg from then on. I was really let down when they let that carburetor go, and I wonder what happened to it. I wonder if some lucky fool is out there driving a car and wondering why his gas mileage just doubled.

The Busted Yolk

Doyalene's dad was a great guy and I loved him dearly. Doyalene and I would take the kids and drive up to Hesperia every time I had a day off from the fire department, and we would spend the day with her mom and dad. Dad and I would grab a six-pack of beer and head out across the desert in his old Datsun pickup. Dad never wasted his time with those puny beers—we always got the tall ones. We would just drive around on the desert, drinking beer and exchanging stories. When I say "drive around the desert," I mean "the desert." No roads—just driving on the desert. The high desert is rock and dirt, and there weren't many homes there in those days.

One day we were out driving around on the desert, dodging Joshua Trees, and he told me about this new cook he had hired. He was watching him cooking eggs, and he noticed him sticking his thumb in the egg yolks to break them. Dad walked over and asked him what he was doing, and the kid said, "They ordered the eggs busted."

Dad looked at the order ticket and said, "You dumb ass! That says basted, not busted." I asked him how long the guy lasted, and he said, "One day."

I have never forgotten that story. Those drives across the desert with Dad were some of my favorite times.

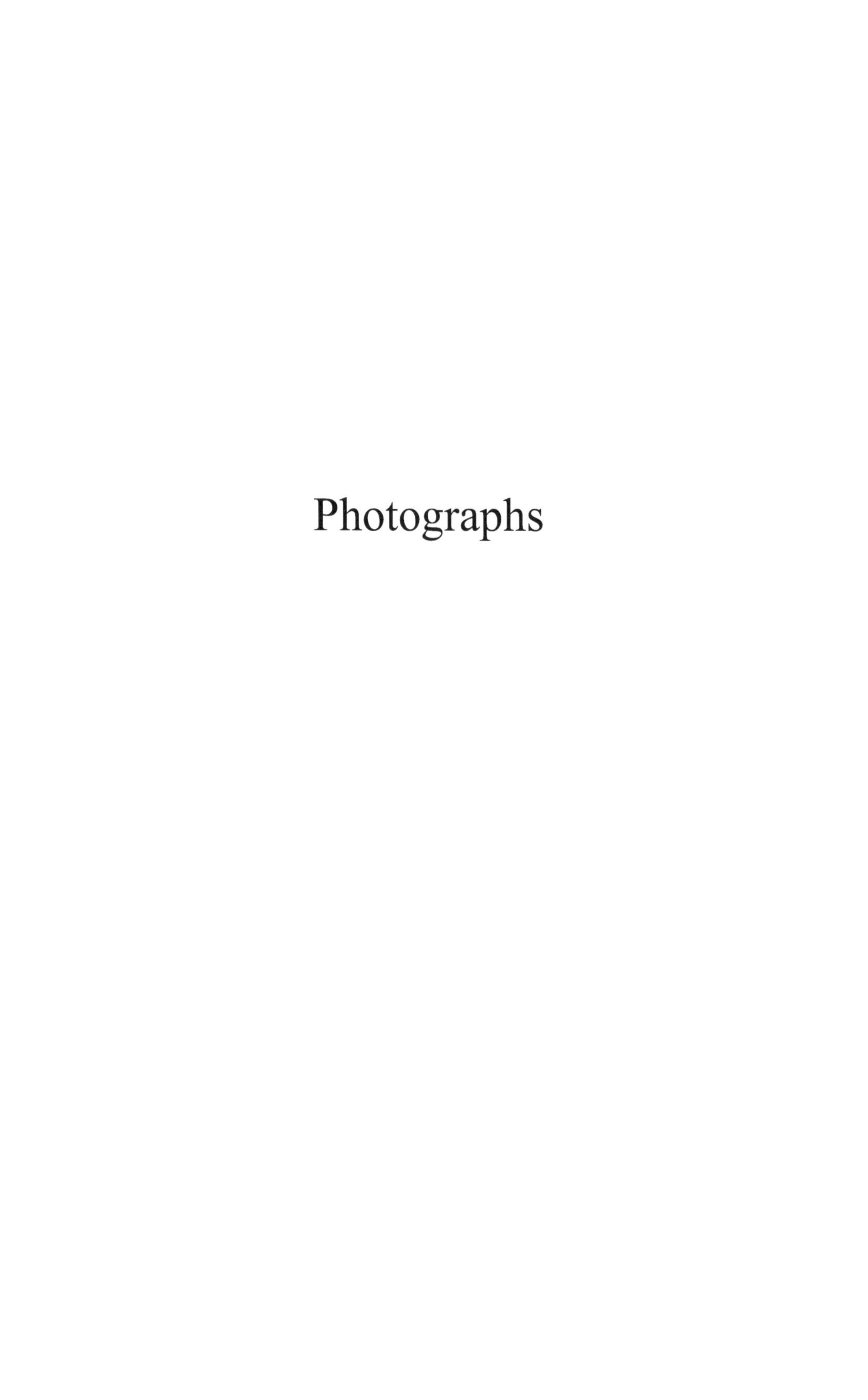

Photographs

Doug standing in lake bed (Now Adulka Park)
December 1956

Gary standing in doorway of burned-out house near Andulka Park. December 1956

Old rotary-style telephone.

Gary Layton and Doug Baker. 11 years old.

Gary and Doug. October 1953

Doug. Cotober 1953

Gary. October 1953

Gary Layton.
October 1953

Hunter Layton.
September 2013

Doodlebug

Doug, Indio Date Festival.
February 1950

**Gary camping in Santa Ana Riverbottom.
About 14 years old. November 1953**

Garys Triumph Motorcycle

1947 Plymouth

Gary's '52 Merc with Dodge Royal Lancer hubcaps.

Doyalene at Riverside Safeway. 1962

Doyalene sitting on the hood of my 1952 Cadillac Coupe DeVille. January 1963

Gary's 1952 Cadillac Coupe DeVille

Versailles series silverware from Sage's Supermarket

Downtown Riverside
University Avenue and Lime Street

Run, Billy, Run

I became homeless after my dad died and my mother decided to pursue a lifelong career of staying high. I stayed with friends and drifted around. I ended up hanging around what was referred to as "Okie Flats" on the eastside of San Bernardino.

Now, Okie Flats wasn't a high-priced neighborhood where you would want to successfully raise a child. There was strife and occasional gang fights. I was shot during one of those altercations, and maybe I will write about that at a later date, but this story is about Billy.

Most of the households in Okie Flats were single-parent households, and although some of the parents were winos or worse, a lot of them honestly tried to raise their kids responsibly, but conditions in the neighborhood virtually prevented it. Billy was a victim of those conditions.

We were at a party on 4th Street one summer night, and everybody was having a good time drinking and talking. Some of the guys were in the street, having a friendly fight. Billy and I were standing in the street, leaning up against a car and watching the excitement. Billy had his girlfriend, Jesse, with him, and a girl named Joyce was with me.

I had dated Jesse for a while, and she was a really sweet girl. She was a lot of fun to be with but was just a little too loud for my liking. I am sorry to say she was killed a few years after I left the neighborhood, and she left behind a small child. This was a common occurrence on the Eastside.

We were all having a good time watching the fight when all of a sudden a half a dozen cop cars drove up with the spotlights on. We heard an announcement from one of the cop cars identifying themselves and telling everybody to stand still and stay where they were.

Billy was on parole, and I looked at him and said, "Are we going to stay here?"

"Hell no," he replied, and we took off running with Jesse

and Joyce in hot pursuit. We ran through some fields and came up to a chain link fence that had us cornered. Billy said, "Hey, let's just hide under these bushes. They'll never see us."

I looked toward the lights and could see all these silhouettes coming toward us. All I could see was the outline of men with holsters and nightsticks. I told Billy, "They're looking right at us and will find us." He kept insisting that we could hide in the bushes, so I said, "Bullshit," and I picked Billy up and threw him over the fence.

I was pretty strong when I was young and could easily pick up 300 pounds and press 250 over my head. I threw Jesse and Joyce over the fence as well. Then I jumped over the fence, and we took off running, the cops in hot pursuit.

We somehow got separated in the melee, and as I ran by my friend Tommy's house, I noticed the door was open and the TV was on. I ran into the house, took off my shoes and shirt, and threw them under the couch. I messed up my hair so it would look like I was napping, and I stretched out on the couch. Pretty soon I heard the cops running around, making a racket. I got off the couch and kind of stumbled to the door. "What the heck is going on?" I asked.

One of the cops asked if I had seen any activity. I told them I had heard some people laughing and running and the commotion woke me up. They asked if I had seen what direction they were heading. I figured Joyce and the others had run to her house, so I pointed the opposite way and said, "It sounded like they were heading in that direction." The cops all took off in hot pursuit.

I don't know where Tommy and Millie were that night. The house was wide open and the TV was going. I waited around for several hours for things to cool down before I left to pick up my car, but they never did show up. Fortunately, I had parked at my friend Benny's house and had ridden over to the party with him, so my vehicle wasn't in question. I just got into my car and drove home.

It turned out that the cops all took off chasing us, so as soon as they all disappeared, the guys back at the party got in their cars and left. The girl who had been holding the party picked up quickly, put her pajamas on, and put curlers in her hair.

When the cops came back, they started beating on her door. She came to the door, acting like they had awakened her, and she denied any knowledge of a party.

The cops were thoroughly mad, and the next week was hell in the neighborhood. We couldn't drive down the street without getting pulled over for some ridiculous reason. They went through our cars, trying to find anything illegal. They harassed us by saying they had seen us at the party, that they knew we knew who the people were who had run away, and it was going to be hard on us if we didn't tell them who it was.

Nobody would ever have told them, even if they had known. That was the code of the neighborhood; nobody was a rat. The cops could have pulled out those kids' fingernails, and they still would not have told. They fought like cats and dogs with each other, but they were extremely loyal to each other and would never rat on anyone in the neighborhood.

One morning a few weeks later I was walking out the door, heading for work, and found cops going through my car. They had the trunk emptied out, the rear seat was out, and everything was scattered. I asked them, "What the heck are you doing?"

They said, "Oh, is this your car?"

I said, "Yes," and they got in their car and drove away. I had to put my car back together before I could go to work. The cops were constantly harassing us, only because we lived in a rough neighborhood. I never parked my car on the street after that. It was always in the yard behind a locked gate.

At that time in my life I was running an automotive repair shop on Baseline Street in San Bernardino, and I carried my toolbox in the car. I got pulled over late one night on the way home, and they arrested me for being a burglar because I had burglar tools in my car. That shows how ridiculous the cops were in those days. The watch sergeant asked them what contraband they had found in my car. When they said all they found was the tools, I told the sergeant that I owned Porters Garage on Baseline Street and they were my mechanic tools, not burglar tools. The sergeant told them to cut me loose.

Needless to say, I never carried my tools in my car again.

Jesse

As I said in the previous essay, I ran around with a group of guys on the eastside of San Bernardino in an area referred to as Okie Flats. Everybody was poor, and it was a struggle to just get through life in those days.

We used to hang around in out-of-the-way places to keep the cops from harassing us. We would get into trouble occasionally, and gang fights were not uncommon. That always kept us under the close scrutiny of law enforcement. We used to hang out in orchards and fields around the Highland area. It was in the sheriff department's area, and they were usually understaffed and didn't bother us as much as the San Bernardino police and the CHP did.

Another place we frequented was an area known as the riverbottoms around the east end of San Bernardino. We used dune buggies to go deep into the riverbottoms where the deep sands kept law enforcement out.

One night as we were standing in one of those fields, drinking beer and talking, and I noticed a pretty girl standing under a tree. I don't know why, but I walked over to her and we started talking. All of a sudden I started kissing her. As I remember it, it was a passionate kiss and she wasn't resisting. In fact I think it was reciprocal. When I stopped and backed up a little, I was holding her arms and kind of stroking them and looking into her eyes.

She asked me why I had kissed her. I was stymied for a minute and didn't know how to respond. I finally said, "I don't know. I just had this irresistible urge."

We spent the rest of the evening together, talking and hanging out. We ended up dating for several months and had a great time running around together. I'm not sure why we parted company. I don't remember it being because of any friction, and we were always good friends after that. I just think I wasn't ready at that time for any serious relationships, and maybe she wanted one. She ended up marrying one of the guys I ran around with.

I am sorry to say she was killed in a horrible automobile accident a few years later and left a motherless young son behind. I think about her often and wonder what life would have been like for her if she hadn't climbed into that car with a bunch of drunken friends. I had five friends in that car that night and lost three of them. As I get older, I reflect upon the fact that one simple choice can have life-altering consequences.

Joyce

I met Joyce when I was about 18. I believe she was about 16 at the time. A bunch of us guys were standing around talking and doing nothing when she and her friends walked up to see what was going on. I was awestruck when I saw her. This girl, barely five feet tall, was breathtaking.

Joyce was wearing a satin, pink polka-dot blouse and Levi's—she always wore Levi's—and had a pair of pink pumps on. Pumps were slip-on shoes in those days; I don't know what they call them now. She had the most beautiful auburn hair with a pink ribbon in it. Her brown eyes would melt your heart, and she had this classic, gothic nose. She was neither skinny nor fat—she was just perfect. She was an excellent example of a perfect woman, and I was instantly in love with her.

Joyce and I started dating and it was serious. We each had a horse, so we took up housekeeping in a little one-bedroom house over on Little Third Street in San Bernardino. I built a paddock and corral in the back yard and moved our horses over. We spent many a day on those horses, running up and down in the riverbottom alongside the house. It was a great time, and I was in bliss all the time.

Joyce and I planned to build a horse ranch, and I did buy some property up in the pass after our breakup to build mine, but after I joined the Forestry Department, I let it go back to the sellers because I didn't have the time to develop it.

Joyce wanted to learn to drive, so I would take her out and let her practice on the back roads in my Mercury. She did pretty well and was a fast learner. One evening while in town she wanted to drive, so we pulled into a gas station and switched seats. She had just pulled out of the gas station when a CHP officer spotted us and turned around. I had her turn the corner, and we switched seats really fast. The CHP guy stopped and walked up to the car. He looked at us and said, "If you're going to teach her how to drive, tell her to turn the headlights on at twilight."

We both said, "Yes, sir," and he walked back to his car and drove off.

I had forgotten that it was just starting to get dark when we pulled into the gas station, and the light in the gas station made it appear as though it was still daylight.

Joyce turned out to be a pretty good driver, so I took her over by the local DMV office. There was an area on a side road by the office that had vertical poles up to designate a parking spot. Everyone who took a driving test had to parallel park as part of the test. If you failed at parallel parking, you failed the test.

I took Joyce over there and showed her how to pull up next to the poles, turn the steering wheel all the way to the right, and start backing up. I showed her that as soon as the driver's side of the car lined up with the inside pole, she should crank the steering wheel all the way to the left and back right into the space. She must have done it perfectly 50 times, so I felt she was ready.

I took her to the DMV Office to take her test. She took the written test and passed it with no problem. Then it was time for the driving test. She climbed into the Mercury with the examiner and off they went. The parking part of the driving test is the start of the test, so I walked down to the corner to watch her park. There were five vertical poles that you had to navigate through, and after watching her back into the space perfectly so many times, I had all the confidence in the world that it was going to be a piece of cake.

Wrong! If you touch one of the poles, you are out. She not only touched one of the poles, but she ran over two of them and backed into the other three. She was five for five. The examiner had her return to the DMV and told her to practice some more. I can't remember if she ever got her driver's license or not.

Joyce eventually grew tired of me and started wandering, so we went our separate ways. Supposedly, she got married and was soon pregnant. Her husband abandoned her as soon as she started showing, and I ended up back in the picture. I helped her through her pregnancy in hopes of rekindling the fire that had once been there.

She gave birth to a beautiful, happy little girl. Things were going pretty well after the baby's birth, and we settled in, but soon the wandering began again. I had an embarrassing conversation with a couple of guys about her appearance at a party, and it almost ended up in a confrontation, but I decided it wasn't worth fighting over.

I finally decided that our life together wasn't going anywhere, so one I night I went over to the baby's crib, leaned over and kissed her on the forehead, and told her to take care of her mommy because I was out of here. I walked out and never looked back.

I didn't realize at the time what a valuable lesson Joyce taught me in learning how to control my emotions and choose the right friends and associates. A couple of years later I met my precious Doyalene and had almost 54 years of bliss and a wonderful family. That would never have been possible without the experiences I had with Joyce.

I don't think a day goes by that I don't think of Joyce. I wonder how her life went. I imagine her living in poverty with seven kids, all from different fathers. I hope not. I hope she found a man she could really love and spent a faithful lifetime with him and had a wonderful life.

The Hells Angels

Throughout my life there have been rumors floating around my friends and family that I was some sort of a badass biker who rode with the Hells Angels. Some members of the family have suggested that I write about my experiences during those times.

You have to understand that I had a less-than-desirable childhood, and I grew up very bitter and angry. I was bent on dealing with my frustrations and anger by hurting people. I feel it best not to write or talk about those experiences. All I will say about the rumors is that they are mostly true.

I was quite innocently introduced to the Hells Angels. One night I was riding my hog around San Bernardino when a bunch of bikers came riding up and closed in around me. They kind of looked me over. One of the bikers was riding double, and the guy on the back was holding a jug of "Dago Red." He asked if I wanted a shot and I said yes. He passed it to me, and I took a couple of good swigs and passed it back.

They said they were heading for a party and asked if I wanted to come. I had nothing else to do so I said ok. They said, "Follow us" and took off, with me riding along.

What followed was one heck of a hell-raising night. The next thing I knew I was attending meetings and parties with them. In those days there was no initiation into the club. You just rode with them, and after you had proven yourself, and they felt they could trust you, they would invite you to wear the colors. It was your option if you wanted to wear the colors or not. Most of the guys would immediately go out and get the emblem—the colors—and sew them on their jackets. Most of the it was a Levi jacket with the sleeves cut off.

I have heard of some people bragging about being card-carrying members of the Hells Angels. I have never heard of a membership card in the organization and never had one myself. I think the people who lay claim to one are just bragging and want to be a bad asses.

I spent a lot of time with a bunch of guys that could really take care of situations, and I never heard any of them claiming or bragging about being a bad ass. They just jumped in when the situation arose and took care of it. It was just the duty of the day.

***

In the mid-'50s, the Berdoo Chapter of the Hells Angels had a clubhouse just north of Highland Avenue on Riverside Drive. We had regular meetings at the clubhouse, and people would be surprised to find these meeting were well organized and followed Robert's Rules of Order. We had officers who maintained order in the meetings. We discussed current events, and there was always legal counsel there to guide everybody in dealing with the constant harassment by law enforcement.

We had parties at numerous locations throughout California. There were always girls who were attracted to bikers and would let the guys hang out at their pads. They were always willing to supply the guys with food, gas, and any favors the guys wanted, just to be able to hang out and ride with them. We would hang out at these houses, and the girls would supply the guys with booze, and drugs, and party favors. I guess the girls were just attracted to bad boys.

We attended a party at one of these houses in Barstow one winter, and the local law ran us off about three in the morning. The ride back to San Bernardino was brutal. I don't know if I have ever been that cold before in my life. You have to remember that most of us rode with sleeveless Levi jackets, and we would have been laughed out of the club if we had worn gloves.

On the way home that night, we would haul ass until we couldn't stand it any longer, then pull off the road and circle the bikes. We would crouch in the center and let the warm air blowing across the hot engines warm us up. We would haul ass again as soon as the engines cooled off, go a few miles, and do the same routine again.

We stopped at a small store and broke into the newspaper

machine and tried stuffing newspapers in our pants legs and shirts. We were doing everything we could to try to stay warm. We finally made it back to San Bernardino, and I think my ears still hurt from that night.

***

We would go to Signal Hill in Long Beach quite often and party until daybreak. We were never hassled by law enforcement at those parties. There were always 40 or more bikers there, and I don't believe there was enough law enforcement at that time to deal with that many. We never caused any trouble, so I think they felt it best to just let us party it out and go home.

We did have law enforcement try to break up parties at other locations. It sometimes got ugly, and a few guys got hurt, including law enforcement. So I think Long Beach just decided to leave us alone as long as we didn't get out of hand.

It was at one of the times on Signal Hill that I attended the last party with the guys. After the party we all rode down to some chick's house—I have no recollection of its location—and all the guys were lying all over the house in a stupor from the night's activities. I remember sitting in the corner of the living room, looking around at everybody, and all of a sudden I asked myself, "What the hell are you doing here?"

I went out, got on my bike, and rode back to the Millers' house in Riverside. I put a "For Sale" sign on the motorcycle and placed it in the Millers' front yard. I sold it in two days for $175.00. (It's a classic now and is probably worth at least 20 grand.)

Four days later I hired on as a firefighter with the California Division of Forestry. This is all I will ever say about riding with the Angels. I won't say I am ashamed of that period of my life, but I am definitely not proud of it. Thinking back, I realize I'm lucky I survived it. Most of my friends did not. I found out later in life that some of them were killed in accidents, some in fights, and some in prison. I believe they are all gone now.

Public Service

I vowed never to write much about my time with the Hells Angels. It is an era I would just like to forget about, but this is a humorous story, so I decided to share it.

We were constantly being harassed by the CHP. We couldn't drive down the road without being pulled over and written up for some BS fix-it ticket. They would constantly harass and insult us, hoping we would get mad enough to swing on them. Then we would be in serious trouble. If we didn't bite and take a swing at them, they would write us up for some BS thing like our taillight being too low to the ground or too high from the ground. They would always find something to write us up for.

Many years later when I was in good graces with the CHP, I talked with an officer, and he told me they could pull another police officer's bike over and find something to write them up for. The idea was if they could get enough tickets issued on you, then they could get your driver's license pulled. If that happened, they would actually sit near your home, sometimes for days, waiting for you to pull out of your driveway. Now they had you for a misdemeanor, and that meant confiscation of your bike and jail time. They could turn you into a felon after enough of these misdemeanors, and that meant prison time. It was their effort to get all the Hells Angels off the road.

We were discussing the problem one night, and one of Hells Angels guys came up with this brainy idea of doing public service to soften our image in hopes of getting the fuzz off our backs. (This guy was obviously in a drunken stupor when he came up with that brilliant idea.)

One day there was a bunch of us riding up the highway near Palm Avenue in San Bernardino when we spotted a young lady holding a baby. Her car was sitting there with a flat tire. She was standing there, looking at the jack, totally confused. We pulled up behind her, and when she saw all the bikes, she screamed, jumped back in the car, and locked all the doors. The only problem was the keys were sticking out of the lock in the trunk.

We went ahead and jacked up the car and changed the tire. We put the flat tire in the trunk and locked the trunk. Big Mike walked around to the driver's-side door and started tapping on the window to get the young lady's attention.

Now, you have to understand that Big Mike was called Big Mike because he was big. He was not fat; he was big. He probably stood six foot five and weighed over 280. When he sat on that big hog of his, it would look like me sitting on a little 80. Mike was a nice guy, but he had a ruddy completion with some acne damage to his face. He looked like he ate children for breakfast.

The young lady was so petrified that she just sat there, not knowing what to do. Mike finally took the key, unlocked the door, and handed the keys to the petrified woman. "Ma'am," he said. "Your flat tire has been fixed, but you need to go to the nearest service station and get a new tire to replace the flat one. You have a nice day, compliments of the Hells Angels Motorcycle Club." He closed the door and we rode off. We watched until we got out of sight and never did see the car move.

We decided that day we had better knock off our public service idea. It didn't look like it was working out the way we expected.

The Levi's

In the '50s when I was riding with the Hells Angels, we would never wash our Levi's. The idea was to get them so greasy that they could literally stand up by themselves. It was a real status symbol if you had the greasiest, stand-alone Levi's. It would take several months to get them in "pristine" condition, and the wearer of them would be very proud of his accomplishment.

I was driving truck down into south Texas once a week to pick up palm trees and needed to take the second truck down on a particular trip. I enlisted the help of one of the Hells Angels riders. Billy and I loaded the bobtail onto the trailer of the big rig so we could ride double down to Texas. We would take the bobtail off when we got down to Texas, load it, as well as the semi, with trees, and head back.

I always stopped at a truck stop in Deming, New Mexico, for fuel, and while fueling, Billy started a conversation with the attendant at the truck stop. In the conversation the attendant asked where we were coming from and Billy responded, "San Bernardino."

The attendant remarked, "Don't you have a lot of Mexicans in San Bernardino?" Billy said he hadn't paid that much attention.

We went on our way, heading east, and then turned south into Texas. The truck route through El Paso takes you right along the border with Mexico. Billy was looking out the windows while we were driving through El Paso and remarked that he was going to tell the attendant when we got back to Deming that if he thought there are Mexicans in San Bernardino, he needed to come to El Paso.

We finally arrived in Harlingen, Texas, after a couple of days of straight-through driving. We unloaded the trucks and took a well-deserved 15-hour sleep. My boss, Woody, had purchased a house with some property in Harlingen that we had set up as our South Texas operational base.

Woody was the kind of guy who had a woman in every port, so to speak, and there was a nice ladyfriend staying with him at the house in Harlingen. I remember her as being blonde and very pretty, and she was always trying to please everybody. She collected our things, thinking she would help us out by washing our clothes.

The next morning she made a nice breakfast for us when we got up. While Billy and I were eating, she announced that she had washed our clothes and remarked about how dirty one pair of pants was. She stated she had to wash them three times to get all the grease out of them.

Poor Billy was horrified and spent days brooding over his Levi's.

Tecate

Every year they used to hold motorcycle races down in Tecate, Mexico. My group used to ride down to watch the races, and although I only rode down with the group once, it was quite the experience. There was a brewery there that brewed Tecate beer, and it flowed like water. I think a bottle of the stuff cost about a quarter in those days. I don't remember actually watching much of the race, and I think the trip was just an excuse to drink beer.

I rode an old army Model 45. It was a smaller bike than the 74s and 80s. Full out I could only do about 85 mph, while the bigger bikes could cruise at around 90 or 100, so I usually lagged along behind everybody else.

Harley Davidsons in those days were not too reliable, and if you could make 50 miles without breaking down, you had a good bike. So every time someone broke down, I would catch up with the group. The group had a stakebed truck loaded with spare parts that followed the group, and the guys would attempt to fix the broken-down bike on the side of the road. (I drove the stakebed on one run when my bike was torn down.) The most common breakdowns were coils, flat tires, and generators. If it wasn't an easy fix, they would load the bike onto the stakebed and continue on. (That stakebed would be pretty loaded by the end of a long trip.)

Back in those days, the in thing was jockey shifts, suicide clutches, and ape hangers. My 45 was equipped with it all, and it was cool! The thing was to get those ape hangers up as high as you could. The higher they were the cooler you were. One guy had used 1/2-inch galvanized water pipe to extend his. Those handlebars were up so high he could barely reach the grips, but he was cool! To say it was a Mickey Mouse setup was an understatement.

I caught up with the group again and they were working on the bike with the galvanized pipes on it. One of the pipes broke loose at about 100 mph, but luckily, the rider was able to keep it under control and managed to stop without crashing. They ended up taking the pipes off and putting the bars back to normal, and we proceeded, with me lagging behind.

The road from San Diego to Tecate went through some mountains, and the road had some pretty hairy turns. It was a dark, moonless night, and I was following along and could see the guys' taillights way up in the distance. All of a sudden I saw brake lights coming on, and riders were going everywhere; it looked like some went straight up. I slowed down, and when I caught up with the group, there were bikes scattered in every direction.

The road all of a sudden made a sharp left turn of at least 90 degrees around a hill, and everybody had been cranking about 90 or so when they realized the turn was there. We got all the bikes untangled and tried straightening bent forks and other items. It was really late, so we decided to bring the wine and beer out and bunk down for the night and try to heal all the wounds.

The next morning we got everybody straightened out and ready to travel. I don't remember for sure, but I think we were only an hour or an hour and a half from Tecate at that point. We headed on towards Tecate and arrived in time to see the start of the races.

We all headed for the saloons to consume mass quantities of beer as soon as the last racer was out of town. We would come out of the saloons when we heard the signal that some of the riders were returning. We would stand on the boardwalks and watch the racers speed by and then go back into the saloon and drink more beer. We spent most of the day doing this.

The bathroom facilities in Mexico at that time were a little primitive. I'm sure there must have been flush toilets somewhere, but I don't remember seeing any. There was usually a trough behind the saloons in the alley and they were wide open to public view. It was a little strange whipping it out and going in the trough with children and women walking around, but nobody paid any attention. It was a little difficult for a modest American like me to do after being used to going in a private stall.

By late afternoon, with all the guys' heavy drinking, the troughs would start to run over, so we would start seeking out dry areas in the alleys—still in full view of everybody.

By evening the guys would start to feel their oats. Fights would break out and things would get broken. On this particular night, things were really getting out of hand and the trouble was really starting. I walked out into the alley to get rid of a little liquid and noticed two trucks full of soldiers come down the hill into town.

I thought, *This can't be good*, and I decided I'd had enough beer for the day. I went in and told my two buddies, Frog and Larry, that things were going to get ugly in a little while, and I was heading across the border as quick as that 45 would get me there.

They insisted that everything was fine and everyone was just having a good time. I told them the good time was going to be over quickly, and I was out of there. I went out and fired up and headed for the border. I looked in my mirror and saw Frog and Larry coming up fast. I'd had premonitions before that had come to pass, so by then I took them pretty seriously.

We heard later that some of the guys managed to get back across the border, some ended up in jail, and we never did hear from a few of the guys again. Some of the guys who got back across the border reported hearing gunfire, so they hopped on their bikes and got the heck out of there. I have no idea what happened to some of the guys, but our entire group finally got back. (A few of them minus their bikes).

I have many interesting stories about my adventures riding with this group, and here's another one. A year before the Tecate run we were at the beach, partying, when it again got really ugly. I can't remember the beach, but I remember I had to ride down a road that went down the side of the cliff to get to the beach.

We had a bonfire going and were sitting around, drinking beer, when three girls came up and started drinking with us. They were really young and were getting giddy very quickly. Pretty soon their bathing suits started coming off, with the encouragement of all the guys.

I thought, *Oh-oh, time to get out of here*. I had Frog, Larry, and Raunchy John with me, and I told them it was a good time to leave. I had a hard time convincing them, but they finally relented and decided to go with me, even though they would miss all the fun. Sure enough, a few days later it was in the news that a motorcycle gang had been arrested for raping three 14-year-old girls.

Pretty soon the guys started trusting my judgment.

Don't Take the Handcuffs Off

I became homeless at the age of 16 due to alcoholism. (Not mine.) I tried everywhere to find a job, but no one would hire me. I was fortunate to be over six feet tall, so I was able to pass for much older, but looking older didn't help me much. Those were the days of the draft, and you were usually called up for military service shortly after your 18th birthday. Nobody would hire you when you were 18, knowing that you would probably be in the military a few months. I couldn't tell them that wouldn't be a problem with me, because if I told them I was only 16, they definitely would not have hired me.

I was visiting with my best friend Doug one day while he was working as a lot boy at a used car lot. I met the owner of the car lot and made a deal with him to fix the mechanical problems on his junkers in exchange for the use of a three-stall garage on his property. Suddenly, I was in the automotive repair business. In less than a year I had two mechanics working for me and we were cranking out repairs.

I had an uncanny mechanical ability that was just a God-given gift. I never had any formal training; I just had the ability to look at something and understand it. It wasn't long before business was booming. I had customers coming in from all over the city looking for the miracle boy who could solve their problems. My shop's reputation was sound. People knew when they came in that they were going to get honest work at a reasonable price.

Unfortunately, I wasn't a businessman, just a kid. I didn't realize that you had to put money away for a rainy day, so every time I had some money, I would go out and buy a piece of equipment. It wasn't long before I had a fully equipped shop but no money in the bank. This would eventually be the demise of the shop.

Most of the cars we worked on were from the late '30s to the early '50s. The larger cars in those days had engines with small bores and long strokes. When you overhaul an engine, you either have to bore out the cylinders or hone them to make sure the new rings will break in. This honing or boring process requires swabbing out the cylinders with solvent when you are done to remove the metal and grit dust from the honing stones. The easiest way to do this is by soaking a rag in solvent and running it up and down in the cylinders, but this is a problem for me. My hands are huge and I had no way of getting my hands down in those cylinders.

One of the guys who worked for me was named Frank. Frank was a normal-sized guy but had the tiniest hands. He could folds his thumbs into his hands and the hands would become smaller than his wrists. Frank ended up being our cylinder-swabber guy. He could run his hands clear to the bottom of those cylinders with that solvent-filled rag and clean the cylinders with ease. Frank turned out to be quite an asset to our shop.

A lot of mechanics are heavy drinkers, and Frank was no exception. I wasn't surprised when Frank didn't show up for work on a Monday morning, but he was usually responsible for the rest of the week.

One Tuesday morning Frank showed up for work and he looked horrible. Someone had pummeled his face, and you could tell he had taken a pretty severe beating. We asked him what happened.

As usual he had gotten pretty drunk on Friday night and been arrested. The police officer handcuffed him to take him in, and Frank slid the handcuffs off and handed them back to the police officer. This scenario repeated itself a couple of times, so the police officer decided to take him in without the handcuffs.

Everything went fine with the booking procedure until the watch sergeant came over and inquired as to why the prisoner wasn't handcuffed. The police officer responded by saying, "I tried, but the prisoner kept taking them off and handing them back to me." He said, "Here, I'll show you." The police officer put the handcuffs back on Frank and told him to show the sergeant how he could take them off.

Frank stood there, looking kind of puzzled, and said, "I don't know what you mean. I can't take them off."

The jail in San Bernardino had the lockups on the upper floors, and after your booking, they would take you up in the elevator to the lockup. By the time Frank made it to the upper level in that elevator, he had been in an awful fight. The jailer locked him up and asked the police officer what happened to him. The police officer responded, "He was drunk and got in one heck of a fight."

The Sheriff's Jeep

I was working on a jeep in my shop in San Bernardino for the San Bernardino County Sheriff's Reserve. The jeep had been donated to the sheriff's department, and it needed work to fix it up and get it running. I was doing the work as a favor, with the labor free and the sheriff's reserve supplying parts. They came up with a couple of old trailer taillights, and I mounted them on the top of the windshield, facing forward. I hooked up a switch and flasher to turn them into red, forward-flashing lights.

They knew this was a spare-time project, so the jeep sat in the back of the shop for quite a while. They had not put any emblems or license plates on it yet identifying it as a police vehicle, and one day while I was out, a CHP officer came into the shop. He spotted the jeep and looked it over. He commented to one of the guys that he was going to keep an eye out for the jeep when it got on the road and was going to write them up for those red lights pointing the wrong way.

The guys told me about the incident when I returned, and I asked them if they had told the officer what the vehicle was. They said, no, that they just smiled and went on with their work. I often wonder how long that CHP officer kept a lookout for that jeep.

The El Paso Incident

Back in the late '50s I drove truck for my lifelong friend Doug Baker's dad, Woody. Woody was in the nursery business, dealing with exotic plants and palm trees. We used to dig up and haul cycads out of Mexico and palm trees and Mexican Gigantea Yucca out of South Texas, mainly the lower Rio Grande Valley.

If you are wondering what a cycad is, it resembles a Sago Palm but is a different variety. They are almost round, come in several different varieties and sizes, and grow in the tropical forests of Mexico. We pulled them out of the ground and removed all the roots and vegetation and would have them fumigated at Reynosa before we could bring them across the border.

We would bring them back to the nursery in San Bernardino and lay them in a bed of fir bark, and pretty soon they would start sprouting this beautiful vegetation. They were very popular and were fairly expensive. We did the same thing to the Mexican Gigantea Yucca. We would just cut the stalks in smaller pieces, lay them in the fir bark, and pretty soon we had these beautiful plants.

We would have a crew of braceros dig the palm trees and yucca for us and load the truck. I would then drive the truck back to California and unload the trees at the nursery in San Bernardino. On some of the hauls, I would deliver the load directly to its destination. I believe I hauled half of the trees you see in Palm Springs up from South Texas.

I always drove the same route back to California. I would come up out of the lower Rio Grande Valley to Van Horn and pick up the I-10 toward El Paso. After you get through El Paso, the I-10 makes a right turn and heads up into New Mexico to the town of Las Cruces. When you hit Las Cruces, you head west and you are on your way home to California.

The turn on the I-10 in El Paso is where the incident I am writing about occurred. I was already through El Paso and traveling in the center lane, approaching the right turn to stay on the I-10. I needed to change lanes to make the turn, but I kept hearing this funny noise that I couldn't understand. I would slow up and check the mirrors but couldn't see anything, so I would speed up and check my mirrors, and still nothing.

I decided the noise must be my imagination, so I put on my blinkers and started changing lanes. All of a sudden the trailer made this horrendous shudder and bounced. I had over 30 thousand pounds on that trailer, so it was hard to make it bounce. All of a sudden I heard all these people shouting in Spanish. I pulled over, and just about that time a Texas Department of Public Safety car pulled up and turned his flashers on. (In Texas the highway patrol is the Department of Public Safety.) I walked back and couldn't believe it, but there sat an old 1947 or 1948 Chevy pickup, and the driver's-side front tire was flat on the ground. The hood, fender, and grill about to the back of the front tire looked like it had been put in a crusher; it was almost flat, clear to the right fender. The right fender was fully intact and wasn't damaged. There must have been 20 Mexican males running around, shouting in Spanish and very upset.

Apparently, when I made my move to the right to turn, my trailer ran over the top of the pickup that had been following too closely and could not be seen.

I explained what had happened to the highway patrolman, and he said the truck had been shadowing me, trying to sneak across the border, and he had been watching them. They were obviously illegals trying to get into New Mexico. I asked him, "What the heck do we do now?"

He suggested that since I was only about five minutes from being out of his jurisdiction, maybe I should climb into the truck and get the heck out of there. Otherwise, he was going to be up all night doing paperwork. I bid my fond farewells, and I was across that border in less than five minutes and heading for home.

The Forgotten Date

We used to hang out at the 40th Street Dance Hall in San Bernardino on Saturday nights. We didn't do much dancing; we usually just hung around outside, drinking and getting into fights.

One night a couple of girls came up to me after the dance and asked if I could give them a ride home. They were both pretty cute so I said, "Sure." My buddy Ted jumped into the back seat with one girl, and the other girl hopped into the front seat with me. She snuggled up real close, so I put my arm around her and proceeded to drive them home. We talked a little during the drive.

I was having a hard time keeping the darn car in its lane; it kept drifting all over the road. I remember trying hard to concentrate on keeping the car straight, not wanting the girl to think I was smashed.

We finally got to her house, and we stood outside and talked for a few minutes. I asked her if she would like to go out with me sometime, and she said, "Yes." I told her I would stop by later in the week and we would make plans.

We took the other girl home, and then Ted and I went out for the remainder of the night and had a few more drinks.

We used to go to a Mexican restaurant after a night of drinking and have burritos with this delicious hot sauce on them. They really hit the spot after a night of heavy drinking. We went every Saturday night and became a fixture for the people who owned the restaurant. They even recognized us when we walked in, and they would have everything ready for us.

The next morning would always be horrid agony for me. I would always take a cup full of Ice cubes into the bathroom with me to try to cool down the burning.

One day I stopped by the restaurant while sober, and the people recognized me and had the burritos and hot sauce ready for me when I sat down. I poured the hot sauce on like I normally did and bit into that burrito. I thought I was going to go into orbit.

I had no idea that being drunk numbed your senses like that. That stuff was so hot I didn't think I was ever going to catch my breath again. No wonder I always had Montezuma's Revenge every Sunday morning.

About the girl ... By the time I woke up Sunday morning and sobered up, I had this recollection of driving a girl home and talking with her, but for the life of me, I couldn't remember her name or where I dropped her off. I asked Ted, but he must have been is worse shape than me, because he didn't even remember the incident.

I wonder if the girl was ever curious why I never came back. (Or maybe she was relieved that I didn't.)

I was relating this story to one of my granddaughters, and she commented that it was probably better that I couldn't remember. She said to me, "You remember the old saying that the only difference between a dog and a fox is a couple of drinks. It sounds like you had more than a couple."

She may have been right. Could that be why the girl seemed anxious to go out with me? Or was I correct when I attributed it to the fact that I had a really nice car?

My Trip to Forest Hills

While I was waiting for a load of trees in Harlingen, Texas, a couple of guys named Ray and Tom offered me $500.00 to haul them up to Forest Hills, Louisiana, and bring a load of gardenia bushes back to McAllen, Texas. Since my load of trees wouldn't be ready for five days, I figured what the heck. They climbed in the cab and we headed for Louisiana. We stopped at Lake Charles, just over the Louisiana border, for dinner.

The girl who waited on us was a young Cajun girl. She had black hair, brown skin, and was the most beautiful woman I had ever seen. I was so enamored with her that I told her how beautiful she was. She must have liked me because she told me she had her own place, and I could stick around and stay with her as long as I liked. I told her I had to take the guys with me up to Forest Hills. She asked if I had anything to write in. I pulled a spiralbound notebook out of my pocket and handed it to her. She wrote down her name and contact information and told me to call or write her. We said our goodbyes and the guys and I headed for Forest Hills.

I don't know to this day why I didn't try to contact her. The time just never seemed right. Several years after I had married, I found that old, spiralbound notebook in my desk and found the page with the girl's name on it. I tore the page out and threw it in the trash, not wanting to explain to my wife who the girl was. Funny thing is, I can't recall the girl's name after 56 years. You would think that with the impression she made, I would have never forgotten it. I remember that it was a French name but just can't recall it.

I often wonder what happened to that girl and how her life turned out, and I wonder how my life would have gone if I had taken her up on her offer and stayed or at least contacted her.

Ray, Tom, and I finally made it to Forest Hills and met up with the owner of the nursery. He ran the nursery with his two sons. We told the owner that we would be back in a couple of days and start digging up and loading the gardenia bushes.

We went up to Alexandria to get a hotel room and did some sightseeing. We played miniature golf in Alexandria, and it was the most unusual course I have ever seen. By the time we got through the first hole and started the second hole, we could no longer see the first hole. The vines and trees were so thick that we couldn't see anything but the hole we were playing. It was absolutely beautiful. Bridges that went over streams with running water separated most of the holes. I had never seen so much greenery before in my life.

We crossed over a bridge with running water after we finished the last hole and came out into the parking lot where the course had started. I was so amazed at the beauty of the place that the memory of it has been etched in my mind for my entire life.

The next day we drove back down to Forest Hills and met up with the nurserymen and made arrangements to return the next morning to get the gardenia bushes. We toured around Forest Hills before going back to Alexandria. It was like a movie set. We saw guys walking around in bib overalls, no shoes, and feet that looked like slabs of meat with toes sticking out. We walked into the general store, and there was a huge potbelly stove right in the center of the store with chairs and benches around it. There were spittoons everywhere and the place stank. I thought it was a movie set. The store, like most buildings in the area, was built up on stilts, putting the building a couple of feet off the ground.

It was getting late, so we headed back to Alexandria to spend the night. We arrived at the nursery early the next morning, pulled out our shovels, and prepared to start digging up the gardenia bushes.

Our shovels were spades we had sharpened all the way around. They worked great for digging up palm trees. We just pushed them into the ground all the way around the tree, cutting the roots as we went. We made the final cut under the tree to sever the taproot and just pushed the tree over.

The spade is about 5 inches wide and 15 inches long and looks quite small when compared to a regular, pointed-nose shovel. The nursery owner showed up with his two sons and pulled out these enormous, pointed-nose shovels. They must have been 15 inches wide and just as long. I had never seen a shovel that big before. They almost looked like snow shovels.

They just about split a gut laughing when they saw our shovels. They were har-harring and making comments as to what we thought we were going to be able to dig with those little shovels. We decided they would start at one end of the field and we would start at the other end and work toward the middle, and we went about our business.

We started at our end of the field, with each one of us taking a row. It only took a couple of minutes to take each plant out of the ground, and we had worked about a third of the way down each row when Tom noticed that the nursery men were just standing there watching us.

We walked down to where they were to find out what was wrong and found they were so astonished at the speed with which we were pulling up the plants that it dumbfounded them. We showed them how simple it was to dig the plants up with the spades and showed them how to do it. They had so much fun doing it that they finished digging all the plants up with the spades by themselves.

We finally got all the plants loaded, and we were heading out when I realized that we hadn't put the shovels in the truck. I mentioned to Ray that we forgot the shovels. He said he hadn't forgotten; that he had sold them to the nurserymen for $10 apiece. I told him they were really going to be mad when they found out they could buy them at Sears, Roebuck for $2.00 each.

The Donkeys

I was sitting around a campfire with a bunch of guys, and we were telling stories. I believe I may have been in Arizona, but I'm not sure, since I have sat around a lot of campfires telling stories since retirement.

I was telling of my teen years hauling Palm Trees and Yuccas out of Texas and bringing them back to California to sell to the rich people. We used to drive around looking for palm trees to buy. If we spotted a home or a field lined with palm trees, we would stop and offer to buy them from the owners of the property. We would offer them 10¢ a foot for the trees and would bring them back to California and sell them for $1.75 a foot.

One day we were out in the country south of Laredo, Texas, and spotted this long, palm tree-lined driveway going back to a home. This driveway had to be 150 yards long. We thought we had hit pay dirt and drove down to the house to introduce ourselves. We met the family—a husband and wife with two teenage boys and a younger daughter. They were typical, friendly country people

They were very cordial and brought out refreshments and we chatted for hours. We told them about ourselves and what we did for a living and what we were doing in Texas. They showed us around the property, which was a small farm/ranch, and described how they made a living so far from the city.

The thing that amazed me was the story about their contract with the Sears, Roebuck and Company. Sears sold donkeys in their catalog, and these people were the suppliers of the donkeys. Sears would send them a shipping label, and the boys would go out and catch a wild donkey and bring it back to the farm. They would build a shipping crate, put the donkey inside, and nail it up. They would put the shipping label on the crate and call the freight company to come and pick up the crate with the live donkey inside for delivery to the addressee. Sears would send them the money for the donkey as soon as the customer received it.

I asked the boys if they tamed or trained the donkeys before they shipped them, and they said, "No, we just throw the wild donkey in the crate and nail it shut."

I often have wondered just how ornery a wild donkey is.

When I was telling this story around the campfire, I could see some of the guys rolling their eyes, thinking, *This guy is full of BS*. One of the guys must have told his wife about my BS story, because a few days later this lady came up to me with a smart phone and showed me an article about an advertisement from Montgomery Ward catalog. It had a picture of a little girl on a Shetland pony, showing it could be ordered. The article went on to state that you could buy a donkey from Sears and a giraffe from Macys.

I asked the lady if I could borrow the smart phone for a few minutes, and I went to everybody who had been around that campfire and showed it to them. I said, "See, I wasn't full of BS. This proves I was telling the truth."

Becoming Citizens of Alice, Texas

As I have mentioned several times that, back in the '50s, I worked for Woody Baker as a truck driver, A-frame operator, on-the-road mechanic, jack-of-all trades, and sidekick. We would go into Mexico and the Lower Rio Grande Valley of South Texas and haul palm trees and exotic plants back to California.

One day Woody got a call from a judge in Alice, Texas, inquiring about an exotic yucca he was looking for. He believed it was called a "Mexican Gigantea Yucca." Woody said he could provide that particular species of yucca to the judge, and they agreed on the price.

You have to understand that this species of yucca was very common in Texas, and it grew in almost every yard in South Texas. I told Woody, "This judge might get a little upset if you don't tell him how common the yucca is." I learned early in life that it is not a good idea to get on the wrong side of a judge. That didn't deter Woody. All he could see was the easy profit in the deal.

Our problem was that we were broke and didn't have the funds to purchase the yucca from a local supplier. It those days banks had stacks of blank checks that you could use to fill in your bank information, so we drove to the local bank in Harlingen, and I walked in and pulled a counter check off the pad of checks on the counter and walked out. I made out a bogus check from a non-existent customer, and Woody mailed it back to California to our friend Helen with instructions to deposit the check into his account at a certain time and date. This was commonly referred as kiting a check and was slightly illegal.

They didn't have computers in the '50s, and the banks had to rely on the postal service to shuttle checks back and forth between banks, so it would take several days to catch a bogus check. This would allow us time to get the funds into the bank to cover it.

Back in California, Helen received the bogus check and deposited it per Woody's instructions. Helen had no idea that the check was bogus and would never have deposited it if she had known.

We proceeded to the supplier to purchase the yucca plants. This guy was a character and looked like he was out of a movie. He was short and dumpy, wore a Hawaiian shirt and Bermuda shorts, and was in slight disarray. He had a pair of flip-flops on for shoes. He sweated profusely and sat in a lawn chair, wiping sweat off his face, for most of the time we were there. He had a Mexican wife who did everything for him.

Woody told him what we needed but said, for tax purposes, we had to pay with a check from our business account. He assured the man that we had the money in the account and gave him the account number and the phone number of the bank. The man called the bank and they assured him that the account had plenty of money to cover the check. The man had his wife bring the yucca plants out, and we loaded them into the truck and headed for Alice, Texas.

It was late in the evening when we arrived in Alice, so we bedded down for the night in the local hotel. Woody called and made arrangements for us to meet up with the judge at the courthouse in the morning.

We arrived at the courthouse early the next morning as planned. We showed the judge the yucca plants, and he agreed they were what he was looking for. We unloaded the plants and went back to his office to pick up the check. We talked to the judge and he thanked us for our excellent service as he made out the check. He got up and handed Woody the check. We talked for a while, standing there in the judge's office, when he suddenly put his arm around Woody and gave him a friendly nudge. He told us they were having elections tomorrow and said, "Why don't you boys stick around until tomorrow and vote for me."

Woody told him we were Californians.

He said, "That's no problem. My brother-in-law is the registrar of voters." He stated several other titles that the man had, but I can't recall all of them.

The judge proceeded to usher us down the hall to the recorder's office and had us sworn in as citizens of the city and county of Alice, Texas, and signed us up on the voter rolls. We told the judge we would definitely stick around until the next day for the election, and we bid our farewells. We pulled around to the front of the courthouse and headed up the road to the hotel. I noticed as we were leaving the courthouse that the front flowerbeds were loaded with Mexican Gigantea Yucca.

My first thought was, "Oh, crap! I hope the judge doesn't walk out front and notice they're the same as the ones we just sold him."

When we arrived at the hotel, I asked Woody if he had noticed the yuccas planted in the flowerbeds in front of the courthouse. He apparently hadn't paid any attention. I told him that if that judge or his coworkers noticed it was the same yucca we sold him, we were going to spend the rest of our lives in a chain gang, so I was getting across the county line before he noticed. We were packed and across the county line lickety-split.

Frank

Frank was the senior foreman at the California Division of Forestry Headquarters on Sierra Way in San Bernardino. I was stationed there in the 1959-1960 fire season as a firefighter. Frank and I were always butting heads, although it was never my intent to do so. It seemed that circumstances just led us there.

Frank was a big, burly man. He kind of reminded me of a bear when I looked at him. He stood well over six feet tall, had a 36-inch waist, and was broad in the shoulders. I would guess he weighed well over 200 pounds. He looked like the type of man you just wouldn't want to get into it with, yet he was a gentle giant.

When we first came to work for him and received our orientation speech, he reminded all of us that there were 20 more waiting outside to take our place if we didn't do our job well. I believed him, and I believe everybody else did too. But I soon found he was all bluff and was just a gentle giant, like I previously mentioned.

One of his absolute rules was if you missed a roll, you were gone. I have actually seen guys jump on the back of the truck on a night response, literally naked and getting dressed while speeding down the road. All in fear of being fired if they missed a roll.

One night the guys were up late in the recreation room, playing cards. I was tired, so I decided to take a shower and go to bed. I was showering when a call came in and I hurried out of the shower, but before I could even towel off, I heard the sirens wailing as the trucks headed out of the barn. My thought was, "Well, I am gone" and I truly believed it.

I finished the shower and dressed in my civilian clothes. I emptied out my locker, rolled down my bed, loaded all my belongings in my car, and waited for the trucks to return. I waited for over an hour before they finally arrived at the station, and here came Frank with the entire crew in tow.

Frank walked down the long hall into the dormitory and

looked at me quizzically in my civvies, sitting on a rolled-down bed. He noticed my locker door was open and the locker was empty. He just stopped in his tracks and paused. He had this look of confusion on his face as if he wasn't sure what to do. He finally pointed his finger at me and said, "If you miss another roll, you're fired." Then he abruptly turned around and walked out of the dormitory. I knew from that moment on that I had his number.

Frank and I got along well after that, and I received praise from him on how well I did my job—quite a compliment, coming from him. Frank didn't say anything when I transferred to the Hesperia Station, but I heard he wasn't happy about losing me.

I was transferred back to the headquarters station in 1961 when I received my promotion to forest fire truck driver, and Frank and I were back together again. That's when the head butting began.

San Bernardino County is the biggest county in the continental United States, and there are a lot of streets and roads. How they could think we could know every street in the county is beyond my imagination, but they did. I always ran to the map and checked out the route before leaving the station. Of course that took some time, and it made the response time slower.

The headquarters station was where all the rangers were stationed, and this brought everybody under scrutiny and added pressure. One day one of the rangers asked Frank why it took me so long to get out of the station. I guess that caused extra stress for Frank. He told me to be out of the station in 30 seconds in the daytime and one minute at night. I told Frank that I didn't know all the streets, and it would be hard to get out of the station that quickly. I think the pressure was on Frank, and he told me again to be out of the station in 30 seconds. I told him, "Ok, Frank, you're the boss."

I don't know why, but I never felt pressure. I just never gave a hoot. I figured if it was here today it would be here tomorrow, so why worry about it. I devised a method of finding out where we were going. We would haul out of the station in the

30-second time period, pull around the block, get the map book out, and figure out where the heck we were going. Then we would fire up and head to the scene.

It worked pretty well, but one day the rangers and Frank were standing out front when I pulled out, and the rangers asked Frank why I was going the wrong way. We pulled over at the corner and found where we were going, so I turned around and drove back by the station. Everybody was standing there, so I waved to them as we drove by. We were on the scene of the fire, and I was standing there running the pump, when a car pulled up and three rangers got out. They walked over to me and asked why I had pulled out of the station and gone the wrong way. I explained the situation to them and they politely thanked me and left.

When I got back Frank came up to me and told me to make sure I knew where I was going before I left the station. I told Frank I couldn't get out of the station in 30 seconds and know where I was going. Frank looked at me and said, "Make sure you know where you're going before you leave the station."

Our second foreman at headquarters was Dave. The foreman at headquarters had an onsite residence supplied by the Forestry, so they could have their families with them. Dave was the foreman riding with me one particular day when we got a call during lunch hour. I ran to the truck and the crew jumped on the back. I fired the truck up and pulled out on the apron, waiting for the foreman. No foreman arrived. I waited for several minutes, and Dave finally came running out of his residence, trying to adjust his pants. (I wouldn't want to speculate why he was adjusting his pants during the noon hour.) Dave finally climbed into the cab and we responded to the fire.

Well, the ever-watching rangers were watching the incident, and when I got back I was told by Frank that I was only to wait one minute for the foreman. If he didn't show up in one minute, then I was to leave without him. I think you can guess what happened next!

A few weeks later Frank was riding shotgun with me and we got a call. Everybody piled onto the truck and I pulled out on the apron. No Frank. I hollered at one of the hose men on the back of the truck and told him to get up in the cab with me. I told him to check his watch and tell me when one minute was up. When he said the minute was up, I pulled out and responded to the fire.

Sure enough, a little later here come the rangers. They came around the truck and asked me if I had a foreman assigned to this rig. I answered, "Yes, sir." They asked where he was and I told them that Frank had told me not to wait more than one minute for the foreman and just leave without him if he didn't show up.

They asked which foreman was assigned to the rig that day. I told them it was Frank. Have you ever looked at a man who was about to burst out laughing but was trying to keep a straight face? They both ran around to the back of the truck. I bet I could have heard them laughing if it hadn't been for the noise of the pump. I never heard any more about the incident.

I found out later in life that Frank passed away from a heart attack at the age of 49. What a shame—he was a really great guy!

Hesperia Station

As a young adult I spent six years in the California Division of Forestry. In those days they were a division of the Department of Natural Resources. I was always a full-time fireman and never served any time as a volunteer fireman. I also spent over five years with the City of Riverside Fire Department. I spent time as both a firefighter and engineer in both departments. I also drove the rescue truck and served for a time as an EMT.

There were a lot of interesting moments during my firefighting career, some humorous and some tragic. I will only dwell on the humorous.

While at the Hesperia Station, we had to contend with the homeless always starting fires in the riverbottom. These fires were usually little more than a nuisance because they could always be contained in the riverbottom due to the terrain and were never be a threat unless there were high winds to blow burning embers out of the riverbed.

One cold morning about 5:00 a.m., we got a call to a riverbottom fire. It was so brutally cold that you couldn't expect anyone to ride the tailgate, so we all piled into the cab of the truck and took off, code three. The driver picked up the microphone and told dispatch we were responding to the riverbottom incident.

We were driving along, all cramped up in the cab of that truck, giving our two cents' worth about riverbottom fires and having to respond so early in the morning in the freezing cold. We were also voicing our opinions about the overhead personnel in the CDF, and it wasn't nice. We noticed our foreman, Kelley, coming up behind us in his jeep. He was hauling. We started making comments about why he was driving so darn fast. We commented about him being crazy, driving so fast in that darn Jeep. Jeeps were very unstable at high speeds and could easily go out of control.

Kelley finally got up alongside us and started shaking his

microphone at us. We said, "Why the heck is he shaking his microphone at us."

One of the guys said, "We got one, too," and picked up the microphone and shook it at Kelly. All of a sudden we heard the repeater kick back in the radio speaker. Kelly smiled, slowed down, and pulled in behind us.

There was total silence in the cab of that truck when we realized we were on the house radio frequency that went through all the fire stations throughout the entire Southern District of the CDF. Everybody, even the rangers, had been listening to our conversation.

It was definitely an "ah, shoot" moment. We knew we were all fired, and we waited for a week, without a word, for our replacements to show up and usher us out the door. About two weeks later a general order came through from Ranger Headquarters. It read, "When responding to a scene, always make sure you get a confirmation from dispatch. If not, make sure your microphone button is not stuck in the transmit position." Not another word was said about the incident.

***

Another time at the Hesperia station a guy came in who had cut off his thumb at the first joint on a table saw and couldn't stop the bleeding. We worked on that thumb for at least a half hour before we could get the bleeding under control enough for him to go on to the hospital.

That evening we were having beans and franks for dinner. We sat down to eat, and one of the guys bit the end off a hot dog and dipped it in the bean sauce. He held it up and said, "Hey, guys, what does this look like?" I don't think anybody ate dinner that night.

The First Borate Drop

It was the first season or early in the second season that I was a firefighter in the California Division of Forestry—so it had to be 1959 or 1960—that we were on a fire near Devils Canyon. We were sitting on the side of the road going up the Cajon Pass, watching the flames moving up the ridge towards Cedar Pines Park and Sawpit Canyon.

Days earlier we had been in a briefing about a new procedure for fighting forest fires. They were going to start using airplanes to drop mud on the fires. We all laughed and guffawed at such a stupid idea. We argued that nothing would ever replace the firefighters on the ground, battling the fire with a shovel and an axe. What would those idiots in the white hats come up with next?

We were all given these airplane identification charts that looked like WWII charts. We were also given forms to evaluate the mud drops on the fires as they occurred. Things like location, terrain, type of plane, and effectiveness of the drop were to be recorded. We all left the briefing in good humor. Everyone was laughing and ridiculing the idiots who had come up with such a dumb idea.

Three days later we were watching this raging fire with 50-foot-high flames rushing towards the peak of Sawpit Canyon. We were advised that a plane would be making a drop on this inferno. We all snickered as the plane approached. We used the charts to identify it as a B-17. (I don't recall the tail number.) We still believed that nothing was going to stop those raging flames; it would be impossible for anything to even slow them down.

The plane approached, made a turn, and headed up the canyon. It came in so low it's a wonder the wings didn't melt. The plane was virtually on top of the fire, and all of a sudden this stream of grayish liquid poured from its belly. The plane lifted up and headed out of the canyon, making a wide left turn.

We were all amazed at the skill of that pilot to bring that

plane in so low over the fire and fly through the heat, flames, smoke, and updrafts with such precision. We looked back at the fire, and except for a few streamers of white, whispering smoke, the flames were gone.

The silence was only broken by an occasional "#@&*" or "son-of-a-b____."

We had been advised to put our remarks down privately and not share them with anybody. They wanted to get accurate, independent evaluations of the effectiveness of this new firefighting procedure. We found out later that almost everyone made the same remark; most of us just put down, "Give us more planes."

That was many years ago, and things have come a long way from the first drop using mud. New chemicals are always being developed that retard the re-burn and seed and fertilize the hillside. New planes are being developed to deliver bigger and faster loads and will continue to be improved in the future.

I am excited to know that I was there to witness one of the first drops and somehow participate in the beginning of a new era of forest fire fighting.

Jogging The Memory

It's funny how a picture will stir long-lost memories. I was watching the news on TV one morning when they showed a restaurant situated on a pier; both were on fire. They had fireboats spraying water and firemen working their way up the pier, putting out the burning deck of the pier as they progressed in an attempt to get close enough to the restaurant to put water on it.

Watching the firemen advancing up the pier reminded me of an incident that happened when I was stationed at the Hesperia CDF station in 1960. The California Forestry Department was always hiring young men just out of high school who were looking for summer work as seasonal firefighters. Some of these kids were real Mommies' boys, and you could tell they led sheltered lives and had no real life experience.

One spring day one of these individuals reported for duty at the Hesperia station. We put him to work, and every time we completed a task, he wanted to go in and take a shower. We told him that he could only shower in the evening with the rest of the guys and was only allowed to take a shower at other times when we returned from an incident with soot on us. This didn't make him very happy. I had my doubts that this guy was going to last.

Late in the afternoon on his first day, we responded to a car fire on the highway that is now referred to as I-15, just north of Victorville. We responded and found the car was sitting right in the middle of the highway and was totally involved in flames. We pulled the inch-and-half hose, and I decided that, since it was just an isolated car fire with no serious threat, to put the new kid on the nozzle to give him some experience. We started approaching the car, with me backing him up. I showed him how to set the nozzle for a fog pattern to protect us from the heat as we approached the vehicle.

Unless you have been a firefighter, you have no idea how hot it gets when you get into a fire situation. It can get really uncomfortable. It takes a lot of self-control and discipline to get in close to the fire, and experience tells you when it is merely uncomfortable or when you are dangerously close to getting seriously burned.

As we were approaching the burning vehicle, the kid kept complaining about the heat. We were nowhere close enough to put the fire out, and I told him we had to get in closer. He kept hesitating and complaining about the heat, so I just put my shoulder in his back and continued pushing him closer, telling him, "We need to get closer."

He started screaming that it was too hot. He actually turned around, slugged me, and ran away. I couldn't believe he had punched me and run off, but I picked up the nozzle and proceeded to approach the vehicle and put the fire out.

Matt was the foreman on the truck that day and asked me what had happened when I returned to the truck. I explained the situation to him, and he just laughed and seemed to get a kick out of it.

We did the report, loaded up the truck, and headed back to the station. The kid didn't say a word on the way back, and I didn't talk to him. I expected him to want to take a shower as soon as we got back. We pulled into the station, filled the truck with water and fuel, and reloaded the hose. We backed the truck into the stall, and we went into the station to relax. The kid didn't say a word; he walked into the dorm, picked up his luggage, walked out the door, and drove off.

I guess he decided that maybe being a banker would be a better career choice for him!

Ringing The Bell

As I have said, I worked for several years for the California Division of Forestry. In 1959 I was stationed at the headquarters office on Sierra Way in San Bernardino. I went to work as a firefighter for the first year, and due to my truck driver experience, was able to take the Forest Fire Truck Drivers exam at the start of the second fire season. I passed the test quite handily and was put at number 19 on the hire list.

In the fall of the second season, I was transferred to the Hesperia Fire Station as a firefighter. (That is where I met my future wife.) Near the end of the third fire season, I was hired on full time as a forest fire truck driver. I was transferred back to the headquarters station as a relief driver between the headquarters station and the Devore Station.

At the headquarters station there was an old Seagraves fire truck. It must have been around a 1935 or 1936 model truck and carried no water, only hose. It carried around 2,500 feet of 2 ½-inch hose. The truck was equipped with siren, red lights, and a radio. It also had this large bell mounted of the right side of the running board so the person riding shotgun could reach out and ring the bell.

This truck was very heavy with all of the hose loaded on it, and the brakes were inadequate for the weight. You had to start slowing down and braking about a block before you expected to stop. Most of the vehicles back in those days ran a six-volt electrical system that was very inefficient, and that Seagraves truck was a prime example of that. The truck was a classic, but even with all of its inadequacies, all who saw it revered it.

The Forestry Department had the responsibility of providing fire protection for the entire county in those days and was responsible for structure protection as well as forest and brush fires. Most of the homes in the outlying areas of the county were one-quarter mile or more from a fire hydrant, so we would respond with the old Seagraves to lay hose from the nearest hydrant to the scene of the fire.

Since most of the responses were at night, we had to run with the headlights on as well as the red lights, radio, and siren. And because the fires were nearly always quite a distance away, about halfway through the run, the old six-volt system would be overtaxed, and the truck battery would start to go dead. The siren would be the first to go, then the radio, and then the lights would start dimming. We would turn off the radio and quit blowing the siren and continue on at what we called responding code 2 ½.

The foreman would reach out and start ringing the bell when we approached an intersection. People in the intersections would laugh hysterically when we rolled through in that antique fire truck with that bell ringing away.

I used to feel sorry for the hose man whose responsibility it was to wrap and hook up at the hydrant. He would have to run all the way to the fire scene after he had hooked up and turned on the water. This was sometimes a great distance.

That old fire truck brings back some great memories when I think about it, and occasionally I will see an old fire truck parked in a fire station or museum, and the nostalgia just overwhelms me.

The A1 Pilsner Can

Back in the '50s I drove truck for Baker Nursery, hauling plants and trees out of the southern border of South Texas and Mexico. The usual route was a two-lane highway, which has been replaced by what is now known as I-8. These were all rural highways at that time that traversed through all the towns in southern Arizona and into the southern part of New Mexico. At Casa Grande, Arizona, the I-8 merged into what is now known as I-10, and I followed the I-10 through New Mexico into Texas to the town of Van Horn, then headed south, following the Mexican border into south Texas. This trip was over 1,500 miles and took about 36 hours. I usually drove straight through, only stopping for food and potty breaks. I understand that now, due to the freeways, the trip can be made in about 22 hours.

Back in those days the trucks had no air conditioning, no air-ride seats, no power steering, no nothing to support your comfort. They did have air brakes to stop the darn things, but there were no exhaust brakes, so you spent many an hour sitting on the side of the road, trying to cool down smoking brakes. I have had brake drums that actually glowed from being so hot.

It was not uncommon to see truckers walking alongside their rigs in those days while the trucks were crawling up steep grades. You would set the throttle and put the transmission in the Grandma gear and just walk alongside of the truck to get out of that boiling hot cab for a while. Occasionally, you had to jump up in the cab and correct the steering, but it was just so darn hot in those cabs that you usually stood on the running board or walked alongside the truck for most of the climb up those long grades.

The only air conditioning in those days was the air coming through the windows while going down the road and a simple fan mounted on the dash to blow air on you in the cab. You had to be a pretty rugged guy in those days to pilot one of those big rigs down the road.

I drove that truck year round, so every weather situation

occurred while I was traveling. Going through Arizona during the summer was brutal, and it was hard to stay hydrated. I remember this huge, A1 Pilsner beer can on the side of the road. That can was a good 20 feet tall and could be seen for miles across that desert. I can't remember exactly where it was located. I have asked several older Arizona residents if they remember the can, but no one can recall where it was. I believe it was near Dateland, Arizona. That can had big, simulated drops of dew running down the sides. Driving by there in the summer in that 120-plus degree truck and looking at that dew-covered can would drive you crazy.

Across the road from the can was a typical tourist trap/trading post with a bar in it. Being underage, I knew they wouldn't serve me, so I had to drive on by, trying to ignore the sight of that can. It was so huge, though, that I just couldn't ignore it.

A few years later I was in the area, and now, being of drinking age, I stopped and walked into the bar, sat down, and ordered a beer. The place was nearly empty, so I started telling the bartender about all those underage years of driving past the place in that truck and going nuts, wanting a beer. He listened to my story with this puzzled look on his face. When I finished, he looked at me and said, "You do know that the legal drinking age in Arizona is eighteen, don't you?"

Crap!

Dick Dale and the Deltones

There have been rumors that I had a sordid past, but I like to think of it as a learning experience. My poor Doyalene had no idea of my past or background when she married me. She was just out of high school and had lived a sheltered life at home. She was as sweet and innocent as a newborn lamb. I, on the other hand, had been around the block and back, and some of my friends had less than desirable personalities. I left the past all behind when I joined the Forestry Department, wanting a fresh start in life. It was at this time that I met and married Doyalene and began my new life as a family man.

We spent the first months after our marriage living in a cabin in Wrightwood, and it was at this time that she got a glimpse of my past life. We were preparing to leave to visit Doyalene's parents, and I went out to check on the car. There was a prison crew cutting down and spraying trees on our property, and they were on a break. I saw one of my old buddies sitting on a log, having lunch. I went over and talked with him to see how he was doing. We exchanged niceties and talked about some of the other guys in our group, and I got an update on their incarceration as well. About that time Doyalene walked out of the cabin to see what I was up to. I bid farewell to my old friend and got in the car and we drove away.

As we were leaving she asked me, quite concerned, "Did you now that guy?"

I commented, "Just from the forestry." I thought to myself, *Boy, if she only knew.*

Several years later, after I had become a fireman with the Riverside City Fire Department, there was a rock group called Dick Dale and the Deltones. They purchased one of the old military warehouses up on Van Buren Avenue near March Air Force Base and turned it into a dance hall and beer-and-wine establishment. We would go up there on Saturday nights and spend the nights dancing and consuming mass quantities of beer.

One night we were out on the dance floor, having a great time, when a fight broke out pretty close to us. I always liked a good fight, so I rambled over, and there was a guy flat on his back with a huge Mexican guy on top of him, pounding him pretty good. I looked down at the fight and saw the guy on the floor was my old friend Arnie. I quite excitedly yelled out, "Arnie, is that you?"

He responded, "Get this fat SOB off of me. He's crushing me."

I nailed the guy in the kidneys a few times and knocked the wind out of him and rolled him off of Arnie. I got Arnie up and we walked away before all the security showed up. I asked Arnie how he was doing, and Arnie, being of few words, just responded, "Ok."

It turned out that the whole bunch was there, with the exception of the ones in jail, and Doyalene ended up meeting them all. Even Joe was there. Now the person we knew as Joe was actually Josephine, and she usually rode with me on the back of my bike. Joe was a great asset, as she fought like a man, and I have seen her put a guy on the ground with one jab from either her left or right fist. You have heard the old saying, "Bite like a crocodile, kick like a mule?" Well, that was Josephine.

We all sat and visited and drank beer for quite a while, and all the time I kept thinking to myself, *Please don't say anything, Joe. Please don't say anything*. Joe left a contact number, we parted company, and Doyalene and I went home.

On the way home Doyalene commented that they all seemed like nice people. That's the last contact I had with the old gang. I just wanted to put it behind me.

Saturday Nights

Every Saturday night in the early '80s, my wife and I would go to the Sportsman Club in Cedar Glenn and spend the night dancing. We would always dance the night away and would usually be run out around 2:30 am. We would then head for the "A" in Crestline for breakfast and to visit with friends, usually making it home just before daylight on Sunday. We had a great time during that era of our life, and I have many great memories of the time.

I had an amazing amount of energy in those days and would tucker my wife out, so I would continue dancing with all the ladies in the place. A lot of the guys would bring their wives, and since many of the guys didn't like to dance, I had no trouble finding dance partners. One night I was out dancing with the ladies, and I noticed my wife was out on the floor, dancing with this guy. He wasn't any taller than she was, and he was smiling and really boogying. It looked like he had finally found a girl for him and was having a great time.

I can only guess by his reaction what his intentions were, but he was really excited to be dancing with my wife and was sweeping the floor with her. We finally worked our way around the dance floor until we were within arms' length of each other, and my wife pulled us aside to introduce us. Father Time and gravity had not yet begun to shrink me, and I was fairly tall in those days. I stood over a foot taller than this little guy, and when my wife said, "This is my husband, Gary," the guy looked up at me and you could see this look of stark terror in his eyes. He just vanished. It was like the Flash. He was just gone. I don't even know what direction he went.

I asked my wife, "Where'd he go?" and she just burst out laughing. I started laughing and we finished the dance together.

We laughed about that incident for months. I spent some time teasing her about her little boyfriend as well. (You couldn't let an opportunity like that go by unused.) Another great memory!

The Stereo Repair Shop

I opened an FM two-way radio repair shop in Crestline in 1972. I did pretty well in business and actually made a profit in my first month, which was a very unusual accomplishment. Layton Electronics built up to two shops—one in Crestline and one in Hesperia—and included the ownership of several mountaintop sites with numerous community repeaters. We had built the company up to 12 employees and five service vehicles before selling in 1985. Our main and only business mission was the servicing and maintenance of FM communications systems, and since we were licensed under the Federal Communications Commission, we were protected from any interference from state or local government control.

We offered 24-hour emergency response service, and I had a business phone extension in my home to receive after-hour emergency calls. Every so often I would get a call requesting stereo repairs. I would politely advise the person that I was not licensed to repair consumer equipment, and they would thank me and hang up. These calls persisted, with some calls being a few weeks apart. I was puzzled why someone would get the idea that I did stereo repairs.

The calls went on for a couple of years, and one day I got a letter from the State of California Bureau of Consumer Affairs stating that it was confirmed that I was in the business of doing consumer repairs without the proper licensing. The letter stated had a violation had been issued against me which included a healthy fine.

In the letter were instructions on the proper filing of the licensing of my business for consumer repairing and the requirements for proper signage and state-required forms for doing business in the State of California. The letter was quite extensive, and the requirements were mind-boggling. With all the restrictions and regulations, I don't know how anybody in the stereo repair business could possibly make a living. Thank God I wasn't in that type of business.

I called the phone number on the letter and asked what the heck was going on and why they thought I was in the stereo repair business? They referred me to page 476 of the local yellow pages. There it was, in bold type, under stereo repair: **Layton Electronics.**

"I don't know how the heck that got in there," I assured them. "I am not doing stereo repair."

They advised me that on such a date a call to my business confirmed that I was indeed in the stereo repair business. I checked my logs and found no one was in the shop on that day. Upon further investigation, I found that my sweet, little 7-year-old daughter, Christine, had answered the phone at the house, and when the caller asked if we repaired stereos, she proudly responded, "Sure. My daddy can fix anything."

I told them, "You have got to be kidding, taking the word of a seven-year-old child." I told them I would check with the phone company about the ad and get back to them.

I was finally able to work through the red tape at the Yellow Pages and got in touch with my rep. His reply was that I had one additional free listing, so he just put it under stereo repairs. I advised him that had caused me to be in violation of state law, resulting in a hefty fine with the Bureau of Consumer Affairs, and if I didn't have a letter of explanation stating that I had no knowledge of the listing in my hands within two days, I would make them responsible for the payment of the fine.

The letter was hand delivered to me with an apology the next day. I immediately called my contact at the Bureau of Consumer Affairs and explained the situation to him. For some reason, he didn't think it was humorous. I sent him a copy of the Yellow Pages letter, along with a letter from me chastising them for not confirming who they were talking to on my business phone. The matter, as well as the fine, was quickly dropped. The ad for stereo repair stayed in the yellow pages until the next publication, but we never received another call for stereo repair.

The Missing Christmas Tree

My wife had this cute way of strumming her fingers. She would start out with the pinky and strum all her fingers down, ending up with the thumb. She would do this quickly and continuously and it made a rhythmic pattern like someone strumming a drum. She would do it on tables, door jams, doors, walls, anywhere there was a flat surface. She did it when she was contemplating something or was upset but not to the point of being angry. The kids knew they were in trouble when they walked into a room and she was standing there, staring at them and doing the finger roll on a door jam.

We lived on the edge of the national forest, and we could walk right out the back yard into the trees. Every December I would walk into the forest and pick out a nice Christmas tree. Then would go back late at night, cut it down, and bring it to the house and decorate it. I didn't dare tell the kids, because it was illegal. They surely would have blabbed to somebody, and the Feds would have shown up at the front door.

One year my business was really booming, and I was too darn busy to go into the forest and pick out a tree. It was late in December, and our younger daughter asked me when we were going to get the Christmas tree. I could have just told her soon and let it go, but no, not me. Being a smart a--, I told her, "I'm sorry, but we don't have the money for a tree this year." I went on my way, not giving it another thought.

A few days later I walked into the house after work, and there was my wife, sitting at the kitchen table, glaring at me and strumming away. I noticed a lot of foodstuffs on the table, mostly stuff we don't use. Large cans of hominy, corn, string beans, bags of flour and sugar, and, sitting in the corner, was this scraggly, Charlie Brown Christmas tree.

"What's this?" I asked.

She promptly replied, "Did you tell our daughter that we weren't going to have a Christmas this year?

I again asked, "What?"

My wife, rather sternly this time, told me that my daughter's classmates were getting up and telling what they we getting for Christmas. When my daughter stood up, she said, "Daddy told me we didn't have money for Christmas this year."

My only thought was, "Oh my God."

I asked Doyalene why she didn't tell them to take the stuff back. She said she did, but they told her they couldn't take it back, that they understood her pride, but some people just fall on hard times, and it was nothing to be ashamed of.

I realized then that my wife was really embarrassed. I thought it was funny until I realized how humiliated she was.

I went downstairs, grabbed the saw, and headed down into the forest and cut down a Christmas tree. I brought it back to the house, and we decorated it that evening. I apologized to my daughter, telling her I had just been teasing, and I assured the kids that we were going to have Christmas that year. The next morning my wife and I loaded up all the items and took them down to the Presbyterian Church and put them into the donation bin for the needy.

You really need to be careful what you say to your children, as they take it literally. Being a smart aleck around your kids can get you into a lot of trouble. I am surprised my kids aren't scarred for life, living around me. Come to think of it, they are a bunch of smart a---s, as well.

How I Met Your Mother

I left my truck-driving job with Baker & Lloyd Nurseries in the spring of 1959 and went to work as a firefighter with the California Division of Forestry. The CDF—now known as Cal-Fire—was a division under the California Department of Natural Resources at that time. I was stationed at the CDF headquarters station on Sierra Way near 40th street in the city of San Bernardino.

I spent the entire fire season of 1959 at the headquarters station on Sierra Way. Firefighters were seasonal employees at that time. The fire season usually ran from May 1st thru November 15th of each year. Most of the guys would get part-time jobs during the off-season, but I just bummed around and had a good time.

I went back to Sierra Way at the start of the 1960 fire season. They were taking applications for the Forest Fire Truck Driver position that spring. You had to have three years' experience as a firefighter to apply for the position, but I found a loophole in the application that if you had truck driving experience, it would fulfill the firefighter experience requirement on the application. I was in.

I filled out the application, and by summer I had taken the written, oral, and driving tests for the position. I was always able to easily pass written tests and usually ace them. (Except English tests.) I passed the written and the driving tests with very high scores, but my lack of firefighter experience knocked me down to 19th on the list.

In the fall of 1960 they asked for a volunteer to transfer to the Hesperia station. I was getting bored, so I requested the transfer. I had no idea how that move would impact my life.

I finished out the 1960 season at Hesperia and returned for the 1961 season. The Hesperia fire station faced Main Street in those days, and you drove out onto Main Street when you were responding to an incident. Across the street was an A & W Root

Beer stand. Every day at about 3:30 p.m., the guys would all gather at the front office window at the fire station and watch as this cute little blonde girl arrived at the A & W parking lot in a really nice, two-tone, 1955 Pontiac Catalina. She would get out and walk across the parking lot and into the A & W to start her shift as a carhop.

All of the guys would ogle and make comments as to their intentions, but I had a strange feeling that couldn't be explained. The attraction was extremely strong and my immediate reaction was to stay away from her because I had no intention of getting seriously involved in a relationship.

Around the 15th of May in 1961, they called the fire season inactive and put us on 8-hour days. It was too far to drive back to Riverside in those days, so Don, the other firefighter at the station, and I would just cruise around the local area in his '57 T-bird. One day we drove into the A & W for a hamburger, and for the first time, I met the cute blonde up close. And she was definitely cute.

The guys would often go across the street to buy hamburgers for lunch and when they came back they would always tell me the cute blonde was asking about me. I just laughed it off. I had no intentions of going back over there.

They reactivated the fire season a few weeks later, and we went about our regular duties. I tried to put the cute carhop out of my mind and continue on with my life. I had no intentions of ever marrying, and I knew if I got involved with that girl, I was going to end up marrying her, so I purposely stayed away from the A & W.

I finally succumbed to my attraction, though. I walked across the street on the 7th of July of 1961 and asked the cute blonde for a date. She accepted, and we decided to go on a picnic in the mountains on the 10th of July. On our picnic, we sat in a meadow on the shore of Lake Arrowhead. At that time the rich people hadn't taken over Lake Arrowhead yet, and you could actually sit on the shore of the lake. The date went well, we seemed to have a lot in common, and the attraction seemed mutual. I had to go back to work the next morning, so any more dating would have to wait for another week.

She came by the fire station the next night, and we sat in the car in the parking lot and talked for hours. She came by the next night, and we sat in the car and talked again. This time I proposed to her and she accepted. That was the 12th day of July, 1961: two days after our first date. She wouldn't turn 18 until the 11th of August, so we had to wait until then to get married. We spent the next few weeks together almost continuously.

On the 1st of August, I was promoted to forest fire truck driver and transferred back to San Bernardino at the Sierra Way headquarters station. We worked a 24-hour-per-day/ five-days-per-week schedule in those days with two days off, so it didn't afford us much time to spend together after the transfer. Most of our correspondence was by mail or on the phone.

San Bernardino is on the other side of the mountain from Hesperia, so we adopted the song "The Mountains High" by Dick and Dee Dee as our theme song.

Nineteen sixty-one turned out to be a violent fire season. I was sent to San Diego for three weeks in August to fight brush fires and was sent straight to the Angeles Forest on the way back from San Diego without any break. I spent almost four weeks in the Angeles Forest before getting back to San Bernardino in September and some well-needed days off.

My fiancé and I headed for Las Vegas with her family in tow, and on the 18th of September, 1961, she became Mrs. Layton. Her sister and brother-in-law, Dana and Dick, loaded up their kids and headed home right after the ceremony. Her mom and dad treated us to a show at the Stardust. The show was Lido de Paris and was a drink show. Doyalene had never had a drink before and ordered a whiskey sour. She said it was terrible and only sipped it. Her mom and dad headed home right after the show and left us on our own. We were flat broke, so our wedding dinner consisted of 15¢ MacDonald hamburgers. We celebrated every anniversary after that by going to McDonalds and having hamburgers.

We spent a couple of days in Vegas, visiting casinos and eating cheap meals. We went out to Boulder Dam and took the tour then headed home to set up housekeeping with our friends Ed and Pat in their parents' cabin in Wrightwood. It is a good thing that my new wife was thrifty, because I didn't have enough gas money to get us home. If it hadn't been for her, I might still be in Vegas, busing tables.

My wife had to leave for heaven a couple of months before our 54th anniversary. She left me behind with four children and numerous grandchildren and great grandchildren. Our life together was great! I can recall on one hand the times we even raised our voices at each other. It worked out for us, but I wouldn't suggest anybody proposing or getting married as fast as we did. The only reason I did it was the amazing feeling that I had met my soulmate. The years have proved that I was right.

Sears, Roebuck and Company

Back in my younger days I was a real Sears fan. If you went through my house or car, you would find that virtually everything came from Sears. Kenmore appliances, TV, iron and ironing board, blankets, everything. In the car you would find Diehard batteries, tires, fan belts, Craftsman tools, you name it, all from Sears. Even my rifles and ammunition carried the JC Higgins brands.

I purchased everything with my handy Sears credit card. That's where the trouble began. They would put everything on my easy, no-money-down, pay-as you-catch-me plan. Boy was it convenient. Just walk into the store, see something you liked, plop down that card, and walk out of the store with your dream item.

One day they decided to put major purchases on separate contracts and accounts. I ended up with three separate accounts after purchasing a new washer, dryer, and refrigerator. My wife was enthusiastically excited about her new appliances, and I was always financially responsible and always paid my bills on time. The problem was with Sears.

Me being a thrifty person—cheap—I started paying these three accounts with one check. (No sense wasting checks, right?) Well, Sears was either stupid or didn't understand—or they just didn't care—and they would put the entire amount of the check on one account, the next month they would put it all on another account, and so on and so on. It wasn't long before I received my TRW Credit Report and found that I was 90 days past due on all three Sears accounts.

Now bad credit in those days was a problem, so I sought out a solution. I called the Sears Credit Department and tried to resolve the issue. I was greeted with the response, " Mr. Layton, you have excellent credit with us."

So I asked, "Why, then do you have me ninety days past due on all my accounts on TRW?" I was assured they would correct it with TRW.

I waited and waited for my next TRW Report, and when it came, there it was, still 90 days past due. I called Sears and got the same response with the same assurance that it would be taken care of. Now another waiting period for another TRW report and same old same old.

By then several years had passed with no resolution of my problem. I was assured by my children who were employed in the credit industry business that Sears was so notorious about reporting bad credit on their customers that nobody in the credit business paid any attention to the negative Sears reports. It still bothered me, having negative reports on my TRW.

I knew I had to do something, so I decided it was time to change buying patterns. We started shopping at Montgomery Ward.

I was always a responsible person and proud of the fact that I was always able to pay my bills on time, and like I said, it still bothered me that I had a negative on my credit report. So I got one of those fancy new credit cards that let you transfer all your payments to it, and I paid the Sears accounts off, figuring that in seven years I would have a clear TRW.

Well, it turned out, it took 11 years and many threatening—and totally ignored—letters to Sears to finally get a clean bill of health from TRW. I vowed never to do business with Sears again and I have held to that pledge for the last 40-some years.

About 20 years ago I was visiting with my sister Joyce and her husband, Bruce, at their Anderson, California, home, when he proudly pulled out his new Sears Revolving Credit Card. I looked at it in total shock and shouted, "Cut it up and throw it away! They will ruin your credit!"

He assured me that he always paid his bills on time and there wouldn't be a problem. I told him, "I don't care if you pay your bill *before* time, they will still screw up your credit."

Well, he didn't listen. The next time we were up there, he told me the story about how he had seen this item in the Sears

Roebuck catalog that he liked, so he ordered it, using his new, handy-dandy, revolving credit card. Well, they backordered it. Thirty days later he got a bill on his new, handy-dandy, revolving credit card for the item. He called Sears and explained that he hadn't received the item yet. The nice lady at Sears told him to just forget the billing and pay it when the item arrived. His first mistake! Come to think of it, his first mistake was not cutting up the card up when I told him to, so I am going to call this his second mistake.

Thirty days later he received another billing showing him thirty days late and still no package. He called the nice lady at Sears again. Same story. Third mistake. Thirty days later, third verse, same as the first. Forth mistake.

After 90 days without receiving the package, he finally cancelled the package. And guess what? His TRW arrived, showing him 90 days past due on an item he never received.

So, I asked him, "What did you do with the card?"

He responded, "I cut it up."

I shouldn't have done it in front of him, but I started laughing. He just sat there with that *I-know* look on his face.

I just saw an article that Sears, who has merged with K-mart, is closing numerous Sears and K-mart stores throughout the country. Do I care? Nah! Anybody that screwed up and incompetent doesn't deserve to be in business.

The Car Dragger

Somewhere back in the '80s, Doyalene and I went to Snow Summit in Big Bear to attend the Dodge Cup downhill races. It was a bitter cold day with ice everywhere.

We arrived at the parking lot at Snow Summit, parked the car, and prepared to go up the hill to watch the races. On the way out of the parking lot, we noticed this beautiful St. Bernard dog tied to a Renault. If you don't know, the Renault is a very small, compact car. The owners of the dog apparently didn't want to leave the dog in the car and didn't want to take him up the hill with them, so this was their best solution.

We proceeded up the hill and found a nice spot near the finish line to observe the skiers as they came down the hill and crossed the finish line. We had been thoroughly enjoying watching the racers coming down the hill for over an hour when an announcement came over the public address system: "Would the people who have their dog tied to their car in the parking lot please come down and get your dog. He is dragging your car all over the parking lot and has already damaged several cars." That announcement received a lot of laughter, accompanied by several people scrambling down the hill to check their cars.

I don't recall what we were driving at that time, but I never drove a decent car in the ice and snow. We always had a clunker on reserve to drive on such days. We always had people coming to the mountains who didn't have a clue how to drive in ice and snow, and they were always plowing into us, so I always had a station wagon—we called it the race car—that was mechanically sound but not too straight in the body. (We called it the race car because we liked to go to the Orange Show on Saturday nights and watch the car races.)

The Orange Show was famous for "parts pickers." If you drove a nice car to the races, you had a 50/50 chance that parts were going to be missing when you returned to your car after the races. The thieves would take one look at our beat up station wagon and just pass it by. It's possible that we drove the race car to Snow Summit that day, so we weren't concerned about damage. We just kept enjoying the races.

The trip home from Snow Summit that evening after the races was unbelievable. The traffic was so bad that I probably would have made better time if I had gone the back way through Lucerne Valley. We would be absolutely stopped for 15 to 20 minutes at a time. Some of the cars would turn their radios up and get out of their cars and dance on the street. It was like a big street party. We got out of the car several times and joined in the festivities. It made the trip down more enjoyable. We finally reached Running Springs after about two-and-one-half hours—normally a 20-minute drive—and hit the cutoff to head across the mountain to Crestline. It was smooth sailing home from there.

It was a long and tiring day, but it was fun and turned out to be a great day. How many people do you know who can tell stories about a dog pulling a car around a parking lot? This was definitely another one for the memory book.

The Rest Stop

Doyalene and I were married in Las Vegas, Nevada, on September 18, 1961, and we tried to make it to Vegas three times a year from that point on. The traffic in Vegas was a lot lighter in those days but was still pretty bad, so I soon learned all the side streets and shortcuts throughout the city to make traveling there easier. Vegas has grown so much that I now need Google maps on the I-Phone to find my way around.

One evening we decided to treat ourselves by attending a show and hiring a taxi instead of driving. That was a major mistake. We were greeted by the arrival of the taxi, and when we got in and announced our destination, we took off on an E-Ticket ride through Vegas. This guy peeled out and took off at 70 miles per hour, cutting through traffic and going down side streets and alleys. Doyalene and I were hanging onto our butts.

The taxi went flying up one alley, and right in the center of the alley, blocking it, were two taxis that had been involved in a head-on collision. They were sitting there with their hoods bent open, water, steam and oil pouring out of both vehicles. We thought to ourselves, "Thank God, now he is going to have to stop." No way.

He slammed that taxi into reverse and sped out of that alley backwards as fast as he had gone in. We finally arrived at our destination alive but totally dehydrated from sweating through our ride from hell. The taxi driver was so mad when I refused to give him a tip that he almost ran over my foot as he pulled out. My quick reflexes were the only thing that saved me. We decided that driving ourselves would be our only mode of transportation from then on.

Being on a budget, we stayed in the cheaper motels to save on expenses, but after a couple of years, we discovered it wasn't any more expensive to stay in the major hotels. Thus began our luxury lifestyle in Vegas. We weren't avid gamblers, so much of our time was spent sitting in one-drink lounge shows, sightseeing, dining, touring the local museums, attending baseball games at Cashman Field, going to the stock car races, and playing all the video games in the children's section at Circus Circus.

Circus Circus had a round bar that rotated up on the mezzanine. We would spend hours sitting in that bar, rotating around while sipping cocktails. There was something really soothing about sitting there, going around in circles. The center part of the bar didn't rotate, and I always wondered how the cocktail girls kept track of everybody's drinks, with them rotating around. The bar was a great vantage point from which to watch the circus acts, and we always tried to get a seat in the bar before the performances started. The place really packed in when the acts started, so having a good seat was important.

Doyalene always loved her breakfasts, so we would head up the strip closer to town to the I-Hop for breakfast. We went there so many times over the years that we became friends with the owner. We were so regular that for a while he thought we were locals. We talked with him regularly, and he almost convinced us to move to Vegas. We probably would have except for the fact that I wanted to keep the kids near their grandparents.

I always thought it was important for them to know their family and be close. Over the years I passed up some excellent career opportunities because I wanted the kids close to their grandparents, but I never regretted any of those decisions.

Doyalene and I were so broke that our wedding dinner consisted of McDonalds hamburgers, fries, and a coke. We kept that tradition up throughout our lives, going to McDonalds for our anniversary dinner every year. We did manage to graduate to cheeseburgers and a large order of fries after the first year. We would treat ourselves to lobster the next night.

I will never forget our 49th anniversary. We were sitting in the McDonalds downtown, having our cheeseburgers, when this wedding party in full wedding attire walked in. We ran over, congratulated them, and told them our story. They were shocked that we had been married 49 years, and they came over and had cheeseburgers with us. I often wonder how they are doing. I hope they are happy and life is good for them.

We used to stop at the roadside rest area between Baker and Mountain Pass on our way to Vegas. Since it was a little over halfway, it was a good place to stop and walk around to stretch our legs. On one trip I walked into the bathroom, and there was a bunch of Japanese tourists standing around the washbasin, wanting to wash their hands. They were obviously from Japan because they spoke no English. They couldn't figure out how to turn the water on and were touching everything while chattering in Japanese. One of the guys pushed on the cap where you put the soap in, and I pushed on the foot pedal and turned the water on. They started laughing and chattering. They were so proud of themselves that they had figured out how to turn the water on. The next guy pushed on the cap, and I pushed the floor pedal. They all wet their hands and soaped up good, but when the last guy pushed the cap to rinse, I didn't push the floor pedal.

They really started chattering then. There they stood, soap all over their hands and no water. I waited a minute and then tapped on the guy's shoulder standing next to me. When he turned to look at me, I pointed to the floor. When he looked down, I pushed on the pedal and the water came out. They all burst into laughter. They knew I had punked them.

They all finished washing their hands and left, laughing and gesturing to me. I went to the bathroom, washed my hands, and walked out, heading for Doyalene, when all of a sudden I heard a horn and a lot of commotion. I looked up and this little car was pulling out, heading up the road, and the guys were all poking their heads out of every window in that car, waving, laughing, smiling, and chattering. It reminded me of a raccoon mother with all her babies poking their heads out of her fur.

Doyalene looked and asked, "What was that?"

I just smiled and said, "Nothing. I just made some friends."

That was over 40 years ago, and I can still see all those

guys with their heads poking out of the windows of that little car. It was one of the funniest things I have ever seen.

The Cute Blonde Bartender at the Rim

Back in the '70s and early '80s, Doyalene was the bar manager at Lori and John's bowling alley, the Rim Lanes. She managed the bar for them for several years. I think she did it more because of the friendship with Lori and John than for the money. I asked her several times to quit, but she kept putting it off.

I seldom went into the bar because of the way the drunks treated her. I almost got into it with some of the guys a couple of times, so Doyalene told me to stay away, as she had the ability to handle them. She never had any trouble with them that I know of, so I guess she was right.

One time I was working on radios for a pipeline construction company that was running pipe down into the canyon off of Lake Gregory drive. It was getting late in the afternoon, and as I was finishing up working on one of their vehicles, I heard the construction workers talking. They were all talking guy-talk while they were working. I heard one of the guys proclaim rather loudly that it was time to pick up and get ready to head down to the Rim for beer and to see that cute blonde bartender!

I kind of felt a little proud of that reassurance that she was indeed as pretty as I thought she was. I thought about making a comment about how they didn't have a chance because she was going home with me that night, but I thought better of it. I just smiled to myself and went on.

The Mozumdar Temple

I moved my family to Crestline in 1970 to start a business, and there was always talk around town about Mozumdar. Mozumdar was an elaborate temple built in the San Bernardino Mountains near Crestline. It had been built by Akhay Kumar Mozumdar, a spiritual teacher who had a dream to build a temple where people of all religious faiths could come together and worship. Akhay Kumar Mozumdar, who became a naturalized American in 1913, was an Indian-born spiritual leader who was associated with the New Thought Movement in the United States. He began construction of the temple and an adjoining camp on the north slope of Cedarpines Park in 1920 but was not able to complete the temple before he died in 1953. After his death the property was sold to the YMCA and then to the Unification Church of Rev. Sun Myung Moon. The property continues to be on private property and has changed hands several times since Moon's death.

One day I drove my family up to the temple to look around. The road was open right up to the temple in those days. It was quite spectacular driving up through the forest and seeing this "Taj Mahal" all of a sudden appear out of the trees. The temple was still in good condition at that time and hadn't started to deteriorate. The place was locked up, so all we did was walk around the area and peer through the windows. All we could see through the windows was open space inside.

I was in the communications business at the time and owned several of the small buildings that you see on the tops of the mountain peaks in the area that have all the antenna towers sticking up, ruining the view of the beautiful mountains.

I had a small site on top of Jobs Peak in the Cedarpines Park area that overlooked Mozumdar. This was during the timeframe that the Rev. Moon had taken over the temple. There was very little in the way of housing in the area in those days, and the area was always quite dark, with very little ambient light at night. Without a full moon it was very difficult to see anything.

I was up on Jobs Peak one night, servicing the radio equipment at the site, and an "escapee" from the Moonies saw the light from the building and followed it to my door. This frazzled-looking young man came in, and the first thing he asked for was a cigarette. I told him, "I am sorry, but I don't smoke."

The poor guy didn't even know where he was. He had run into a bunch of Moonies in LA, and they promised him a life of peace and tranquility. He was dumb enough to climb into a windowless van with them and ended up at Mozumdar as a pledge. I told him I would be finished in a few minutes and would take him down to the main highway when I was done.

The trip down the hill into Top Town Crestline was quite amusing and interesting. The young man talked of his treatment as a new Moonie. Apparently, they are sleep deprived and fed only gruel. They are worked quite hard and constantly bombarded with brainwashing. They are allowed no beverages except water, and definitely, no smoking.

The Bra Tree

The Mojaves were a tribe of Native Americans who lived along the Colorado River in California, Arizona, and Nevada. Myth or legend has it that the Mojaves were great runners, were noted for being able to run a hundred miles without rest. They were used regularly by the military to run dispatches between Fort Yuma and Fort Mojave during the Arizona Indian uprisings in the 1850s. The legend was that their feet would get extremely sweaty from the desert heat, and there would be trees along the way that they would hang their wet moccasins on, grab a dry pair, and continue on their journey. There was supposedly one tree near what is now Highway 95 just north of Quartzsite, Arizona.

Some people decided to keep the legend alive and started a shoe tree in the area of the supposed, old moccasin tree, and it became so popular that people started hanging their old pairs of shoes on this tree. It turned into such a tourist attraction that the road department made a parking area in front of it and actually put a marker up to designate the area as point of interest. The local Quartzsite Chamber of Commerce had a write up on the history of the shoe tree and directions to its location in the points-of-interest section of their flyer. That's where my family and I first learned of the shoe tree. We decided to stop by and look at it, but I can't say that we were overwhelmed by it.

I had heard that some jokers decided to spoof the shoe tree by starting a bra tree a mile north of the shoe tree on Highway 95. I wanted to go see it, but Doyalene was quite reluctant to do so. I finally talked her into it, and we drove up the highway and arrived at this new monument to women's undergarments. There it was, standing in its entire, majestic splendor, by itself, all alone on the side of the highway along a stretch of lonely, barren desert. It was a sight to behold with hundreds of bras of all shapes and sizes hanging from all of its branches. I got out to take in the sights, but Doyalene was so taken aback by the disgusting display that she refused to even get out of the car.

There was one bra on the tree that was huge. I haven't a clue what the size was, but the woman to whom it belonged must have been very large. I swear you could have used it for a pup tent. It had writing on it with a felt tip marker saying, "For a good time call Martha at 1 800 864 xxxx." I was very curious as to whether this was a good number and what would happen if someone called it. My curiosity was getting the best of me, but Doyalene was quite emphatic in her opinion that I was not going to call that number.

I decided that satisfying my curiosity wasn't worth going without dinner that evening, or possibly more than one, so I never made that call.

This incident occurred approximately 15 years ago, and I doubt that the tree is still standing, but if it is, it's unlikely, with the harsh desert environment, that the writing on the bra would still be legible. If any of you stopped by the tree and called the number on that bra, please call me and tell me the results. I am still curious.

The Unknown Road

There were rumors that back during the prohibition era of this country, a speakeasy was in operation in the north part of Los Angeles County, somewhere on the ridge route. The ridge route was the main road down from the Bakersfield area into Los Angeles. The road followed the ridge down through what is known as the San Gabriel and Tehachapi Mountains. It was replaced many years ago by Highway 99 and is now known as Interstate 5.

It is also rumored that a bordello was being operated from that speakeasy, and clients would be driven in limousines with blacked-out windows to this bordello. It is also rumored that the feds finally found the bordello, picked up all the ladies of the night, and drove them to the Nevada border. They dropped them off at the Nevada state line and told them not to come back into California.

The ridge route still exists in part, and some nostalgia buffs still drive the open portions of the road. Some of Los Angeles County's radio sites are located on peaks in this mountain region and some of the county communications people explore the region, looking for possible sites to set up communication equipment.

During explorations near the Sandberg area, some of the guys found a large cement foundation with obvious plumbing and signs of a building being on it at one time. It is a common belief that this foundation is the location of that speakeasy from back in the '20s. Nobody ever reported finding the location of the bordello.

Los Angeles County had a communications site known as Bald Mountain near this area. There was a private road that accessed the Bald Mountain site just on the other side of the ridge route where Pine Canyon Road meets with the ridge route. I drove that road many times to access Bald Mountain to service the radio equipment. The site was a main hub to relay signals back to Los Angeles for the sheriffs, fire, and the road department radios.

A private road meandered around the peaks, went over a ridge, and ended up at the radio site's location. There were two dirt roads leading off to the right of the paved road about 100 yards before the payment ended. The first dirt road led up to a private site, and the second road led up to the county communications site. There was an old farmhouse on the right side at the end of the paved road, and the dirt road extended farther up and veered to the left where a telephone company site was located. There was also an FAA beacon site located near the telephone company building.

I never paid much attention to the old farmhouse because a lot of cattle were ranged in the area, and I thought it was possibly a ranch house for the local rancher. One day, while waiting for another crew to arrive with some equipment, I walked down and looked the farmhouse over. I thought it was strange. There was no sign of habitation. There were no rabbit hutches, chicken coops, or pens for small animals, things that were always seen at a ranch or farmhouse. I didn't think any more of it and went on my way.

Over the years the road started deteriorating, and chunks of asphalt started coming out of the road. As the senior technician for the area, the engineers would always come to me for information and advice about the condition of the communications sites. They were getting concerned about the condition of the road to Bald Mountain and wanted to pave it. Since this was a private road, they didn't dare pave it without getting permission from the owner. I told them I had no idea who owned the road, but there was the phone company, the FAA, and a private site that I had no knowledge of the owners, all of whom could possibly own the road. They checked with all the parties mentioned and reported back to me that none of them claimed ownership of the road. I told them I had no idea who else to contact.

Several years later, as I was about a month away from retirement, we had a trouble call at Bald Mountain. One of our technicians, named Scott, went with me to the site and we discovered there was an antenna problem. As we were not allowed to climb the towers, we always had to call the line crew to come out and do the antenna repairs. There was always a two-plus-hour wait for the line crew to arrive, and I, having little patience, and having my own safety belt, would climb up there and do the repair myself. I would be severely reprimanded if I had ever been caught doing this. Since Scott was with me, I didn't dare let him see me climb the tower, so we called for the line crew.

Scott was a very adventurous and curious person like me and loved to hike, so instead of sitting around waiting for the line crew, we went on an excursion around the site. We discovered two or three small houses in a little valley over the hill right behind the site. (I can't remember if there were two or three houses, but I know there was more than one.) These houses were situated where they couldn't be seen except from an airplane.

We definitely went exploring through those houses. They were all collapsed, but we were able to access some of the rooms. We found women's clothing of the risqué variety. There were bodices and sexy underwear, but, not surprisingly, no men's items in the houses. Since the buildings were a short walking distance over the ridge to the farmhouse, I have deduced that Scott and I possibly found the *Ridge Route Bordello*, and the builders of the road.

My 75th Birthday Facebook Posting

I posted this on Facebook on my 75th birthday:

"Here I am, celebrating the day of my birth again. If you had asked me 50 years ago if I was going to live this long, I would have replied, no way! Yet here I am, pondering my life. I am indeed one of the luckiest men on earth. I am, with the exception of a few hiccups, in great health and shape for a man of my age. I had the good fortune to marry a beautiful woman who has given me more love than most men would get in two lifetimes. I raised four beautiful children who are full of love and whom I love dearly. They have given me beautiful grandchildren who are loved dearly as well, and now those children have given me beautiful great-grandchildren. I am not a wealthy man of coin, but my wealth is overflowing. If someone asked me if I could go back and do it over what I would have done differently, I would tell them I would have done nothing more than worry less, laugh more, and practice more patience.

They say you must measure life by quality not quantity. I am blessed to have both. I am truly blessed, and to all of my friends and family who offer a birthday greeting on this day, I thank you, and with the grace of God, I will be accepting more greetings in future years."

Stories from My Elders

Throughout my childhood I was told or heard stories from my elders, and when I am gone, those stories will be gone. This is my attempt to keep these stories alive for the generations.

***

Mother's Uncle Jim was an ornery old cuss. My only recollection of him was being at his cabin in Big Bear as a very young child. The cabin was not very large. It probably measured 20 by 30 feet in the main room. It had a kitchen area and a large room attached that was full of firewood. A fireplace was the only heat source and was used for cooking as well. This was a rustic log cabin that he had built himself. Jim fought in the Civil War and came to California sometime after the war, settling in what is known as the Erwin Lake area of the San Bernardino Mountains. Jim probably built the cabin in the late 1800s when he settled in Big Bear.

We were at the cabin, visiting Uncle Jim one day, and there was a table in the center of the room. Several men were sitting around the table, playing what I assume was poker. There was always a large pile of newspapers in the corner that were probably used for starting fires in the fireplace. Every once in a while, old Jim would take two fingers and press them against his lips, and you better get out of the way, because a large stream of brown spit would shoot out of his mouth and land right on the newspapers with a large splat. I was amazed at his accuracy.

Jim was always busy doing something. He was very active, and even as he was getting into his nineties, he always had a project he was planning or working on. The family kept trying to get him to slow down and relax, but he was just not capable of it. They got this brainy idea of having him committed to Patton State Hospital for a few weeks. They figured he would have to relax then. The men in the white suits came and picked him up and locked him away. About three days later the hospital called and asked the family if they had come and picked him up. It seems old

Jim escaped. They scoured the hospital grounds and the roads without any success—he was just gone. They sent out search parties but were never able to locate him.

By this time the family had built a nice house with running water and all the conveniences about a block up the road from Jim's cabin, but Jim hardly ever stayed there. He said he just wasn't comfortable in there, so he always stayed at the cabin. About a week after he disappeared from Patton, someone smelled smoke and walked down to the old cabin. Sure enough, there was smoke coming out of the chimney. They opened the door, and there was old Jim, sitting there in front of the fire, warming up. He had walked from Patton in San Bernardino through the forest to the cabin in Big Bear. It was winter, and all he had on was the hospital gown. They asked him why he left, and he said he didn't like it there. "They were just too darn bossy."

I guess the family decided to leave him alone after that excursion.

Several years later I heard the family talking about the demise of old Jim. He was 102 years old and was out late at night, walking his two dogs, when a drunk driver came peeling around the corner and ran over him, killing him and one of the dogs.

Many years later, after my Mother's passing, I ran across a newspaper clipping confirming the accident in my Mother's belongings. I still have that newspaper clipping in my possession.

I had always wondered why he walked down the center of the road, and finally, one day the mystery was finally solved. I was talking with a man who lived in Big Bear who, as a young boy, remembered old Jim. He said Jim's eyesight was so bad that he always walked on the line in the center of the road; otherwise, he couldn't tell where the road was.

***

My Aunt Mabel was always my favorite great aunt, and I visited her regularly. Many years later, while going through my mother's things after she passed away, I found a picture of my mother wearing this really old, 1800s-type clothing, and I wondered what it was all about. I discovered by the note on the back of the picture that it was actually Aunt Mabel as a young lady. I think that may have been the reason for the closeness to her I always felt, because she was an older version of my mother.

For as long as I can remember, Mabel lived in the old cabin that Jim built. I guess she didn't like the big house either. After Jim's demise, the family had put plumbing and a bathtub in the cabin. I don't remember if there was a flush toilet or not. I only remember the bathtub because, one day when I was visiting Aunt Mabel, her daughter Billie Ann was washing out the tub for her, and I was surprised to see it. I remember on one visit she talked about the grandkids never coming to see her. She asked me about running electricity to the cabin so she could put in a TV, thinking the children would come if they could watch TV. I told her I didn't know if it would help because there wasn't any television reception in the mountains. I think she just dropped the idea after that. That was the era before VCRs and satellites.

Right after Doyalene and I married, I took her to Big Bear to meet Aunt Mabel. We arrived at the cabin and she wasn't there. I looked around and blew the horn a few times. In a little while I saw this tiny figure hobbling across the mountain ridge. Now Aunt Mabel was in her seventies, but she could probably outrun me, so I thought, "No, that can't be Aunt Mabel," and I wondered, "Who could it be?"

There were five sisters, and I knew it had to be one of them. Pretty soon the figure came into view and it was definitely Aunt Mabel. I introduced her to Doyalene and asked her about walking with a cane. She responded by saying that she and Aunt Lucy were gathering pine nuts, and she was up in the tree shaking it and a limb broke. She fell out of the tree and bruised her hip. She said she was all right and it was feeling better.

We had a nice visit, but heading home Doyalene asked, "What the heck is a seventy-five year old woman doing climbing a tree?"

I told her, "Honey, they live on piñon nuts, so they have to go out and gather them."

"But, my God, a women her age should not be climbing in trees," Doyalene said.

I just smiled and thought to myself, "She doesn't understand my family."

Doyalene talked about Aunt Mabel for years after that, but I don't remember ever seeing Aunt Mabel again. I guess I just got busy with my own family. I talked with my cousin Donna, Mabel's granddaughter, a few years ago. Donna is still living in Big Bear and is doing fine. Donna is the same age as me, and I wonder if she climbs trees to gather pine nuts.

About the Author

Gary Layton was born in the late 1930s at Saint Bernadine's hospital in San Bernardino, California to third-generation California parents. He has always been a very active individual, starting as a young boy seeking adventure through exploring the areas of his childhood around Highgrove and Riverside, California.

Gary started writing essays about his adventures at a very young age and has continued writing throughout his life. Now living in the Mojave Desert, he continues his adventures—and writing—while traveling in his recreational vehicle throughout the western half of the United States and Canada.

Gary and his wife, Doyalene, raised two daughters and two sons in the Riverside and Crestline areas of Southern California, and he is now blessed with numerous grand and great grandchildren.

Growing Up in Riverside is his first published book.

Made in the USA
Middletown, DE
08 December 2022